PAST THE PAST

Book II: Upon a Time In France

I0143304

JAMES I KEPNER

Flying Phoenix Press

Printed in the United States of America.

For more information, or to book an event, contact: jimkepner@gmail.com

Book design by Dawn Black
Cover illustration by bookcoverspro.com

ISBN - Paperback: 979-8-9881149-3-2
First Edition: November 2025

Dedicated to my grandchildren, so they may know that their legacy crosses time itself.

Contents

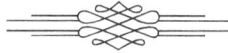

Part II: The Robere Cycle

The Soul's Eye
by Édouard du Bourguignon[1]

How much is required
To open the soul's eye,
That we may see,
What we are called to see?

How much love? Is
600 more years of love enough?
And, how much love is that?
More than *you* ever imagined,
mon amis.

That much love,
And that many
loving companions.

All the loving companions
Gathered about you, right now
Filling more dimensions
than you know.
Right now.

And, of course, much Light,
By which I mean God's Light.
Streaming from
An infinity of stained-glass windows.

By which I mean,
From an infinite number of souls,
Each with its own
Patterns and colors,
Becoming beauteous form.

So that everyone and everything,
All you can apprehend
Is so stupefyingly beautiful
That you could believe the same,
Even of yourself.

To the third eye,
The eye of the soul,
It is so.

Preface

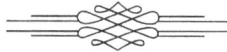

You are not here to look back in time. You are here to immerse
yourself in the Sea of Time, that you might glimpse your soul's
most curious project.
— Édouard du Bourguignon

[2]This series is a memoir carried by two currents: one flowing
through the past, the other through the present. It tells, as faithfully
as memory allows, of a life once lived in fifteenth-century France
and of the strange unfolding in this life that led me to remember it.

Past the Past is divided into two parts. The first finds Étienne
returning from Brittany after his confrontation with the Old Man,
emerging from months of darkness into sunlight. He travels across
France, reflecting on the lessons he received and how they have
changed him. His arrival at the Château brings both dangers and
discoveries. And love.

The second part brings the story into contemporary time, when a
mysterious painting awakens memories I could not have imagined—
challenging everything I think about myself and the nature of the
soul. These recollections lead me to travel to France once more,
where unexpected places reveal further threads of the past.

The two parts speak to each other, though not in sequence. Memory—especially the soul's memory—does not follow clocks or calendars. It arrives in flashes and floods. I could not impose a novelist's order upon what the soul revealed; I could only bear witness.

You don't need to believe in reincarnation or past lives to walk with me through these pages. Maybe you'll see it as allegory or as a spiritual-romantic journey of remembrance. However you approach it, I hope it finds a place in your own landscape of meaning.

Anyway, recollection of past lives is no badge of spiritual attainment. The ancients warned that such visions could distract the seeker from true contemplation. Yet when these memories arise, they do so with startling intimacy. We try to listen to what they might show us, but no life can be reduced to some tidy lesson. They are windows into a long endeavor. The deeper challenge is to glimpse what a life means in the vast tapestry of the soul. The intellect cannot encompass this, though it will try. The soul simply invites us to follow.

Throughout these books, I refer to my teacher as "Rose." Her real name is Reverend Rosalyn Bruyere, and I used a pseudonym out of respect, not secrecy. Telling one's own story is delicate; telling another's, especially a respected spiritual teacher's, requires humility. Rosalyn's teachings on energy, healing, and the architecture of spirit shape my work. Decades later, her words still resonate within me. The work my colleague Carol and I teach grows from Rosalyn's foundation—my gratitude for her runs through every line of this book.

Ultimately, these books are less a story than an invocation—a quiet calling to what waits within us. They are a kind of incantation, an Open Sesame that stirs the sleeping memory of the soul. You need not recall other lives to feel their echo. Simply trust that something within you—older than your name—still listens.

—Jim Kepner
Cleveland, Ohio • 2025

SYNOPSIS OF

About Time, Book I of Upon a Time in France [3]

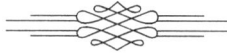

About Time, Book I of Upon a Time in France, is the author's memoir of a past life as Étienne in 15th-century France, and his contemporary journey to remembering it. While pursuing his career as a psychologist, the author explores meditation and subtle energy practices and eventually meets Rose, a renowned healer and clairvoyant. Immersed in Rose's extraordinary energy field, he experiences vivid past-life memories, confirmed by others' independent recollections.

The story unfolds in late medieval France, where he lived as Étienne, an orphan rescued by Édouard, a master alchemist and magician. Édouard is part of a secret Order opposing dark sorcery, gathering a ragtag "Army of Light" beginning with Étienne. Alongside Édouard's allies—the formidable Abbess, the wise cook Matilde, and the warrior François—Étienne and his fellow orphans embark on adventures to learn magical arts, counter evil magicians, and rescue others from dark purposes.

To have his Army of Light, he must first heal and train them. The Maestro Édouard must use every principle of alchemy he has gleaned to transmute the lead of Étienne and his fellows into the gold of higher purpose.

Eventually, Étienne is sent to Brittany to study with the last living Druid priest, the Old Man, a powerful yet flawed High Priest of the Moon Mysteries. Enduring months of training in complete darkness and initiation by the Goddess, Étienne discovers the Old Man's secret: the Old Man is dying, and plans to manipulate Étienne into becoming his successor. With guidance from the spirit of the Old Man's High Priestess, Étienne masters the test of Moon travel, confronts the Old Man, and refuses his coercive plan. Protected by the Goddess herself, Étienne breaks free and reclaims his independent destiny. He reclaims his horse and begins his return journey across the width of France, and back to the Chateau and home with Édouard.

PROLOGUE:

Impossible Things

❖

"I can't," said Alice. "There's no use trying. One can't believe impossible things."

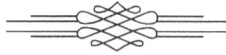

"I daresay you haven't had much practice," said the Queen. "When I was your age, I always did it for half-an-hour a day. Why, sometimes I've believed as many as six impossible things before breakfast."

— Lewis Carroll, Through the Looking Glass

By the final day of my first residential retreat with Rose, I had certainly encountered some impossible things. Far more than six of them, I'm sure, though keeping track of numbers in an altered state was a beyond-impossible thing for me. I'd again felt Rose's potent, non-subtle energy; I'd witnessed evening sessions where Rose "channeled" truly wise beings in spirit; I gained more insights into energy healing work in a week than I had from years of reading and workshops; and I discovered a sense of community I hadn't realized was missing, with people who seemed very unlike me.

Oh yeah, and my third eye opened—big time. That last part—the third-eye opening—had led to experiences my mind hadn't entirely accepted yet. It started to unfold on the second day.

While I'd experienced Rose's powerful energy firsthand, observing her on someone else was underwhelming, akin to watching grass grow. She described her sensations and actions, but only her hands resting on the body and the client's subtle physical changes, such as breathing and skin color, could be observed.

Then, on the second day, as I observed her demonstrating a technique on an eager volunteer, I noticed images forming in my mind. They were identical to what I saw with my physical eyes, yet they also revealed the internal organs and the energy streaming from Rose's hands.

I was sure that I was imagining this. Could this picture reflect anything real? I was compelled to ask.

"Uh,… Rose?"

"Yes, Jimmy. You have a question?"

Lord knows, I hadn't been called "Jimmy" since I was seven years old, but Rose started to refer to me this way from the first workshop, and I wasn't going to tell her otherwise.

"Um… yes, Rose. Are you using pink energy to work on her pancreas?" I asked hesitantly.

"Uh-huh," Rose confirmed, without further comment.

Hmm... she hadn't told us what color she was using before. Or that she was specifically working on the pancreas —just put her hands there.

After I asked, she said nothing for a bit, then explained why she was using pink, mentioning it had anti-inflammatory effects or something like that. I wasn't really paying attention since her confirmation of my internal image shook me up.

A minute later, the picture in my head changed. Her hands hadn't moved physically, but my picture showed something different from what she had done before.

"Uh… Rose?"

She glanced up at me. "Yes, Jimmy?"

"Did you change to work on her stomach and duodenum?" I asked breathlessly. "Uh…, and change your energy from pink to blue?"

She squinted at me, a habit she had when checking out someone's aura.

"Uh-huh. That's right," Rose said.

She had one of those secret smiles on her face, like she knew something about what was going on with me that I didn't. She said nothing about her smile but went on to explain why she was working on the client's stomach and duodenum, which are where the pancreatic ducts empty. Shortly after, she finished the work, answered some questions, and then announced that she'd give another demonstration with another volunteer.

From the very beginning of this second session, images formed in my mind of what she was energetically doing. It felt so disturbing to me! I'd hungered to see energy, but this wasn't how I expected it to look. These were just images in my head!

How could I be sure I wasn't just making them up? If this were real auric sight, shouldn't I be seeing the energy outside, just as I see with my physical eyes, but with auras added? These pictures in my mind didn't fit with the books I'd read about clairvoyance.

I didn't want to keep interrupting Rose, but I couldn't help myself. I was making myself crazy with my doubts. I had to check whether these pictures meant anything.

Each time I asked about what I was "seeing" in my images, she said, "That's right, Jimmy." A few people in the group, known for their ability to see auras and energy, exchanged glances. "Should we tell him more?" one asked aloud.

The other woman nodded and spoke up, elaborating on Rose's monosyllabic confirmations. "Can you see how Rose is wrapping the bone in a spiral, Jim?"

I could, kind of. Now that she mentioned it. At least it was added to my inner picture.

Someone else added, "And look how Rose is using her other hand to calm the client's heart and keep it steady as she works?"

Darn, these pictures hadn't shown both hands. Maybe because I was only focusing on the hand I thought was the working one. Now that it had been pointed out. My subsequent images "widened the lens" to include both hands as the demonstration progressed. And that was just the morning.

During the afternoon session, Mary, a nurse practitioner with a sharp ability to see inside the body, kindly suggested that I sit with her during any demonstrations. She said she could help me "tune up" my clairvoyance, and it would be helpful if I were in her auric field. I gratefully agreed and felt relieved that I wouldn't need to keep interrupting Rose to check things out. I bet that others in the room were hoping that Mr. Big-Mouth might be quiet for a while.

Mary's ability to see the body's insides in detail, and at will, was quite remarkable. It was just an everyday thing to her. Salt of the earth, she was a die-hard Red Sox fan and used her talent to scan her favorite pitcher's arm clairvoyantly while she watched a game on TV, to see if his throwing would be up to the task! She narrated what she was seeing until I could make it out, and her skilled third eye helped increase the detail and acuity of my inner pictures.

Then, on day four, things got even stranger. At lunch, I started to see images of people's spirit guides. It began in the dining room when the woman sitting across from me mentioned that she could *feel* the presence of her spirit guides; she had no idea what they looked like. This kind of thing had become typical dining conversation by that point.

As I listened, an image instantly appeared in my mind of the woman with two people hovering just behind her on either shoulder. In my mind, they seemed to be looking at me, as if trying to convey a message. I took it as something like *"Tell her!"*

"Hey," I said, "would you like to know what they look like to me?"

She didn't look at all surprised by my question; I guess people expected this kind of thing from me by this point. On the other hand, I couldn't believe those words actually came out of my mouth.

No matter, she said, "Yes, please do!"

I uttered my standard disclaimer, saying, "I'm not really seeing this, but…" and then told her what I saw in my image anyway. "There are two. There's a man over your right shoulder. He looks like someone from the Middle Ages, nicely dressed. I see a woman on your left. She has an Asian appearance and is dressed in animal skins. I mean, I'm not really seeing this. It's just a picture I get, really."

Someone else asked who I saw with them, and I told them, always adding the caveat, "I'm not really seeing this, but…" Apparently, one part of me thought the whole thing was so outlandish that it had to be dismissed. The rest of me seemed pretty happy to straddle two realities and see people's spirit guides as if they were the most normal thing in the world.

As the week went on, it got worse, or better, depending on which part of my mind was asked. Along with images of energy, spirits, and X-ray vision, I sometimes heard words—names or bits of information. It almost felt like a conversation at times. I was hesitant to share this unless I was sure they wouldn't think I was crazy. Hearing voices? Really? But it didn't seem like that.

While this clairvoyant faculty stayed with me, it was never as acute as this first opening. The exception was when I was in a similar group energy field. Left to my own devices, I had to learn about and refine my energy to achieve anything even close to these startling visions.

Later, some friends told me their guess about what caused my third eye to open so unexpectedly. Just guesswork, you know, but they knew Rose well and had observed her interactions with me from the beginning.

Rose's indigenous teacher would assess personality style by animal types. The animal you resembled revealed your strengths, weaknesses, and tendencies. By way of example, he told her she was a 'Bear,' which clearly highlighted her significant need for sleep, her tendency to overindulge in sweets, and how grumpy she would get when rushed, disturbed, or interrupted. Also, Bears get annoyed with Crows, who are always poking at things and incessantly squawking their questions and comments.

Guess what animal an intellectual Jewish guy like me is? With a beak nose too, just in case you missed the bird thing, a guy full of smart questions and comments? You got it in one. Crow.

My friends speculated that Rose, the Bear, found my Crow nature quite exasperating. Those constant, annoying questions! "Rose, what are you doing with the energy?" "Is that an aura?" "What do you mean by 'energy'?"

To a Bear, it sounded like "Rose, caw, caw, squawk…," "Caw, squawk, Rose?" and "Awk, awk, squawk!"

But my friends went on, "Rose knew that Crows just *love* shiny things!" They guessed Rose had popped open my third eye like a champagne cork, hoping to keep Jimmy-the-Crow preoccupied with pretty-shiny-things so maybe he'd shut up for a change!

I recalled the secret smile Rose would give me sometimes. Hmm. Maybe their story was plausible.

If this is what happened, I like to think that her ploy backfired. Instead of all the shiny images quieting me down, my Crow nature simply had more to squawk about!

"Pretty, pretty images! Caw, caw!" "Ar-r-k, a-r-rk! Pink energy in the pancreas? Squawk, squawk!" "Oh look, squawk, squawk! I see spirit guides, caw, caw!"

By the end of the week, all of this had quite "blown my mind," but the most impactful moment was waiting for me in the final hour of the retreat. One of the participants who had worked with Rose for several years had asked for a blessing ceremony. The woman, Jan, credited Rose's influence as a vital part of her recovery from childhood trauma. Jan was starting a service project to assist others who had similar childhood trauma. She requested a blessing from Rose to invoke protection and success for her new initiative. Rose decided to use this as the retreat's closing.

I'd seen Rose do a lot of things, but I'd never witnessed her in her ministerial or ceremonial capacity. Rose sat on the floor with

Jan, and we all formed a large circle around them of about seventy-five people. From where I sat, it felt like we had created a kiva, a circular, sacred space to hold the ceremony.

Rose explained why we gathered, emphasizing Jan's healing journey and her choice to serve others who experienced similar trauma. She described Jan's work, including giving talks and counseling, with the ceremony symbolizing her commitment to this new purpose.

I watched and listened raptly as a congregant, but even beyond that, I was so attuned from the week that I could even register a bit of what Rose was doing with the energy. As a good leader, Rose was bringing us on board with the purpose of the ceremony, but it was much more than mere words. As she spoke, Rose also enveloped the entire community in her subtle energy field, bringing us into a state of connectedness and coherence.

There can be no 'audience' in this kind of thing. From an energy field perspective, anyone present either contributes to or takes from the ceremony's energy; there is no "neutral" stance. We all influence the field, and therefore, we are all participants in creating the best conditions for Rose to call in the blessing.

Rose took a moment to gather herself, closing her eyes. The room fell into a deep silence as the community tuned in with her. Then, she opened up, in a big way, through her crown chakra. There was a connection with something from "above," sacred, and beyond our earthly realm.

Opening her eyes, she began to pray aloud. She spoke spontaneously, without a set liturgy or script, asking that Jan and her service to others be blessed. With every word, an energy poured down from above. Each word carried this powerful energy, flowing through Rose and wrapping Jan in its protective mantle. It was unmistakable, unlike anything I'd been part of before.

My jaw dropped open at this. I was utterly stunned.

This, *this* was what blessing was. It was the answer to a question I'd carried all my life, without realizing it.

Scenes from childhood flashed through my mind when I was six or seven years old in synagogue. My mother helped me read the ritual words the rabbi was reciting from the prayer book. Throughout, I felt that something was missing in all this. They were just words, I thought. Where was God? The congregation praised and beseeched through the liturgy, but I sensed that something essential was missing.

And now, during the ceremony with Rose, I realized what was missing. It was the energy that made the Sacred tangible; the officiant's connection with the Holy was brought into the prayer.

Among all the impossible things from the retreat week, this unexpected answer to a childhood mystery was the most astonishing one. I'd been waiting over thirty years for this. I wasn't going to let it go until I could reclaim what Rose was showing me. And here, also, was a bridge to that precious little boy, who was far more spiritually attuned than I'd previously credited, the boy who knew and longed for what was missing, yet couldn't quite name what that might be.

As all this cascaded through me, Rose completed the ceremony, closed the connection above, and grounded herself before announcing a short break. People stood, crowding around, to honor and embrace Jan.

I couldn't yet move, so I sat there, feeling as if everything inside me had been rearranged. Knowing now the difference between a true blessing and mere recitation, I would never see ceremony or ritual the same way again.

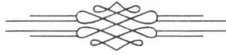

Part I:

Filling the Cup

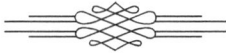

CHAPTER I:

The Return

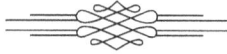

The Mother was merciful to me that first day, and the sky was gray and overcast. Gloomy and fitful, the growing daylight would not have seemed much brighter than the usual dawn to anyone accustomed to daylight. I was not one such. It had been months since I'd been exposed to full sunlight, and my body and senses rebelled at its intensity. The Old Man had required me to live in a pitch-black cave, arising only at night for instruction and ceremonies. The only light I'd seen for many months had been that of the cook fire, the moon, and the stars.

This ancient and challenging custom had rendered me exquisitely attuned to the subtleties of perception usually masked by the glare of the day. Living in the dark, my senses absorbed every possible impression, and I became sensitized to every oblique nuance of the night. As I began my journey into daylight, my whole body felt raw to the onslaught of the day's impressions.

Sensory impressions in daylight are myriad and much more amplified than at night. My mind had to work overtime to sort the riot of sensory impressions into a coherent whole. The rustle of a deer through bushes seemed to blare as loudly as a horn; the soft beat of birds taking wing was an ear-shattering drumbeat compared to the silent flight of night owls; even the wind startled me with its pressure upon my already overburdened senses.

I squinted in the beclouded and subdued light of this day. Even hidden behind a bank of clouds, the sun felt like hot and searing pressure against my pale and unprotected face, so I averted my gaze from the sky.

Fortunately, my horse had remained a creature of the day and was not as taken up as I was by a mere flock of starlings. He turned his head and eyed me as if to say, "You are acting strangely, Étienne; it's only birds." I hooded my face in my cloak and shrank back in the saddle, seeking to withstand the sunlight as best I could.

I had succeeded at the Old Man's premature test of Moon travel despite, rather than because of, him. I'd used up every ounce of power I had accumulated or received and was exhausted. Despite this, I knew I must put out more effort to escape his presence, though usually one should rest after such an extraordinary effort. Only sleep, food, rest, and prayer would help me recover, but I couldn't bring myself to stop. Though I was exhausted, my insides buzzed like a beehive from my confrontation with the Old Man, and I hoped this would fuel my ride. I would not rest until I was beyond the territory where the Old Man held spiritual authority.

Prayer, however, I could do from the saddle. I cocooned in my cloak, opened myself to the greater beings who had aided me, prayed my gratitude, and asked for guidance.

Over the course of the day, Brittany's hills and dense forest thinned into meadows bordered by trees. The land had once been cleared but had since reverted to the wild, a not-uncommon result of the waves of plague that had decimated the population, leaving too few farmers and peasants to plant and tend the fields.

My horse needed little direction as he ambled along the track, which wound gently down the hills. I held the reins slackly. My mind also ambled. The shade of my hood gave little to occupy my vision, so I rested my eyes.

I awoke in the saddle with a start. I roused myself and sensed around me, noticing that the spirit of the land no longer had the mark of the Old Man's authority. It was time to stop and make camp. I drifted to sleep in the saddle again before finding a suitable grassy clearing where my horse could graze. I removed his saddle and rubbed him down with handfuls of dry grass. When he had settled, I hobbled him and left him to graze. Finally, I wrapped myself in my cloak against the damp, curled up at the base of an old oak, and descended into exhausted and dreamless sleep.

When I awakened, the day had ebbed into the sunset. The coming darkness had become my customary wake-up with the Old Man, and although my impulse was to saddle my horse and get going, there were things to do before I even broke my fast.

Typically, the Old Man would have me out of the cave and into the night immediately upon waking, no matter the weather. He said that the keenness of my senses should not be dulled by food until after I had done my foundation practices. I followed this custom as I stood in the meadow, settling myself and letting the pull of the earth's power act entirely on me.

Something didn't feel right at first. I realized that, having lived barefoot for the past few months, I was still wearing my boots. They felt a needless barrier separating me from the earth's energy.

Having fallen asleep with them on, sweat had glued them to my feet, and I pulled them off with some difficulty. Finally, barefoot, I felt comfortable and could enjoy the damp, cool meadow grass with my toes. The Old Man had taught me how to let the rocks resonate in my bones. He called rocks the bones of the earth, demonstrating his tradition's principle, the Law of Similars.

The Old Man showed me bones, some dry and picked clean, and fresh bones about to be tossed into the stew pot. He said that dried bones were like rock, illustrating how our bones are similar to the earth's rocky body. He told me that our living bones are moist and somewhat pliant, like stone would be if it could be softened and made flexible by water, which allows them to grow and heal, unlike rock.

In that way, he joked, our bones were more like tree branches made of rock instead of wood. Even old people's bones grew, as evidenced by their knitting back together after being broken and reset properly.

He asserted that living things share the solid substance of the earth from which they originated, as well as the lighter essences of water and air. In the Old Man's Druid lineage, since living things grow from and upon the earth's substance, Nature's elemental forces are reflected in the structure and substance of our human bodies. Everything within our body, similar to some aspect of Nature's more excellent substance, can draw on that part of the earth's immense power once we learn how to do so.

The Old Man's gaze fixed on me in the dim, flickering firelight inside the hut. "There are many bones in your body, boy. Some say as many as two hundred." He looked at me and grunted, "Hmph! You will do this practice until you can sense every single one of them vibrating with the rock in the earth's body beneath you."

Of course, he had no interest in keeping count, but said this with his customary threatening tone to impress upon me the level of detail he expected. After letting me absorb his seriousness for a moment, he continued. Over time, he insisted that this practice would strengthen my health and prolong my life, and that his advanced age was partly due to it. At another time, he'd asserted that he was over a hundred and twenty years of age. I scoffed at his claim, although I admitted that he was more physically vigorous and stronger than he looked for his age. Only later was his claim affirmed to me by the High Priestess, who said this was normal for the practitioners of this tradition.

A benefit of being sequestered inside a pitch-black cave during daylight hours was that such practices became my sole form of entertainment. I could sleep for only seven of the ten or eleven hours of darkness, and working on my assignments helped to fill the rest of the time. One can make considerable, rapid progress when one has nothing else to do but sleep. I readily evoked the sensation of the big bones of my body, like thigh bones and pelvis. Surrounded by the rock of my cave, I could sense and feel its natural resonance, letting it vibrate the bones within me until they seemed to match and vibrate in kind. But even to sense the smaller bones required work, and only repeated movement and touch allowed me to discern one from another. The number of small bones in my hands and feet needed even more time and practice to sense, let alone find, how to get them to resonate with the rock.

However, momentum developed over time as I practiced. The more resonant my bones became with the rocks and stones in the earth, the more the rock seemed to reach everything in my body that was similar to it, lighting up these less palpable bones and aiding the process.

The Old Man was naturally suspicious when I told him I had completed the task. Traditionally, he said this practice took months for an apprentice to accomplish, yet here I was claiming completion in only weeks.

I knew this was because the practices the Maestro had us doing for years made the discipline familiar. The Maestro had us harmonize our bodies with the landscape around us when he taught us the 'magic of concealment.' It was similar to what the Old Man required, even if the Old Man's practice was more anatomically detailed. I knew the Old Man would never credit anything I'd learned before him, so I kept silent about these thoughts.

He tested me, of course, expecting to catch me out in a lie. His test was to show him the location of the smallest bones in the body. These were little known to anyone but anatomists and would only be discovered when one was advanced enough for the rock's vibration to highlight them. His eyes widened with surprise when I quickly pointed to the inside of my ears.

I told him that my discovery of these tiny bones, vibrating through the rocks, had allowed me to hear animals moving beneath the earth. I added that I hardly needed such a sensitive ability to hear his thunderous stride, as even the rocks found his steps too loud! He responded with a mean-looking squint, communicating that he'd make me pay for the pleasure of my disrespect.

Now barefoot in the meadow where I had slept, with the clamorous calls of birds quieting as twilight set in, I began the familiar ritual of resonating each bone in my body with the earth's. I started with the larger bones in my legs so their stronger resonance could spread downward to the bones of my feet and toes and upward to the pelvis. The thick bones of my spine gradually took up the song of the bedrock beneath me, spreading this more and more to ribs, collar bones, and skull bones as this vibrance gained ground. The procedure had occurred more quickly over time, which the Old Man attributed to the bones becoming purified of anything that did not match the fundamental hum of the earthly rock.

I renewed this deep connection with bone, rock, and earth, feeling the cool evening breeze as the sun dipped below the horizon. The blessedly familiar energy of night surrounded me, shielding me and bringing a sense of relief as I was supported by the earth's solidity resonating from below. As I'd hoped, this practice helped buffer the oversensitivity I'd been overwhelmed by previously.

By the time I completed the practice, the sky was fully dark. I rummaged through my saddlebags for food, finding a piece of rough farm bread with its crust hardening and a chunk of fragrant cheese. This, along with a couple of apples, filled out my travel feast. I set aside a portion of each item, knowing I would need to break my fast again before sunrise and my next full day of travel. I would need to watch for farmers along the way to obtain supplies. I was not ready to brave the tumult of some village market day.

Having eaten, I was now fully awake, as I would typically be, living in the cave and rising at dark for practices. My horse might be chivied into traveling for a few hours at night, but then I'd have to find and make camp in the dark, a thoroughly unpleasant thought. It was best to stay until dawn and travel in the daylight, though my body would be desiring sleep by then. What to do?

If I engage in vigorous physical activity, I might exhaust myself enough to nap before dawn, allowing me to stay awake and ride longer in daylight. The most physically demanding activities I knew were the blade drills François taught me. I had only been able to do these drills infrequently. As the Old Man was jealous of any activities he did not assign, my skills were rusty. I knew I'd be sore from such vigorous exercise the next day, but I hoped it might tire me enough to encourage a nap.

Ah, what a pleasure to take up the art again! I rediscovered my fluid movement and my body's memory of the fighting forms, which made me think fondly of François and his long mentorship of me. Working my body to the point of physical exhaustion did indeed tire me. I performed some of the Old Man's practices to induce relaxation and drifted into a deep, well-earned nap.

When my eyes opened again, I could sense that sunrise was only an hour or so off. I was happy I had slept so thoroughly until I tried to get up. Mon Dieu, I was unbelievably sore! I levered myself reluctantly to my feet, feeling and looking like a creaky old grandfather. I ate the remaining apple, cheese, and bread, imagining it would help wake me up. It contributed nothing to this goal. Then, I thought to use one of the Old Man's practices to warm my sore muscles, recalling how much it had heated my body against the night chill in Brittany. It was a practice called the "Fire of the Earth."

The Old Man told me that the Earth was not flat, as it seemed to our senses, but an immense globe, round as an apple. Furthermore, it was not built solely of dirt and solid rock, but had a molten core of liquid fire upon which the cooler, solid land and ocean floors floated. I thought his notion fanciful and outlandish; how could solid rock float upon molten fire? But he insisted that the ancient seers had spoken this as a truth. Then, I recalled the history of the ancient city of Pompeii. It had been destroyed when Mount Vesuvius, upon whose slopes it was built, erupted in flames, pouring down molten rock that burned and buried everything in its path. Perhaps the Druid was not speaking complete rubbish, although I still thought he stretched the point too far.

The Old Man insisted further that the earth floated on this molten liquid rock, burning deep inside it, even under the oceans. This meant that, just as our bones mirrored the rock, the molten fire deep within Earth could resonate and amplify the fire within our own bodies.

His notion seemed to me ridiculous. By logic alone, it is evident that if one covered a fire with earth or water, the fire would be put out! Much as we smother a campfire. The rocky earth and water he claimed floated on this liquid fire would do the same. Nonetheless, I withheld proclaiming this obvious truth aloud to avoid the Old Man's ire.

The Druid ignored my stubborn expression and added that all this was mirrored in our bodies: the fire of red marrow surrounded and contained by the rock of cooler, denser bone—our body's fire within the rock coating made for our qualities of vitality within solidity. Likewise, the molten, fiery core, covered by the Earth's rock, is what makes our world's vital energy and solidity possible. He added that our blood was the counterpart of lava, flowing within us like lava from a volcano, carrying the fire of vitality. And just as molten lava does, our blood forms clots and scabs as it cools when exposed to air, much like molten lava cools into solid rock.

It all seemed fanciful, but I did the practices as he prescribed. Eventually, I found these parallels precisely as he said, despite their seeming illogic. This took me longer than the bones because dispelling my stubborn disbelief took extra time.

I followed these familiar steps to utilize this natural heat source to soothe my overtaxed muscles, connecting my achy bones with the rock deep within the Earth. Stretching my attention further to Mother's fiery core, I held the connection until the marrow of my bones matched it. After a time, I became warm enough to sweat, even in the cold morning air. My body was visibly steaming in the cool air, and I felt energized. I began to stretch and move about with increasing force as my muscle aches gradually eased with the warmth. I saddled my horse, got back on the road, and worked on adjusting to the cycle of daylight once again.

Although I was warmer and ready now, my horse was not. I gave us a gradual start to our ride, letting him figure it out on his own. When he found his usual morning enthusiasm, I gave him his head and let him run as he wished. After a while, he settled into a comfortable travel pace.

We proceeded along the road at an easy walk, and once again, I reflected on the Old Man's teachings. The intense pressure he exerted on me before the Moon traveling ritual, combined with my decision to depart after my confrontation with the Old Man, left me with minimal time to sort everything out. The Moon's teachings had preoccupied me, but he'd taught me so many other things, and I'd not sorted through them.

The Old Man had always been relentless in his pressure to complete the practices he taught and for me to move on quickly to the next step. He was adhering to a traditional sequence prescribed by the sages of his lineage. He would not skip any steps, even if they were already familiar to me, and he pressed me to speed through each step, even when I'd just mastered it.

At that point, I still attributed his inflexibility to his Druidic tradition, as Édouard had told me that the old ways were often harsh and demanding. Much later, I received a dream visitation from the High Priestess of his lineage, who informed me that the Old Man's harshness and disdain reflected his failings and were not a reflection of the tradition itself.

I was glad to sort out the lineage itself from what I was coming to understand as the Old Man's profoundly distorted teaching method. As I reflect now, it was clear that the mentor's generous help was essential in any esoteric study. No apprentice, no matter how talented, could reach these higher dimensions without being augmented by their teacher's power. But the Old Man had been miserly in affording me such help, only doing so when he felt forced to. Only towards the end of my time with him did the High Priestess and the Moon Mother herself step in to circumvent his improper goals and generously provide me the augmentation the Old Man would not.

As usual, no sooner had I gained facility with resonating my bones with the earth and then resonating the marrow with the earth's molten rock than the Old Man pressed on. He announced that the next step in his tradition's teachings from the natural world concerned a new and challenging aspect of similars.

The Old Man noted that our flesh, other than that of bone, is part of a principle that all living things share.

"Every living thing needs," he asserted.

At first, this seemed little more than a foolish contrivance, but the Old Man challenged me to name a living thing that did not need. Humans? Animals? Insects? These were obvious even to me. All needed... food, water, their like kind to mate, and so on. Plants? They need sunlight, soil, and, of course, water, as well as bees to carry pollen. What of the mold that stained the stable walls and fermented our cheese? Of course. One needs wetness, as the other needs milk. The black mold stains diminished in the dry weather, and the cheese needed milk to ferment.

Of course, I was intentionally being contrary by arguing and looking for exceptions. It was a way to maintain my self-respect in the face of the Old Man's harshness. Eventually, he would be baited no more by my exhaustive search for exceptions and told me to "just fucking do what I say." I smiled secretly at having pushed him to his edge.

He took me to the trees surrounding the sacred hill and had me stand. As before, he instructed me to start with my bones and have them resonate naturally with the rocks. After this, I added bone marrow, along with its resonance, to the deeper molten rock.

Then, he said to put all my attention on the rest of my flesh, and while holding the sensation of my flesh firmly in mind, sense its likeness to every living thing I could apprehend. One at a time, first the grass, then the bushes, followed by the leafing trees, I was to find what my flesh shared. I saw little of note, though I had moments when I sensed that each had its energy. The Old Man dismissed this and pushed on to more forms of life.

What of the hopping night bugs and the unnamed animals rustling through the brush? Again, he had me ask, "What did our flesh share in resonance?" And what about the beings of the air? What did my flesh share with that of the ghostly owls and acrobatic bats? At some point, he even demanded that I put my nose to the loamy soil of the forest and breathe it in.

"Smell the life in it, boy! You smell the aroma of living beings. Their flesh is not less than yours, which shares the same force of need as yours. It's everywhere… feel it!" He kept me at it, sensing and searching, discovering the need in each and never letting me settle on any living thing in particular, insisting that all shared it. On and on. I was not done, he said, until I could sense the flesh of life in its primal need, in me and everywhere it was located around me.

The practice was both tedious and trivial to me. Tedious in its exhaustive cataloging of living things, one after another, and trivial in that I could neither sense nor imagine the result to have anything like the power of the earth's rocks and molten core, immense forces to be sure. Yet, over many nights, something began to form that belied my initial expectations.

Reluctantly, I began to understand what the Old Man was driving at. The likeness of our flesh to everything living did not mean that the literal substance was identical, nor did it refer to a similarity of shape or design. It was not that all living things had some form of blood or appetite, or that living substances rotted when that indefinable force of life left. My lists of characteristics could never make sense of the Old Man's assertion that "All things need." But what was similar was a force of hunger that only living flesh had, that could be known even if not enumerated.

Slowly, as I had learned before, resonating with the rocks and fire of the earth, my flesh found harmony with the chaotic mass of living things around me. It didn't matter whether this was at night on the hilltop or hidden away from daylight in the dark, quiet of a seemingly isolated cave. Once I grasped it, I could sense it everywhere. In truth, every living thing displayed this force, driving its existence and fueling hunger and desire, as collectively powerful as that of rocks or fire.

In the silent dark, I realized there was nothing "dead" in "the dead of night." All living things are driven to explore and expand into their world, through every crack and crevice—whether mountain, cave, forest, desert, or ocean—all propelled by what he calls "need." The rocks and molten core of the Earth are enormous forces, true, but they simply exist. They are not going anywhere or doing anything. But this need in living things, which some mystics and alchemists refer to as Motive Force, drives them to go everywhere it can, urging all life to move and grow.

The world grew more alive as my flesh resonated more deeply with it. Before understanding this force, I would complain that the Old Man was depriving me of life by keeping me in this cold, dark cave. Now, I had to admit that he had given me access to the core of life, and its power was all around me. How could I be cut off from this great, hungry, vibrating, and flourishing need that my flesh shared with everything alive, shared with life itself? It was always there, even in my cave. Perhaps there, especially in its quiet, as I only needed to settle my bones on the rocky floor and feel my flesh's need to realize that, even here through the rock walls and earth of the surrounding hill, the hungry grasses and living woods beat in sync with the need within me.

I no longer felt isolated. It required no light to recognize the needs of the silent mice that rummaged through my piled clothing, seeking crumbs caught in the *seams or the powdery crust of a soup stain to lick. Their hopeful foraging shared the same force that my flesh did. The centipedes scurrying along the floor and up the dark cave walls were no less driven by the needful fabric of living things than I was, even if their hunger was more singular. Even the low rocky ceiling, against which I often banged my head, glowed with a crust of living, hungry organisms. Mold or lichens, I did not know, but I understood my flesh recognized their living nature and that constant soft impulse of need.*

And while "need" was probably the most common term, it wasn't the word that mattered to the Old Man or to me. I understood that this was a powerful, secret, even sacred force. A force that did not originate from any individual hunger or the appetites of specific beings.

It was something primal, embedded in the act of creation itself, that gave life its original impetus, an invisible foundation upon which the threads of life were woven. It vibrated in the air so intensely that I was astounded it hadn't been obvious until now. The ancient Druids understood this as a power source, a sea of energy to be harnessed. The Old Man's branch of the tradition saw it even more profoundly. They recognized that it was of the Divine, driven by the need of the One that compelled the impulse to create, that it was Divine creativity itself, constantly expanding throughout creation. They knew it as a glimpse into God's mind and the fabric of the Divine.

My horse shook the reins and snorted to get my attention, and I realized that the sun was high overhead. I broke from my preoccupied review enough to notice the smell of water in the air.

"Good lad," I said as I patted him on the withers to thank him for letting me know he was thirsty.

As we rounded a bend in the road, I could see and hear a shallow stream flowing across the road ahead. When we reached it, I let my horse take a long drink and dismounted to do the same.

A splash of cold water on my face helped refresh me from the dust of the road and the increasing heat of the day, but I was still tired. It was time to find shade from the noonday sun and give both my horse and myself a rest.

There was a clearing nearby, so I led my horse over and tied his reins to a sapling so he could reach fresh grass on the bank. It felt right to practice what he had shown me, which was related to the lessons I had been contemplating all morning before taking a nap.

Like all such practices, the traditions of the Old Man held that they were best performed outdoors, barefoot. The Old Man and the Druids of his lineage avoided human-made buildings and other enclosures in their worship. This was not because they cannot sense the immense forces of nature within such structures, as some believe; nothing can make them unreachable because they are... immense! However, while one can still feel the rocks and molten core standing in a building, the Druids considered human-made structures to be akin to sacrilege: they add nothing, and their form distracts from the understanding that Nature's temple is everywhere. Without such distractions, I always found it easiest to connect outdoors in natural surroundings.

Standing barefoot in the clearing, I followed the expected sequence. First, I connected my bones to the earth's bones and their resonance. Then, I linked the molten rock and its resonance with my blood and marrow. Finally, I reached out to the shared resonance of my flesh with that of all living things in their need. Everything I could sense was included: the grass, the wood of the trees around me, the herbaceous plants rustling in the breeze, the animal body of my horse, and all the small creatures stirring in the woods and fields.

While my bones, relatives of the rocks, made me part of the Mother's unimaginable depth and vastness, my fleshly kinship and likeness to living beings spread my awareness horizontally. In this thin coating upon the earth of various living flesh, I felt as if I were part of some vast, tissue-thin wing spread over the planet and scintillating in the sun. I gradually felt completely merged into this dimension of Nature's living and ceaseless movement. Its power lay in reflecting the Creative force and its origin in the Divine will. Let there be life, indeed.

When I first learned this practice, I worried it would make my already highly sensitive nature unbearable. I feared being overwhelmed by the chaotic, swirling noise of life when opening myself to the multitude of fluttering, buzzing, breathing, and moving things. But I didn't need to worry. The outcome was entirely different. Instead of becoming the noisy, chaotic whirl of countless particles I anticipated, Nature's body appeared as a fabric woven upon the earth's surface through time and space, made from all of life's stories.

Each creature's life was not a particle but a thread, weaving a story—big or small—through the cloth. Many similar threads, such as groups or species moving in harmony, would gather together, forming scenes like those woven by medieval maidens in their wall hangings. These collective stories expressed something within the skein of life, appearing and fading as each story reached its natural end, only for new threads to fill the space. My flesh, my life, was just another thread woven into Nature's fabric, along with everything about me—animal, vegetable, insect, or seed. To be born was to join in Mother's project of adornment, the rippling, elegant movement of cloth weaving itself.

I opened my eyes and returned to standing in the clearing before lying in a leaf pile to nap.

I slept for a while and eventually woke up. I stretched, not realizing until later that the sunlight no longer felt overwhelming. Eventually, I untied my horse and walked back to the creek, where we both took a long drink before resuming our journey. I let him walk to loosen up before settling into a steady trot. I'd had enough recollecting and reviewing for the day, so it was time to focus on riding to cover more miles in the afternoon.

I had been traveling for several days, avoiding villages and towns as much as possible because my faculties were still too delicate to handle the raucous bustle of human activity. By sticking to the back roads, I was fortunate enough to meet farmers and peasants working the fields, who were willing to trade coins for sausage, bread, and other food. I discovered some real treasures, like a dripping piece of honeycomb at one point and a slice of freshly baked fruit pie at another. I had to willfully restrain myself from devouring these treats all at once, as it had been months since I had eaten anything so sweet, and I deeply longed for the pleasures of Mathilde's kitchen.

Occasionally, I would encounter rougher characters than the generally gruff but usually friendly farmers. One grizzled, unkempt man watched me from his perch atop a stile as I rode past. He looked no stranger to violence, with scars on his face from blade work and a crooked nose that had been broken more than once. Shoeless and dressed in tattered clothing, he carried a few possessions in a small bundle tied to a stick, ready at his side. He observed me watchfully, taking in the riches of my horse and saddlebags to decide if I would be easy prey. I looked back at him intently to show I wouldn't back down from a challenge.

I watched him quickly assess the risk of challenging me, then drop his eyes and look away, his slumping posture signaling submission. Although I was relieved to avoid confrontation, I was surprised to be seen as someone to fear. What was it that he had so easily noticed, which made him not want to draw my attention? On my trip to Brittany, I usually had to show the steel of my knives to signal that I wouldn't be an easy target. What is different about me now that this thug sees me as a predator instead of prey?

I hadn't seen my reflection during the months I'd been with the Old Man, and I decided to see how I looked now. An opportunity arose soon after when the road crossed a clear stream, and the backwaters deepened into a peaceful pool. I noticed that the water there seemed still enough to reflect the sky and trees, so I led my horse a little downstream to it. I directed my horse toward the banks, dismounted, and knelt by the water to look at myself, holding the reins loosely.

There, staring back from the mirrored surface of the pool, was no boy but a man. My face had filled out and become firm with muscle. My expression had a new hardness, with a set jaw and steel in my eyes, neither of which had been there before I set out for Brittany. My 'beard,' which had been so sparse that I only titled it so from wishfulness, had also filled in.

While with the Old Man, my clothing had become tighter; I thought it was due to the normal cycle of outgrowing familiar clothes over the years. I hadn't realized until now that what had strained my blouse was the muscle I'd developed.

The man reflected in the water appeared tough and prepared, and indeed, he did not seem like a pushover. He seemed capable of taking action to defend his resolve if necessary—no wonder the ruffian had tried to avoid any confrontation.

My horse lapped at the water, creating ripples that disturbed the image and freed me from Narcissus's spell. As I got to my feet and saddled up, I realized I was only beginning to understand the changes brought on during my time in Brittany.

I had ridden the first half of the journey at a modest pace, needing recovery and review more than speed. It took about ten or so days to fully become a creature of day again and readily sleep at night, and another two days to reach the halfway mark by distance. Less sensitive and more replenished, I had less need to avoid the chaos of towns, and I decided to stay at an Inn when one presented itself, as my horse and I both needed a full day of rest. I was in great need of a bath, a home-cooked meal, and provisions for the road.

I found an inn at a crossroads and decided to stay two nights, enjoying the luxury it offered. I headed back to the road feeling refreshed and ready to move at a more efficient pace. I hoped to reach home in eight to ten days, weather permitting.

My faster pace required more attention, but I no longer felt as occupied with recollecting and sorting what I had learned. I still needed to review a few things from the higher teachings to complete his tradition's teaching of similars.

In his tradition, power from nature is gained through the principle of similarity. We are a product of the natural world and its forces; so much of our nature comes from them.

According to this principle, the main practices involve bringing the resonance of these larger natural forces to empower what is within us that is similar to them, whether elements of our body or aspects of our spirit.

The progression of his teachings had taken me from feeling my bones resonate with the rocks, or "Bones of the Earth," as the Old Man called them, to my bones and blood resonating with the earth's molten, fiery core. The next step was to understand the similarity of our flesh with all other living beings, which he said was reflected in the shared quality of motive force, that of need.

Another aspect of this teaching of similars required deeper reflection and would occupy me for the remaining half of my journey home: the quality of spirit.

The Old Man had been simultaneously teaching practices related to the Moon, as well as those of the earth, fire, and flesh, from the Druidic tradition. The mother Moon was part of my nightly practice, but the time devoted to this usually varied with the proximity of the full moon throughout her cycle. In between, I practiced Druidic work to become more skilled at merging my flesh with the body of nature and to develop another way to gather power untethered to the moon. The Old Man also used these exercises as preparation for the "higher practices" involving the moon and other mysteries, so he had me do them before anything else.

One night, as I performed Druidic practices on the hilltop, the Old Man watched me from his perch on a stone. I had reached a deep connection to nature's essence when he began to question me from his spot. By now, I was used to how he would unsettle me by stirring my mind, especially when I was in deep meditation. I ignored him for a while until one of his questions finally caught my attention.

"So, boy, riddle me this. You understood that our bones are most similar to the rocks and dirt of the earth and therefore connect us to her body."

I opened my eyes and saw that he was looking at me for a response. He was being pedantic to annoy me, since he thought it mimicked Édouard's educated methods. It was too ludicrous to comment on, so I stayed silent and nodded.

"And you know that our flesh is most similar to all living things, through the likeness of need, and this connects us to the force and power of the whole alive world."

I nodded again at his querying look. It was easier to play the part of acolyte to his high priest than to speak unasked, which he'd no doubt pick apart just for sport.

"So, what is our spirit similar to, boy? And what does our spirit connect us with, huh?"

Our spirit? Did he mean the élan vital, the animating force of living things? I knew this was incorrect, but I tendered it as an answer, partly to buy myself some time, because he expected wrong answers from me, and partly to annoy him.

"Don't be an ass!" He relished this almost obligatory dismissal as the expected confirmation of my insufficiency.

"Such merely animates flesh and bone. It is not the same as our spirit, our essence, don't you see? If what is most similar to our spirit is the animating force of life, then when the body dies and the élan vital disperses, our spirit would also disperse!

"The fire in the hearth can heat the soup in the pot, nothing more; it does not make the nourishment in the broth. Otherwise, we would eat fire, not soup! Vital force is only what animates flesh; it cannot be the spirit that inhabits it. What is your spirit? Think!"

The Moon Mother glimmered with her first light as she edged above the horizon. As I had become so sensitized to her, her shine upon me felt like a physical pressure, as definite as a heavy wool blanket would be. In that instant, I grasped what our spirit most resembled—Light.

Well, not literal light. I had come to know her through the increase, peak, and ebb of her moonlight, and I had come to use "Light" as a shorthand for something that I had come to know in these cycles of moonlight but was much more than that. I knew from Édouard's astrolabe that her literal light was reflected sunlight, but her "light" was another thing.

What did I perceive in the Moon Mother's light as the innate force of her spirit? It was something I had not expressed before. Using "light" as a shorthand, the literal and the metaphorical became intertwined. Her spirit possessed qualities similar to those of actual light—her presence was radiant, and when she focused her mind on me, I sensed a physical power, much like sunlight warming whatever it touches.

But the moon's cool light warmed nothing, yet it carried something as palpable to me as the warmth of sunlight, which my initiation had revealed. The Old Man was properly pushing me to reach beyond the obvious and claim what I had experienced, though not yet fully articulated.

I grasped it like turning a corner to see something anew. Her light carried her force of mind, which I call her Intelligence. Her immense and knowing mind, which I experienced as <u>conveyed</u> through her light, had come to penetrate my being.

Having come in innocence and offered myself unhesitatingly to her service on that first night on the hilltop, she had turned her gaze and the immensity of her conscious intent to me. Her literal light had shone upon me as on everyone, but until that moment, it was not the force of her mind. It still boggled me that she responded to my tiny voice and blessed my minuscule and seeking heart. Or that she deigned to notice me at all. Yet, mysteriously, she chose to radiate her intelligence to me. The power she seemed to grant me was that of her Intelligence, but my small mind had grasped it only through the symbol of her literal light.

I was unsure how long I had been thinking, but the Old Man seemed uncharacteristically patient as he waited for my answer, letting this work through me. I turned from the moon's shining presence to look at his shadowed face.

"So, what is our spirit most like? Our spirit is most similar to this greater Intelligence, and like the moon's light, our spirit is but a tiny reflection of the greater light of Intelligence we are from. And this Intelligence or consciousness has its distinct nature, whether embodied and animated by a life force or not," I answered.

"Our spirit is most like light," I continued, "especially Her light," gesturing to the rising moon. "Like Her light, our spirit acts on commands and is felt as a force, but is not the force itself."

The Old Man grunted ambiguously. Dismissal or acknowledgment? It wasn't clear to me. He responded as if he found my answer a bit too ready at hand or too sophisticated for his liking.

"Like her light, eh?" He continued, "Some say her moonlight is not her own but merely a reflection of the Sun's light. What do you say to that, lad? Do you mean our Lady is but a bauble, a mirror shining the essence of another? If she makes no light, is she empty?"

As usual, he was merely baiting me for a reaction, so I paid it no mind and kept to my point. "No more nor less a reflection than you or I, Old Man," I countered. I looked up at the magnificent presence of the Moon as I spoke further. "I would never commit the sacrilege of calling the immense gift given to her by the Creator a mere bauble, but suit yourself, Old Man. Everything with spirit is but reflected light, the sparkle of the primal Intelligence of the Nameless One, so my Maestro has said."

I intentionally added the part about Édouard to goad him. I hoped mentioning my Maestro would rankle, as the Old Man wanted my loyalty for himself and often undermined the value of my benefactor's teachings. His efforts only hardened my resolve to resist his manipulations. He seemed as tired of that game as I was this time and offered no reply.

"At any rate," I continued, "I was intending to answer your question, not argue theology." This, at least, he snorted at. "Our spirit is the intelligence that *directs our animated flesh, not the force that animates it. Our spirit, and the Mother's, is not like light; it is better described as Radiance, something intrinsic to the mind and consciousness that radiates from all sentience. Her literal light shines on all, but her spirit must be turned to us to feel its radiant presence. Only then is it more than mere light. Only then do I apprehend her consciousness, will, and unfathomable spirit."*

Even with his face invisible to me, I could sense that this rendition had brought him up short as if he wasn't expecting me to grasp the answer truly. He paused for some moments before responding. When he did, he was uncharacteristically mild in his rejoinder. I had not expected that, and it made me feel off balance, as if I had been leaning against a wall that suddenly was not there.

"Radiance, eh? Not a bad word, as words go. Better than 'light,' which is easy to mistake for power or vital force and the like, and that leads down a false path if you were to interpret the teachings that way," the Old Man mused as he looked at the rising moon.

He looked directly at me for some moments in silence. His tone shifted back to the familiar, preemptory, as he gave me his orders.

"You will spend the rest of this night learning the difference. This night, you will not call on her first. Instead, as I have taught you, you will join your bones to the rocks and flesh to living Nature. Then, you are to discern Her, ahem, 'radiance,' and compare it to your spirit, your... radiance, such as it is."

"When this is clear, then and only then, you will perform your supplication to her, and when she turns her attention upon you, ask her to show you your spirit. We will see if her Intelligence, as you have called it, reveals if there is anything like intelligence in you."

He turned and left me to it, walking silently down the path to the hut and cave on the hill.

Bathed in her light on the hilltop, I was already acutely aware of how her shining light carried on it her vast and overwhelming intelligence. At the same time, it was underlined that moonlight was not the same as her intelligence, her extraordinary mind. Indeed, her phase and the amount of light she shone amplified the energy available for magical practice; the greater the light of her phase, the greater the energy one could gather. But I could see now that my connection to her Intelligence did not intrinsically require moonlight. The differences that varied over her phases were something I clearly did not yet understand. Still, her radiant being could grant something to mine by the Law of Similars and by the fact that my small intelligence has been increasingly similar to Hers.

Heartened, I performed the steps in the exact sequence the Old Man had ordered. Having already discerned the constant of her radiant intelligence, it was of another order when she responded to my supplications and turned this intelligence intently on me. It was like the difference between seeing the light of a bonfire and being abruptly blasted with the furnace of its light and heat when the wind shifts towards you.

She did, indeed, reveal my radiant spirit to me. It is no surprise that mine felt like the tiniest spark in comparison to hers. Without words, it was conveyed somehow that my life's task, from her view, was to grow my radiant mind until it shone to its fullest. Other things were also communicated that night that were impossible to put into words.

I reflected deeply on these lessons during one of my last days of travel, recognizing the importance of fully claiming the insight and knowledge I had been granted. It was the first time since I'd left Brittany that I truly appreciated what the Old Man had taught me, no matter his motives. He was my teacher and had given his gathered power to bring me to initiation. He had granted me access to a lineage of knowledge whose teachings held great light —the radiance of so many who had gone before me —and I could feel that they all walked with me now and guided me. In some small way, I was a vessel that carried the light of this lineage, though its priesthood would pass from the earth when the Old Man passed on.

I made camp just below a hilltop from which I knew there would be an open view of the moon that night. I hoped to reach the Chateau by the end of the following day and wished to be fully prepared so that the familiar habits of home would not pull me off myself, or at least the self I'd developed in the time away.

Calling on the ancients of the lineage I'd joined who had practiced their devotions back through the shadows of time, I opened myself to the rising sliver of the new waxing moon. I offered my gratitude and love for all she had given me and thanked her for the strength she had instilled in me. In answer, she turned her gaze toward me, flooding me with her radiant Intelligence. My spirit was effortlessly pulled from my body to be held within her mind like a drowning man is pulled from entangling seaweed. Everything rooted in my animal nature remained behind: all the churning, scheming, and noisy needs I shared with all alive on the earth seemed to shed, including my thoughts. It became apparent that human thinking was an outcome of this force of need. Among all living things, we had become specialists in talking to ourselves to pursue our needs, and we had confused our internal dialogue with our essence. Only what was intrinsic, my radiant spirit remained, and minuscule though it was compared to Hers, she blessed my radiance by holding me, for an eternal moment, in the light of her immense mind.

I basked in her spirit, feeling bright and clear under her aegis, knowing this was being given to sustain me through the many challenges ahead. Many things occurred that remain beyond any words. Then, all at once, I was dismissed, released from my enraptured connection to her, and washed back to my body as if sent tumbling down through the rapids of a great river.

I suddenly found myself back in my physical form. I had to work hard to stabilize myself by settling my bones into the earth and drawing on the ever-vital connection of my living flesh to the living world. I had received her blessing and knew she had equipped me to face whatever was required.

Chapter II:
Arriving Home

Eventually, I rode over the familiar hill and looked down into the valley, the winding river bordering the Chateau, and the far hills on the other side. The setting sun over those hills broke through the clouds, streaming gold-cast light over the autumn trees and the Chateau set on the rise in front of the river. There was a sense of the land beginning to turn inwards as the Fall season proceeded. The russets and golds of the leaves still clung to the trees. I chivvied my tired horse along, impatient to reach the courtyard gate before it became dark. Turning into the old familiar lane, the harvested fields greying in the dusky light, tears welled in my eyes as all the disciplined focus and the severe requirements set upon me by the Old Man began to lift from me. Arriving, I could finally let all my pent-up homesickness rise within me.

To my dismay, the gate was untended. I dismounted and walked my horse to the stable, where I had to rouse the boy assigned there from his nap.

"Why so quiet, Jon?" I queried.

He didn't quite flinch at my question, but I could see a tenor of fear in his eyes.

He only shook his head, silent as he led my horse to its stable and began to remove the bridle.

"You'll see," he ventured, and busied himself with the saddle and hanging up the tack. "Best to let the older fellows catch you up."

I was preoccupied with my relief at being back and my excitement to see my fellows, so I did not press him further. He helped me feed and rub my horse down, first things first, as they say. I pressed my forehead into my horse's neck as he munched some oats, thanking him for his steadfastness on my journey. Assured he was cared for, I took up a lantern and walked into the courtyard to ring in my return.

Édouard had declared a "tradition" before anyone left for apprentice time. Each boy was to proclaim his return by ringing a large bronze bell hung on a post in the courtyard. The bell had been rung to call us in from the field or to alert us to emergencies. Now, a special sequence had been assigned to announce returns.

Taking a deep breath, I grasped the short rope that hung from the clapper and remembered the sequence.

Clang, clang, clang-a-clang!

I paused to take another breath and let the echoes fade before striking the note again.

Clang, clang, clang-a-clang!

And then a third time, as we had been told.

Clang, clang, clang-a-clang!

Even before the last run was completed, there was a commotion of opening and closing doors and running footsteps echoing off the house's stone. Then a shutter from a window overlooking the courtyard banged open. An outstretched head, the face indiscernible in the dark, peered out.

"Is that...?" A boy's voice exclaimed loudly.

The head thrust itself further out the window to peer down at me. "Étienne? Is that you?"

"Aye," I yelled. "Who's that?"

My request for identification was ignored. I only heard a voice exclaiming, "Thank God," and the shutters were banged closed as the figure retreated. By this time, a small crowd had assembled, and my fellows were leaping upon me to embrace or to slap my back. A few adult household members had arrived but were standing back. My friends, however, were wholeheartedly enthusiastic in their greetings. I glowed back, grinning with pleasure. Still, the faces of the householders, such as Mathilde, the kitchen maids, and the gardener, while pleased to see me, betrayed the strain of worry in their eyes.

Then someone, perhaps the figure from the window, raced out of the dark and flung themselves at me, almost knocking me off my feet. Only being wedged in by the press of hugging bodies saved me from a fall. Well, now I knew who it was.

"Louis! Oof! Get off me, you lunk!" I could not unwrap his grasping hands, but at least I was no longer falling, as a tree trunk braced me from behind. Who was that big?

"Yes, thank you, Petan," I muttered, "I missed you too. Mon Dieu, lad! You have gotten even bigger!"

Hard-muscled shoulders absorbed my hearty slap. "You're like an ox! What is Mathilde feeding you?" Petan laughed with pride and pleasure at my acknowledgment.

They pushed and shoved me from one boy to another, each loudly peppering me with insistent questions.

"Why are you back so soon, Étienne? "We thought you'd be months more!" "You've grown too, Étienne." "What was it like, Étienne?"

And then I heard in the dark the unmistakable, eager voice of Tonton. "Where is your saddlebag? I will carry it for you, Étienne. I won't steal anything either!"

It was all heartwarming and familiar in its commotion of home, but I still detected a note of strain behind their voices. I looked around their heads as I felt the homecoming greetings were incomplete.

"So, where are Édouard and Francois?" I called out.

At this, it all abruptly ground to a halt. It was like throwing sand in a clockwork. Embracing hands seemed to hesitate, and then they withdrew, and their voices quieted. They all looked to Mathilde to answer me, who stepped forward and took hold of my upper arm with her broad and rough hands. I knew those beloved, strong hands well from the many times she had comforted me as a child, but now it was clear that she needed comfort and strength from me.

"He's been called away for a bit, Étienne, and Francois with him," she added, letting out a breath.

Reassured by my solidity under her hands, she pulled me abruptly into her embrace. I wrapped her in my arms, resting my cheek on her head. She seemed much smaller than I remembered.

"It is so *very good* to see you, Étienne," she sighed. "We've all missed you. We've needed you." Her face was buried in my shoulder, underlining that I had grown noticeably taller during my months away. Buried as her face was in my clothes, her last comment seemed to be intended for my ear only.

I eventually released my fervent hug and pulled her away to see her face. Tears ran down her plump cheeks as she looked back at me.

"Mathilde, something is wrong? What has happened? Tell me."

She looked away briefly, then unwound further from her embrace of me and pushed herself back. She gathered herself and spoke in that authoritative voice I remembered so well.

"Where are our manners? What are you all doing standing here in the dark?" She shooed everyone with her hands as a farmer herded his ducks to the pond. "Go on with you! Étienne has been traveling. He is hungry and in need of rest!"

She turned, and I was compelled to go with her as she hooked my arm with hers and gripped my bicep firmly in her hand. We headed towards her kitchen, where she rattled off orders right and left to staff and boys alike. So forceful was her intent that I'm sure she would drag me behind her had I resisted. I knew her well, though, and it was apparent that bigger concerns took her attention.

"Joseph, bring the ewer so he can wash the road off his hands and face. Irma," she said, gesturing to a shy kitchen maid peaking her head around the corner, "bring him a cloth to dry his hands so he may break bread."

"Louis, Bora, and Antoine," she commanded. "You will attend Étienne at table. The rest of you go about your business, now. When he has supped and rested, there'll be time to hear about his adventures."

Matilde had selected the most senior boys present to bring me up to date. There was expectable grumbling from those dismissed, but Matilde ignored them and guided me out of the chill night air into the warmth of her kitchen.

As I sat at the bench with a bowl and bread, Louis, Bora, and Antoine sat upon the warm stones before the hearth, hugging their knees. When my hunger was sated, they began to unwind their tale, others filling in the details should the current teller leave something out.

The long and short of it, then. Édouard and Francois had been called away some weeks ago. They left quickly, excited that a prospect for success in something long desired seemed to be coming together. Little was said other than there was an opportunity to clear "a nest of snakes," and that they would be traveling at least a week and would likely be incommunicado for a time. Protocols that had been in place to run the Chateau and the estate were put into effect.

Some weeks after they had been called away, a messenger arrived in haste under the Maestro's seal. Things had grown considerably more complicated, Édouard wrote, and it would take more time to see the task through to its conclusion. The same messenger also carried a missive from the Maestro for the Abbess, resulting in her and the Major joining the messenger for the return to join Édouard and Francois and render their assistance.

The Maestro's hurried scrawl and words in his message conveyed an unspoken air of anxiety, leaving the whole household distracted and worried, their attention drawn to mysterious events far from home. As the saying goes, the fox can raid the henhouse now that the guard dogs are lured away.

There was a boy among us named Eustache. He was not an orphan but had been fostered at the chateau. His fostering provided the unique tutelage that only the Chateau could offer, along with the added benefit of security. Eustace's father, who played a high-stakes game against certain enemies of the Order, had drawn his enemy's wrath for his efforts. Eustace had been secretly removed from his home and taken to Édouard for protection to prevent him from being a target for reprisal.

Shortly after the Abbess was lured away to assist Édouard and Francois, Eustace was kidnapped, and in broad daylight. A group of uniformed men, badges identifying them as serving a specific Baron clear upon their breast, swept through the grounds of the Chateau, separating Eustache from his fellows like a lamb from the flock. Only a field man dared to fend them off with his wooden rake, his weapon, but they rode him down and knocked him into a ditch. Eustache was carried off screaming in rage while the men laughed, leaving the rest of the boys in the dust from their horses.

As I listened to this account, some things stood out clearly. One was that the brash daytime assault signaled that they knew those remaining at the Chateau were powerless to stop them. The second was that they were the Baron's men, and not the particular villains with which Eustace's father had been at odds, indicating that the kidnapping was directed at Édouard, and that Eustace was simply the opportunity.

Mathilde finally spoke up at this, her voice quivering with strain and fear. "Twas only then that we understood the enormous efforts that lured the Maestro away. They knew much about our strengths and weaknesses, and took advantage of both to bring about this ploy."

The boys pooled their psychic and practical skills to gather intelligence with thoughts of a rescue. Our master thief, Tonton, and some of his "apprentices," as he called them, attempted to scout out a possible entry into the Baron's stronghold. They had found the approaches well-guarded. The only unguarded door was stout, locked, and barred from the inside, requiring assistance from the inside to gain access.

Even if they had gained entry, locating Eustace in such a large castle was challenging. Some of the boys, who could identify people through psychic means, discovered that a kind of magical protection prevented their efforts. A mental fog surrounded the keep, and no one could sense their friend's trace, despite knowing his psychic signature well. Their spying revealed clear visual proof that he was held there as Eustace's captors paraded him about the top of the parapet daily under guard, as if to dangle their prize as a challenge to Édouard.

Bora affirmed their conclusions. "It is clear," he said," that all had been arranged as a direct challenge to the Maestro and the Order. No one else has the skill and knowledge to surmount all these barriers. To try with regular military means would risk them killing Eustace outright."

As I listened to their story, I was utterly dismayed by what I heard. I'd thought to be returning to my familiar and comforting home after my testing with the Old Man, and I sorely wanted the counsel of Édouard and Francois about my decision to leave Brittany. Now, I'd arrived to find the Chateau a place of worry, uncertainty, and chaos, and without the expected parental figures. I was being called to put aside my doubts and concerns and serve my family. It is said that one can't return home again, but I think it is more accurate to say that one cannot return to *childhood*. My memories of home had indeed helped me weather the many difficulties of my trials with the Old Man. Now it seemed my turn to serve my home in like kind.

Lost in my thoughts for a moment, I realized that Bora, Louis, and Antoine had all fallen silent. The usual clatter of the kitchen around us had similarly gone quiet. The maids, who had pretended that they had not been listening, were wringing their aprons from anxiety. It came to me that they were all looking expectantly at me for a response to their tale. It was the moment I first understood what it meant to be called to lead, regardless of whether or not I believed I was capable. It was a weighty one. It became clear that I couldn't respond as a fellow to another boy, because my words could either break or make their hearts and hopes. Dare I don the mantle being proffered to me? Dare I not?

I pondered deeply, allowing the silence to linger as much as possible before replying.

"I do not know what course of action remains to us," I said, "short of the Maestro's return." I could see disappointment creeping into the faces around me.

"But…" I continued, hearing Mathilde's breath catch with hope. "But," I repeated, "I will pray and think it through deeply before seeking my rest."

I took a deep breath to give myself a moment to see what else to say, as it was clear they'd not heard enough quite yet.

I looked through the unshuttered window at the night sky, realizing that there were more than the four at the table and the anxious kitchen maids. All the boys Matilde had dismissed earlier to their duties gathered outside and listened. They huddled together for warmth in the evening's chill, their collective breath steaming into the night air.

It was time for me to step up. With far more confidence than I felt, I spoke with all the sound of authority I could muster.

"I have not spent these long months past in a cave to learn nothing. I shall bring all the magic I have acquired, and everything else the gods will provide to search out a way through for us."

I stiffened my back and spoke even louder than before, making sure my audience could hear me.

"And in the morning," I declared. "We shall convene a Council of War and lay our plans to rescue Eustace!"

The boys outside, who had been pretending to be silent with little success, I might add, broke into an unrestrained "Hurrah!" They crowded through the kitchen door in a rush to express their enthusiasm. Bora, Louis, and Antoine surged to their feet and beat them to me, embracing me with great relief.

Matilde looked on, trying to conceal her pride in us by scolding everyone for lack of decorum and shooing the kitchen maids back to work, who had been hugging each other in relief.

I was not as confident as I sounded, but I knew I had been given power that I had not yet tapped. After all, powerful teachers had taught me, the Old Man included, despite or even because of his many failings. A glimmer of a plan was forming in my mind, and I believed we could turn this foundering ship away from these shoals.

As I'd said, I would pray on it and think deeply, calling on everything I knew and more. In the morning, we would find a way and see it through.

CHAPTER III:

The Rescue

"So," I offered in summary to those who had gathered in council, "if I can find a way to get into the Keep and open the unguarded door, are we equipped to free Eustace and fight our way out if need be?"

A dozen of us, including Mathilde, who had gathered to decide a course of action, sat around the fireplace in the Great Hall. We had been discussing the ins and outs of the situation for what seemed like hours. Everything hinged on gaining entry into the Baron's guarded and magically warded Keep without discovery. The boys' scouting had not revealed an exploitable gap in the Baron's defenses.

But an audacious idea had been brewing in my mind as all other practical solutions had been dismissed, and it was time to offer it.

I believe I can get inside the Keep to let others in," I said, "if the Moon is right and the gods are with us. The energy I need will have to be gathered. I will also need a specific focus that I'm sure is located inside the Keep. I have an idea that will depend on others to figure out."

They readily accepted the possibility I offered, so we shifted the discussion to our tactics for locating Eustace and escaping once we had access. Previous observation from outside the fortified walls revealed that the Baron had garrisoned several squads of armed troops there.

"We are going about this all wrong," Louis had said, the light of insight glimmering in his smile. "We have neither the power nor the numbers to do this directly. We must ask what the nature of our opponent is, as Édouard has taught us, and how we can lead his nature to crack itself?"

His question launched us into a discussion of precisely this. We considered what this assault and kidnapping in broad daylight revealed about the Baron. He was a man who felt he had all the cards and was, therefore, prideful and arrogant. This was all to show his dominance. He believed he had the upper hand over the Maestro and would never admit to having a fault. He certainly would not think that mere *boys* could succeed in challenging him when he believed that even Édouard could not.

Further, it was clear that his trap was set for the Maestro and the Order, not for us. The Baron *needed* to demonstrate to Édouard how he had tricked him. He would need to lord it over Édouard to prove his dominance over him.

The alchemical solvent for the Baron's particular metal lay here. He believed in himself as gold and that, above any other substance, he could not allow another metal to be alloyed. But gold alone is weak—it shines untarnished but is too soft to hold by itself. All this was precisely why he underestimated us. We must convince him even more of our weakness, even as we were shattering his plans.

"I must confront him," I said. The others gasped in dismay at this. Louis just grinned excitedly and urged, "Go on, Étienne!"

"He will be off balance that I, a mere child whom he believes is only the Maestro's "catamite," have mysteriously gained access to his sanctum without being able to detect how. He'll know it was magical, but unable to imagine how, as what the Old Man taught me is completely outside anything the Baron knows. By offering myself to his inquiry, I can keep him occupied long enough for others to find and free Eustace. He will not see me as any significant danger."

"But Étienne, how will you get away?" one of the other boys said worriedly.

"Well," I said, smiling broadly. "That will be all your job, won't it? You and the rest outside the Keep will have to create a diversion or two, diversions big enough and urgent enough to distract the Baron and his men so we can all escape. We've all worked to outwit the Maestro, a far more wily opponent than the Baron. And for this task, we have an unlimited license to do so in far more destructive ways!"

I paused until I could see that notion sink into the boys on that team. Louis, their leader, nodded, and I could see his mind was already at work on the problem.

I turned to our master thief, Ton Ton. His ability to infiltrate every seemingly secure place in the Chateau had once driven Édouard to distraction, until the Maestro turned Ton Ton's talents to stealing from those we fought on behalf of good!

"Ton Ton, my friend? I will need to trouble you for some help with finding a focus object within the Keep."

He leaned forward excitedly, knowing I'd have thought up just the kind of trouble he loved. "What do you have in mind, Étienne?" he said.

I leaned towards him across the table conspiratorially until we were almost nose to nose.

"How might you feel, Ton Ton, my friend, about using your talent for theft... but in reverse?"

Ton Ton looked puzzled for a moment before he thought it through. Then, I saw the light dawn in his expression, and he grinned wider at me.

"Oh, yes, Étienne! This shall be great fun!" he boasted.

So I arrived on the night of Mother Moon's fullness, some days after our planning session, at a place atop a nearby hill. Ton Ton had used his skill to conceal an object of focus that was very well known to me within a bag of grain destined for the Baron's stores in the Keep. He and his acolytes had worked on their "reverse theft" method to bring an object *into* the Keep rather than removing it. The object must not bulge or be felt on the bag's surface, or it would raise curiosity and be discovered.

The object for my focus was a thick, cast-glass vessel, perhaps eight inches in diameter. Édouard had required that I clean it after every alchemical procedure, which had been challenging. I had to scrub the thing until it was pristine, so no residues remained to sully the delicate procedure that followed. It took me hours! So I'd come to truly hate the thing! I'm sure the Maestro intended to teach me something by requiring this task of me, and *only* me, but whatever the lesson was supposed to be, I only recalled how much I hated it.

Nonetheless, my dislike of it made me intimately aware of all its features. I could see it as clear as day in my mind, recalling its heft and the rough texture of its impossible-to-clean surface.

They were all happy that some proper theft would be required. They located the granary on one of his estates, identified the Baron's stock of sacked grain marked to be delivered to the Keep, and purloined a bag. Then they developed a method to suspend the alchemical vessel within the grain bag. They arranged the laboratory vessel in the sack and restitched it, proving that the added contents were undetectable, even when the vessel was thrown around during loading and unloading from a cart.

Once tested and proven, they marked it in a way known only to themselves and carefully tracked it to ensure it was loaded into a cart and entered into the Keep.

In the meantime, Louis and the others devised and rehearsed plans and contingencies to provide misdirection, allowing us to escape. With the new moon upon us, I entered the dark, as I had with the Old Man, to gather the power I would need for moon travel upon the next full moon. I reflected wryly as I closed the cellar door to enter my new "cave" that I was now willfully doing two things I'd declared to myself I'd never do again. The first was living in the dark, and the second was making Édouard's favorite alchemical laboratory vessel the center of my focus and effort!

The Moon Goddess's shine could be seen as she rose over the horizon. I'd been living in the dark again, emerging only at night during the waxing cycle to practice the devotions for absorbing her power. My arrival at the Chateau had occurred just a few days after the new moon, giving us less than two weeks to mount the rescue. Now, as the Goddess was mounting to her fullest expression, it was time for me to make my bid and risk the most difficult of her tests. It was something that I'd done only once before when I was tested in Brittany. If I failed to "moon travel, "as the Old Man had called it, the rescue would fail before it could even begin. Everything hinged on this.

I calmed my doubts and began the ancient chant, asking for the boon of her power as a blessing to me, her initiate. I asked her to transport me, body and soul, to the place of my intent. As she rose over the horizon in her fullness, I reached for the filaments of her power and drew them to me.

I was surprised by how easily this occurred. Then I recalled what the moon priestess had said when she came to me in my dream before my test in Brittany: "The Goddess does not stint those who serve her," she had said. "To those who serve her, she gives as naturally and completely as she gives light." So it was.

I could picture the Keep in detail, as I had observed it many nights, and I held the image of Édouard's alchemical vessel within its walls. Fixing this rigorously in my mind, I reached out to the Goddess and began to draw on her. The Old Man's initiation had revealed to me the tendrils or filaments of her power, the threads made up of pure energy that extended from her until their accumulation began to vibrate my naked body. I continued to gather her filaments of power, and my body began to shake more and more. I had nothing but my will to maintain a focus on the Keep and the glass vessel we'd smuggled there as my body vibrated and shook violently. The filaments of her power I'd gathered now wrapped me, drawing me to her. So immense was her power that it seemed she was shaking me from my flesh. Her pull on me grew until it became colossal. I could hold on to only the merest thread of my intent until even that thread parted, and I could do naught but yield to her so entirely that my body was flung out into the night.

The Night of the Rescue—*Bearding the Baron*

Flung into the void by the Moon Mother's power, I opened my eyes to find myself in pitch dark, naked and shivering upon a cold flagstone floor. It was so dark that I had to blink before I was sure my eyes were open. I sat up and felt around the stone floor about me, encountering a rough sackcloth, which I recognized as the grain bag in which Ton Ton had hidden my focus object. I had arrived in a windowless storeroom within the Baron's Keep. Success!

Fumbling, I untied the heavy string that cinched the bag closed and dumped the grain contents onto the floor. My fingers quickly found the lumpy form of the alchemical vessel that was my focus object, which Ton Ton had cleverly padded with a soft bunch of puffed, steamed, and dried grain. Thank you, Ton Ton, you clever boy! I needed fuel after such a significant expenditure of my will and energy, so I stuffed my mouth with nourishing grain. When I'd had enough, I put the glass vessel back into its protective inner sack and the remainder of the puffed grain and cinched it closed.

Feeling immobile from the act of Moon Travel, I had to coach myself to get going before I sank further into lethargy. "Come on, Étienne, my lad, it's time to get a move on!" I muttered quietly to myself while I hauled myself to my feet. Slinging the grain bag over my shoulder, I felt my way to find a door.

Using all the craft of concealment that Édouard had taught us, I found my way out of the cellar where I had arrived, thankful that the Baron had not been concerned about locking his larder. It spoke of wealth and plenty, likely combined with a threat of severe discipline, that the Baron saw no need to guard his supplies from internal theft.

I had hoped that other items, such as uniforms, would be stored nearby, and this proved to be the case. An adjacent room, with grates to admit air and keep things dry, also shed a faint light from the still-risen Moon. I found leggings, blouses, and tunics stacked on tables, grabbed what I needed that looked close enough in size, and found a pair of worn boots I thought would serve.

I emerged from the cellar into the interior yard of the Keep and quickly assessed where the door to the outside would be located. Carefully creeping along in the shadows, I reached it. The place was quiet at night, and the Moon was already lowering in the sky, making it easier to find cover. It took longer than I had planned, and I was sure the lads would get impatient!

The door itself was unattended and looked long disused. It was built of stout, heavy oak and triple-barred at the top, middle, and bottom, which is undoubtedly why they thought it needed no guarding. Slowly and carefully, I lifted each one from its slot, straining against its significant weight and sweating despite the cool night air. Now for the dangerous part: As a little-used door, it would likely squeal like a banshee when first moved.

It was stuck! The damned thing was going to be the death of me: if I yanked it too hard, its momentum could force it open faster than I could control. Then I heard Louis's insistent whisper through a crack between the planks. The fellow had read my mind.

"Étienne? Étienne! We'll push from this side, but you must resist it so it doesn't move too fast."

Shortly, the door was unstuck enough to scrape along the stone. We paused whenever we heard the hinges start to squeal, but eventually got it open enough for Louis, Ton Ton, and the others to slip through. I handed my bag to Louis, who was to guard the door to ensure it went unnoticed during our escape. Gathering with the others, I pointed out the cellar stairwell I'd come out of and the layout I'd discerned so far.

Ton Ton had brought his "finder," a boy named Rob, who was skilled at locating objects and people. He knew Eustache well and had his psychic signature. Rob had briefly checked the direction of Eustace's location, now that he was inside the protection of the Baron's magical wards. I was always amazed at the powers the Maestro discovered in small packages like Rob, who was even smaller than the "Wee thief" Ton Ton, as we all called him. With confidence, many magnitudes greater than his small stature, Rob pointed to one of the stone turrets, saying, "He's up there."

At that, Ton Ton whispered, "Let's go," and his break-in team moved off into the shadows and about their business.

Now, for my next act, I will confront and distract the Baron himself.

I'd spent much of my preparation time gathering the power for the Moon travel and strategizing how to approach bearding the Baron in his den. We figured that once inside the Keep, I needed only to look for and intentionally breach the *second* most magically warded room I could find to gain the Baron's attention. I also knew he would attend to this personally—his whole scheme had been assembled to lure his nemesis, Édouard, to a place of the Baron's most significant power and defeat him.

It was telltale to me that the Baron's men continued to refer to Édouard as "Comte," as if the Baron needed to attribute greater power to his enemy to make his triumph greater. Édouard was certainly no Count of the realm. In noble terms, Édouard was little more than a manor holder of a minor line. Any license he had from royalty was granted for his services in the esoteric realm he'd provided, not for traditional service to the crown.

However, the Baron seemed to need to justify Édouard's previous victory by granting him more status and power than he had, which would also make his domination of Édouard sweeter and grant himself greater self-importance when he would defeat the Maestro by luring him to Eustace's rescue. This gave me something predictable to play with.

Since the Baron expected Édouard's aim to be the rescue of Eustace, that location would be the *most* protected place for the Baron. Ton Ton's break-in team could not safely do so unless the Baron's power was focused elsewhere. I was betting that the _second_ _most_ warded room would be to protect the precious treasures the evil man had collected. Breaching that storeroom would draw him to me and distract him from where he was keeping Eustache as bait. For the rest of it, we worked to concoct a story to sell, so to speak, that I believed would play upon the Baron's cupidity and natural arrogance. I would keep him distracted until others defeated his magical power source, and my fellows could extract Eustache. Then diversions would be sprung so we could make our exit.

I took a breath to prepare myself, knowing everything would happen quickly, and I breached the warded doorway. Entering swiftly, I gathered the best of the magical treasures I could see on the tables inside, knowing that the Baron himself would be with me shortly.

I barely had time to place a few choice items in an empty bag I'd brought when the door was pushed open with a bang. The Baron and a uniformed guard rushed into the room, and I was grabbed by my collar and yanked down onto the floor. I was held down by the guard's boot on my chest, and a sword point held against my throat, making it clear to neither speak nor move. I maintained a calm expression and gazed past the guard at the fat and sweating face of the Baron peering down at me.

"Hah!" the Baron exclaimed. "The Count has sent a boy to do what he is not man enough to do. He must be more desperate than I thought my plans would have made him. Let him up, guard; he is no threat to me."

The guard released me and backed away. I rolled to my side, facing the Baron, who had stood his ground, smiling gleefully at me.

"You are just one of his boys," he declared. "Did you think I would be so focused on my bait, the boy Eustace, that I would leave my magical treasures unwarded?"

I smirked back at him and shrugged as I got to my feet. "I thought it was too good an opportunity to pass up," I said. "Others can be noble rescuers, but I decided that you, a man of wealth and discernment, would have a few treasures I should take advantage of." I shrugged again, indicating I had taken a chance, though it was not working out now.

The Baron laughed and slapped his thigh at my conceit. As planned, I had given him a motivation he could understand best— selfish greed.

"I will admit," the Baron responded, "that I have not yet figured out how you got into the Keep in the first place, as it is too well protected to be easy. But once here, you have no finesse. You blundered into every ward I'd set!"

I worked to harden my expression and resist smiling at this, as I had looked carefully to identify the wards he had set so that I could violate as many of them as thoroughly as possible to ensure I'd get his attention.

"Now, let's see what you thought was valuable," he said, picking up the bag I'd dropped.

He pulled out the magical implements I'd grabbed, placing them back on the table from which I'd taken them.

"You chose these few items well enough, so you've been taught a little. Too bad your master hasn't instructed you how to deal with wards set by a *real* magician, but perhaps he did not know any better himself."

He dismissed the guard to underline further that he saw me as no threat to him. He pondered me for a minute, tapping his finger on his chin. I waited, hoping that I'd correctly predicted his next move.

"You seem to have some hidden talents, young man. I could have you executed as a mere common thief, but you somehow managed to get into my Keep without my detecting how you did so. Whatever your talents, you were betrayed by poor training in magic, which made you unequipped to reap any rewards."

His tone had become almost cordial, and I knew I had him then. I had hoped that his cupidity would lead him to dismiss me as any real threat, but I also hoped that he would want to take advantage of my greed to recruit me to his side. The Baron could see others only as a reflection of his selfish motivations, and I had surmised that he would dangle access to power and riches to milk me for information.

Then I suddenly sensed Eton and Bora, the two other legs of our Tripod, and knew they had successfully found their way to the central wards that guarded the Baron's source of magical power and the power source itself. Suddenly, a constant pressure of mystical power that hummed in the background was gone.

Just then, a strident call came through the open door. "Baron! Come quickly! They have broken in and freed the boy!"

The Baron rushed to the doorway and exchanged words with his guard. The Baron gestured at him to be gone. "Go, fool! I will be right after you!"

In the very act of turning back to me and summoning the magic to obliterate me on the spot, the Baron appeared rocked and weak, having had his source of power cut off. I reached under my tunic and grasped the package Louis had given me that I'd kept hidden for this moment. Tearing off its protective wrapping, I covered my face and held my breath, throwing it hard into the Baron's face. The blue, finely ground, and caustic powder exploded in his face. A cloud of blue dust surrounded the Baron. He gasped in surprise, inhaling the stuff into his lungs. Coughing violently, he collapsed to his hands and knees, eyes closed against the burn they must have felt. He was reduced to little more than pain and spite.

I leaped over the Baron, briefly peered out the doorway to find the hall empty, and rapidly made my way through the Keep in the opposite direction from all the shouting.

No sooner had I found an exit than flames arose from the ramparts of the Keep. Yes! One of the diversions we'd planned to make our escape! I oriented myself amidst the chaos and proceeded to the hidden doorway where Louis and others were already urging boys out in singles and small groups. As I passed him to exit, he slapped me on the back, saying, "Just a few more now, Étienne!"

Another fire blossomed across the compound, further deflecting attention from us. Elated by our success, I headed toward our prearranged rendezvous.

***

The night of the rescue seemed like it had occurred months ago to us, though only two weeks had passed. We'd kept a lookout from the parapet atop the turret of Édouard's laboratory and watched the expected cavalcade approach the Chateau. We were eager to see how we were met when they reached our walls.

The hoofbeats became thunderous as the riders turned from the main road onto the minor lane through the fields leading to the gate. As they hastened towards us, we could begin to make out the individuals on their horses.

I glimpsed a glint of blue from the lead figure, the familiar color of one of Édouard's favored travel capes. His roan stallion galloped, his tail up, and the scent of home caused his nostrils to flare widely. François followed closely, his spare, whipcord, sinewy form atop his dapple-gray horse. Trailing behind them were another five or six mounted men. All had military bearing and were unfamiliar to me, though I could surmise from the particular aura surrounding them that they were likely troops of the Order.

Pursuing this first grouping at a slight distance, as they'd not yet turned onto the lane, I could make out the Major upon his charger. He was keeping pace with the Abbess's carriage, galloping just outside the cloud of dust thrown by the churning wheels. The Major held his drawn sword out at the side, the trained posture of a cavalry soldier going into battle. The position was to ensure his mount was protected from the blade's edge while leaving the sword ready for a fight.

I descended the circular stairs inside the turret and stepped into the courtyard to meet them. Judging from the tumult I heard outside the courtyard, the first troop must have pulled up and taken positions around the Chateau's walls. Édouard and François rode through the gate into the courtyard, where we all waited. They both swung out of their saddles and slid to the ground in unison, tossing their reins to whoever was nearest, so intent were they to reach us. Both men were breathing hard and dripping with sweat from the ride's exertion.

The Maestro was wide-eyed with concern, looking as close to overwrought as I'd ever seen him. He strode directly to me and clapped his hands on my shoulders, bracing them. He looked to be needing the feel of my solid muscle under his hands to assure himself that I was real. He stared at my face with his intent, hawk-like gaze, taking in every detail to assess how I had fared. I met his gaze just as intently, noting that I no longer looked upward to meet his eyes, as my growth while away in Brittany had brought my face almost level with his.

His fellows shoved Eustace to the front of the crowd, directly into François's path. Out of the corner of my eye, I glimpsed François, taking hold of Eustace's shoulders and examining him, much as Édouard was examining me.

Barely a few breaths later, another thunder of hoofbeats heralded the arrival of the Major, his sword now sheathed, followed by the rumble of the wooden wheels of the Abbess's carriage. François and Édouard released us and stepped back to receive our honored guest.

The Major unhorsed and, giving his reins to Joucain, went to help the Abbess down from her seat. He guided her over to us as she lightly clasped his bent arm. Édouard and François respectfully stepped aside to give her a sufficient view of us. She released the Major's arm and paused to survey the scene. The Abbess's eyes rested briefly upon me to give a nod before turning to take in Eustace, her gaze narrowing as she gave him the once-over. She then shifted to look at the crowd gathered behind us before sending her pointed glance over everyone's heads to Mathilde, standing behind the crowd, leaning against the door of her kitchen. Feeling a tension in the air, the gathered throng came to a hush.

I watched the two women conduct one of those silent yet thorough conversations. Back and forth it went, each nodding sagely to the other's soundless queries, assessments, and comments, conveyed through subtle eye shifts and a few pursed lips. Eventually, Mathilde gave forth her summary, apparently condensed into a singular shrug, and the Abbess responded with textual commentary, though it looked to me to be through one raised eyebrow. Both women finished with an almost imperceptible shake of their heads, indicating their agreement on the shambles of things men made, thus closing the conversation.

The Abbess then turned back to us and addressed François and the Maestro.

"Gentlemen, I will assess for myself the sufficiency of Eustace's well-being," she announced.

Releasing them from her gaze, she looked to me. "I see that the Mother has left her mark on you, Étienne. You have quite a story to tell us."

Though seeming still to address me, she looked pointedly at Édouard as she continued.

"And, of course, Étienne," she said, holding the Maestro with her eyes, "you shall venture not a *single word* of your story until I have completed my business with Eustace. Don't you agree?"

Édouard nodded his agreement as if she had spoken the question to him. I surmised that she was not asking for my opinion on this, so I took it as marching orders needing no confirmation. She gestured to Eustace to approach her, and, taking his arm, she guided him into the Great Hall. Having been in his position before, I smiled as she bent her considerable powers to him, blanketing him in her concern. It was pretty heady stuff to an innocent, as I recalled.

It was clear to everyone that we had been dismissed, including the Maestro and François.

As if we had been released from a spell, the crowd rushed forward to crowd around and embrace the homecoming arrivals. Some went to clasp François's hands or slap his wiry shoulders as he eschewed anything as sentimental as an embrace. He smiled broadly at their warm greetings, looking happy to be home, as long as no one became too effusive.

Édouard had no inhibitions and welcomed every embrace with his typical gusto, loudly proclaiming each by name and lifting those he could in his enthusiastic embrace. Édouard almost met his match when the big-bodied and big-muscled Petain tried to lift Édouard off his feet with a great bear hug of greeting. The two tussled back and forth like boys wrestling each other, stopping as they broke into laughter at their game. I smiled joyfully at all this loving commotion.

I looked on with pleasure when I felt a gloved hand smack me firmly on my back with a gruff, "Ahem!" I knew it was the Major, so I turned to greet him, embracing him with similar gusto and clapping his back with both hands as I hugged him.

We were both quite pleased to meet again. I got to know the Major when he joined me on the first leg of my journey to Brittany, which seemed like an age ago! I'd grown quite fond of the man and was grateful for the guidance he had given me on the journey.

"What the Abbess said goes for me as well, Étienne," the Major declared. "You will tell no story until I am ready! We must all have a breather and a chance to wash the road from us before we are fit for a tale or ten." He grinned even more broadly at me and continued in a conspiratorial tone but an even louder volume. "By God, man, we had the devil's own time getting here! I could tell you a few stories myself!" he laughed.

"And here we are, riding heroically to save you all," he said, striking a pose of exaggerated dismay, "only to arrive and find the crisis has already been resolved! That was your doing, I'm to understand, my lad?" He ruffled my hair affectionately as I protested that it was a massive group effort and that everyone should share the credit.

Ignoring my protests, the Major looped one arm over my shoulders and wrapped the other arm over the shoulders of Louis, who had joined us in the interim. He swung us both around to face the Chateau. He raised his nose to the air, sniffing like a hound, looking for the scent trail.

"Now, where could food be in this menagerie?" he queried. He sniffed the air again, then queried, "Must a man who has sacrificed his nourishment to speed his way be required to eke out sustenance by himself? Where is my ale, bread, and meat?"

Louis snorted, pulling back from the Major's grasp to glare at him. "You old fraud!" Louis said, poking the Major's ample girth with a finger. "It doesn't look like *you've* sacrificed your victuals much! What do you think, Étienne? No starving man I've ever seen would have such a belly."

"Silence, boy!" the Major protested. "I'll have you know that the belly you are poking is nothing but muscle! Pure muscle!"

Louis dismissed this and said, "Come on, Major, you know *exactly* where the food will be found. It's the same place you always find it. Every time you are here!"

True, and the seasoned campaigner had been guiding us toward Mathilde's kitchen even while declaiming his suffering.

The Major always had a place at Mathilde's table and was familiar with its location. He did not need a hound's nose to find it! When he rode through the gate, I expected a flagon and platter to be set for him. I only desperately hoped that Mathilde had allowed Louis and me to join the Major for sustenance.

A few hours later, Eustace, Louis, and I assembled with the Abbess, the Major, François, Édouard, and The Reichardt, who was the war leader of the Order's troops, to recount what became known as the *Great Rescue*.

Eustace told of his surprise, terror, and rage when he was plucked from the field and kidnapped. He displayed admirable aplomb as he recounted his ordeal. He was taken to the Keep, where the Baron strutted and gloated over him. Eustace said he was utterly confident he would be rescued, having come to know our orphan band's fierce camaraderie and loyalty. Other than being taken out daily to be displayed on the parapet so that any observers would see him in good health, he was captive but well cared for. He commented that he was utterly bored and trusted we would not let him languish long in the Baron's evil hands.

I recounted the story of my return to the Château, where everything was in chaos after Eustace's kidnapping. I expressed my dismay upon learning that Édouard, François, the Abbess, and the Major were all unreachable. The Maestro and the Abbess looked quite sheepish and admitted they had been tricked by the urgent call to help others. Only afterward did it become clear that the "emergency" they rushed to was just a trap.

I continued my story, telling of the Council of War the morning following my arrival, and how we laid out our tactics and plans. I gave no specifics about my method of getting into the Baron's Keep, noting only that I utilized what I had learned under the Old Man. My reticence stemmed from the need to maintain the secrecy of my initiation and from the fact that I had taken a considerable risk without a mentor to provide a margin of safety. I knew they would likely see it as unnecessary, even if I gave the Abbess and Maestro more details.

Both the Abbess and Édouard exchanged glances at my cursory description. The Abbess silently mouthed "Luna" to him, causing the Maestro to look a combination of astonished and horrified. François also silently raised his eyebrows, not in astonishment as Édouard had. He shook his head in a way that conveyed, "The boy did what? God in heaven!"

I was reassured that the Major, aware of this silent commentary, grinned and nodded approvingly at the risk I took. Old soldiers have taken bold risks and live to tell the tale. Of course, many a soldier *didn't* get old having taken bold risks. But I knew the Major approved of bold acts taken by a leader. He would think my choice was valid because I lived to tell the tale, and the proof was in the pudding.

I continued the story, which grew more exciting as others joined in, sharing their teams' activities after I unlocked the door and granted them access. Eventually, I finished the tale.

... then I leapt over the Baron, leaving him choking on the caustic powders. I found the way out to be clear, as the Baron's troops were well distracted by my compatriots' diversions, Eustace's rescue complete, and headed to our prearranged rendezvous.

There was a pause in silence, then, to my complete surprise, the Major stood up and started to clap. He turned around and directed his applause toward everyone involved in the rescue, including the house staff standing in the background. Everyone had contributed to the rescue effort in their own way. His muscular hands thudded together repeatedly without losing enthusiasm for what seemed like an endless moment, surprising everyone.

One by one, others in the gathering stood and joined him—François, smiling proudly, followed by the Maestro and the Abbess. They were immediately met with a louder burst of applause from those listening outside the open windows and doors. I was already on my feet, clapping just as enthusiastically. I looked from one to another of my fellow adventurers, praising them for stepping up together to this unprecedented success.

Eventually, the applause faded naturally. By then, it was late in the day, and the Maestro dismissed everyone to rest or work, as needed, so the Hall could be prepared for a celebratory meal large enough to host all our guests.

As the hall emptied, Édouard looped his arm through mine and led us to walk around the courtyard walls to look at the fields, as if to survey his domain. Neither of us spoke, happy to bask in each other's company and feel our unbreakable bond. He was nearly bursting with pride for me, for all of us. No words could better express this than our linked arms and synchronized steps. Eventually, we returned to the gate, where he embraced me, kissed my cheeks, and went to wash up for supper.

CHAPTER IV:

Marcella

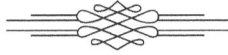

While we were full of pride in our accomplishments, that did not mean Édouard saw no room for correction and improvement. He referred thereafter to the Rescue bluntly as that "idiotic and risky use of fledgling powers by Étienne" accompanied by "your ridiculously overconfident fellows" and on numerous occasions to "the extremely dangerous sorcery you all ignorantly and blithely chose to confront."

He managed to sound, in equal parts, admonishing and proud. It could go either way, depending on whether you focused on the scathing look in his arched eyebrow or the upturned corners of his mouth.

Having preached the necessity of rewarding success, the Maestro announced that he had meditated deeply on the appropriate recompense for us. He declared that, since we all had stepped up to take responsibility in his absence, our reward was that we were all now "rewarded" with even greater responsibilities!

I suppose there is a spiritual principle in this somewhere — perhaps "Be careful what you ask for?" Or famously, "No good deed goes unpunished?"

The result was that I was given the "privilege" of taking charge of my fellows and guiding many aspects of their training. We all were "granted" more work of "managing" care of the property and lands, and additional magical studies.

As the Maestro put it, stroking his mustaches with an air of an old man pronouncing great wisdom, "If you would decide the fates of others, then by all means continue, Étienne. And if you all hunger to prove your talents more, it shall be so!"

Of course, standing behind the Maestro as he made his pronouncement was François, who looked far too smug that our triumph was leading to the "privilege" of even greater toil.

This put me in the unenviable position of directing my team members to take on additional responsibilities *and* training. I felt particularly put upon after returning from my long, solitary ordeal with the Old Man. I had looked forward to a cosset at home and time to joke and gambol about it as before. Now I had to be in charge, and it rankled.

The intended result was that Édouard and François were left unencumbered by routine to see to affairs *outside* the Chateau now that the duty of managing this Asylum for the Adventurously Insane was turned over to us, its inmates. We'd proven too well that we could handle the significant demands ourselves.

And so, as had become more and more common, both Édouard and François were absent from the Chateau to negotiate with the estate's tenants in the next village, and I was now "in charge."

Since we weren't expecting visitors or planning any magical battles, it was my duty to coax my fellows to perform the exercises and tasks assigned to us as part of our daily routines. While François had no trouble organizing us efficiently for these training exercises, my friends made me work much harder to get them to cooperate. François had given us physical exercises designed to strengthen both the body's physical and psychic energies. These involved unusual movements synchronized with specific breathing patterns, which François stressed must be followed precisely. Our primary motivation was to test our skills by knocking our partner off balance without physically touching him, a move François demonstrated effortlessly. It was so enjoyable that we gladly endured the constant corrections needed to practice the exercises.

I finally got my brethren to engage with this, and we were all intently working on this task in the yard on a bright spring day. Suddenly, hoofbeats broke our concentration, and a horse and rider charged through the gate. His horse's mane was lathered, and the rider was in a panic. I recognized him at once as the Abbess's stable hand. He was red-faced with exertion. I ran over to help him get out of the saddle and discover the emergency.

"Come quickly!" he cried out, clutching the dangling stirrup to balance while he tried to catch his breath. "Highwaymen attacked us on the road to the east. The Major won't fend them off too long!"

I slapped his back for reassurance and yelled to Louis to saddle a horse, then dashed to the armory for my weapons. Petan, although younger than I, was nearly twice my size, had already stepped forward and grabbed a mattock leaning against the garden wall, bridled a bareback mare, and swung himself onto her back by the time I was back with weapons and upon my horse. We charged after the stable boy, who had recovered enough of his breath to remount and lead us to the trouble.

They had been waylaid only a short distance from the Chateau, at a natural dip in the roadbed that left them vulnerable to ambush from the crests of the road, where the robbers must have awaited them. We could see the scene before us as we rode up the first crest. The Abbess's carriage was stopped near the low point of the dip where debris and bracken had been strewn to bring the horses to a halt. One man lay still in the road behind the carriage, no doubt the work of the Major, who had been following in guard position. The Major had driven the other marauders back across their impromptu blockade, putting himself between them and the carriage so that their backs faced us as we rode towards them.

The Major half-stood in his stirrups, displaying his cavalry training. He used his sword and battle-seasoned horse to fend off the attacks by the three ruffians, who, between them, were armed only with a short sword, a couple of knives, and a staff. They were used to working in concert—perhaps they were once soldiers who had done battle together—and the Major was tiring, and the robbers had been gathering themselves to take advantage of that fact until we showed up.

Our charge over the hill certainly caught them off guard, but their dismay lasted only long enough to see that we were boys and not grown men come to challenge them. The Major, however, was heartened by our appearance. Reinforcements, no matter how young, are enough to give an old warrior an edge as he redoubled his efforts. The highwaymen were now forced to rearrange themselves to deal with threats from two directions, as their plan to wear down the Major's superior ability until he became tired and careless was no longer tenable.

Hoping to dispatch us quickly, two of the ruffians broke off from their one swordsman, who seemed tasked to keep tiring the Major with feints and forays, although without engaging him fully now that it was no longer three to one. I slid off my horse about ten yards from them as my knives gave me no advantage atop the animal. The stable boy stayed on his horse and circled warily, rock in hand, clearly having no fighting skill but eager to help if given the chance. Petan slid off his mare and hefted his tool to confront the attacker, who was wielding the staff, while the knife-wielding partner split off to engage with me. A brief silence settled, broken only by the scuffs of the Major's horse and the nervous hoofbeats of the circling stable boy.

I held both knives in my hands: my left hand holding the curved blade in reverse grip with the blade edge facing out, and my right hand holding the straight, double-edged blade in forward grip. Despite this being the first actual application of my battle skills, my profoundly ingrained training habits swiftly took over. I whispered a prayer of thanks to François and gave myself to the teachings.

I'd been trained by a master who embodied the physical art of fighting and its inner secret dimension, teaching me how to shift my mind and state. The charged-up, racing feelings that are the typical response to danger, even in hardened soldiers, were replaced by something quiet and calm, a focus without thought, little else but the sense of my body, my weapons, and my opponent.

Accustomed to working with the kingdom's most fluid warrior, my opponent's roughness and discontinuity between thought and action were jarring. When he abruptly attacked, hoping to dispatch me quickly, I did not even need to counter him. The direction of his movement was so evident that I effortlessly stepped aside so that he stumbled past me. He turned to slash at me, perhaps hoping through his sheer aggression to drive me into retreat, but he was off balance. It was a trivial matter for me to dance aside as he overreached and stumbled.

Had I had more combat experience, I should have dispatched him in either of these poorly executed moves, but I was still assessing my opponent. Though used to fighting, he was poorly trained, more by the crude requirements of survival on the battlefield than any refinement of the practice floor. His gambit to dominate me with an all-out attack had failed, so he settled into a serious fight and awaited my mistakes.

I realized I did not have that same luxury. Petan, fending off his opponent's more extended staff with his shorter pick, would not last long unaided, even with his brave efforts. I heard François's voice: "When you must press the attack, open your senses and slip through his guard where Light is absent from his body."

I shifted my perspective to "Battle Sight" and attacked the shadowed area on my opponent's left side. I closed, with a feint, shuffling my left foot forward as I slashed my curved left-hand blade forward towards his head. He stupidly brought his blade high to block, but I'd already stepped in with my right foot while dropping low into a graceful crouch and slashing with the straight blade in my right hand through the shadowed area of his left side. My blade sliced cleanly into the space between his ribs, stopping his motion abruptly. My movement continued naturally into a complete rising turn counterclockwise, which brought my curved blade in the lead to slash across his throat, severing the artery. The ruffian dropped to his knees, clutching at his spurting neck, and gasping for air from the lung I'd slashed.

With my opponent no longer a concern, I looked to Petan, who was on the ground, about to be given the *coup de grâce* by his staff-wielding assailant. The man drew back the staff for the final blow, and I let his movement suck me towards him as does a river's vortex. I flowed along the staff inside its arc, curved blade corkscrewing around the shaft to meet his grip, cutting deeply into his fingers. He let go of the staff with his hand, pulling it to his chest in pain, but attempted to swing the staff at me with his unwounded right hand. His effort was useless, as I'd already pinned the front of his staff to the ground with my straight blade and brought the sharp edge of my curved blade to his throat. My opponent dropped his staff and fell to his knees, cradling his wounded hand and whimpering in pain and fear as he yielded, begging for mercy.

The Major gave a gusty "Hurrah, lad!" at my success and moved in full earnest on his opponent. They engaged in a flurry of swordplay, and then the Major struck down the robber's sword and laid him low with the butt end of his sword handle, knocking the man as senseless as a rag doll. A sudden silence fell, broken only by the nickering of the horses and the Major's labored breathing.

The Major looked us over, eyeing me in a way that contained surprise and respect. He broke the silence, ordering Petan to tie up the still-conscious robber who was groveling at my feet.

He spoke again with that odd accent the Swiss have when they talk Mother French.

"Well, my young friend," said the Major, "it seems you have grown some real teeth." He swung a leg over his saddle and dropped off his horse, pulling a rope from his saddlebag to tie up our prisoners.

"François has passed his Way on to you, I see."

I nodded to him. I'd not yet realized I'd put my skills to their intended use. It all happened so quickly, guided entirely by the habits of training, without any conscious thought, and it did not seem quite real. Even the blood on my blades seemed false, like stage paint, perhaps, or maybe just the glint of sunlight refracted from the blades.

I looked over at the crumpled body of the man I had slain and blinked. He looked as lifeless as a scarecrow fallen from its perch. The Major walked over from binding up the live but unconscious prisoner and turned the dead body over with his boot. The dead eyes stared up at me from the bleeding corpse, and I was suddenly sick. I lurched over to the ditch by the road and violently threw up.

When I had emptied my stomach, the Major spared me a sympathetic look and clapped me reassuringly on the shoulder.

"First real fight, eh?" he said appraisingly.

He slapped me firmly on the shoulder again, this time in a way that drilled my feet into the ground to brace me up, a command skill I'm sure he'd found helpful for his young troops in the past.

"Come on, lad, let's see how my passengers have fared," he said.

Picking up the staff to disarm the man who was trying to staunch his half-severed and bleeding fingers, the Major grabbed the scruff of the man's collar and marched him over to the carriage.

Passengers? It had not occurred to me that he was escorting anyone, but why else would he be personally guarding the Abbess's carriage? I accompanied him to it, where, peering back over the seat, was the most stunningly beautiful young woman that the world had ever witnessed. This vision of beauty was dressed in courtly attire, replete with rich embroidery. Her dark and lustrous hair was twisted into a braid and coiled around her head, over which she wore a fine linen scarf against the dust of travel. Her bewitching dark brown eyes glinted with amusement as she watched us walk toward her. For all her youth, hers was a worldly look, a confident attitude that could only come from the privilege of wealth and high station. I was so taken with her that I barely noticed her lady-in-waiting sitting next to her; the poor girl was still shaking in fear from the close brush with the violence.

"Well, Major," said my angel in a measured tone, "I see you have finally dispatched our unwelcome visitors."

He bowed. "With the help of my young friends, Milady."

"Do introduce your handsome warrior to me, Major," she fluttered. "I should like to thank him for his brave assistance."

He smiled and gestured expansively towards me and Petan.

"Allow me to introduce my friends, Étienne and Petan, to you, Milady."

Petan gave a curt bow at the mention of his name and busied himself helping the stable boy put the horses in order. Then, he worked on wrapping the wounded ruffian's hand tightly in a cloth.

"Étienne," the Major continued. "I thank you for defending and protecting milady Contessa Marcella, daughter of Count Dessine, and her companion. The Contessa bears tidings from her father to your Master."

He pronounced the Contessa's name in the Italian way, using a hard "ch" instead of the softer "s" sound of our native French, so it sounded like "Mar-Chella."

I covered my embarrassment at having prissily retched out my insides in front of all concerned enough to recall my instruction in courtly behavior from François.

"I am most honored, Milady, to be of service." I bowed to her, only then realizing that I still held my blades, which I'd not cleaned and were stained with drying blood.

"My apologies for offending you with this unseemly sight, Milady!" I sputtered while attempting to conceal the blades behind my back.

The Contessa brought her gaze haughtily to the battle scene with an air of detachment. Smitten as I was, I mistook her lack of emotion as evidence of majesty.

"Oh, that," she said dismissively, turning her gaze back to my blushing face. "It is really of no account."

I was impressed by her air of command. I was in post-battle shock, and I did not feel in control of myself at all. I had killed a man and wounded another, who had then begged me for mercy. It all happened so fast, without hesitation or thought, and I was not yet in my right mind. Despite my victory on the field of battle, I had yet to conquer myself.

And while thoroughly trained to fight, I had no prior instruction for handling a skirmish with a Contessa. It was all moot anyway, as the overwhelming weapon of her charm left me already defeated.

The Major intervened, grabbing me by the arm and pulling me over to assist in sorting out affairs. I cleaned my blades and yielded to the Major's instruction to tie up the ruffians. We loaded them onto the back platform of the carriage, meant to hold packages and trunks for traveling, along with the body of the one I had killed. That last made me face the reality of the fight again, sobering me. Then, the Major, Petan, and I mounted and headed to the Chateau.

It had not occurred to me why a Count sent his dear and beautiful daughter as a messenger, nor why she had no escort save the Major in such rough times. A hundred other questions worth considering didn't occur to me either because I was preoccupied with riding alongside the carriage so that I might catch a glimpse of her. Without appearing to be doing so, of course, making it even *more* apparent that I was trying so very hard to do so. Without a doubt, I was the *only* person in our party unaware of this fact.

The Contessa did not show that she noticed me at all. She chattered away glibly to her lady-in-waiting as we all traveled down the road at a brisk trot. Only the fact that her lady-in-waiting was still white as a sheet from the crisis and thus incapable of responding to her mistress's conversation gave away this chatter as an act.

Not that I noticed. I was simply aware of being ignored, as I'm sure it was intended, to set the hook better. I was desperate to find a way to attract her attention. The only available gambit seemed to be to look manly and in charge, which I achieved by sitting straighter in the saddle and squaring my shoulders. My efforts only gave Petan, riding alongside me, a chance to poke fun at me. He rolled his eyes at my manly posing and aped my excessive posturing. The Major gave me a toothy and overly solicitous grin, the kind one gives the daft, and drifted back to his customary guard position following the carriage.

Then the Chateau appeared ahead of us, and even I was distracted as we passed through the gates and were greeted by the clamor of orphans and household staff as they descended upon us, calling out for us to tell them what had happened. No sooner had we arrived than we were interrupted by more hullabaloo as Édouard and François thundered through the gate, followed by a detachment of men-at-arms from the local garrison. The crowd around us momentarily scattered like a flock of birds startled from strewn grain, only to crowd around the feed again, realizing their fear was needless.

Édouard explained that he had sensed a crisis at hand, which was reinforced when he encountered Louis, who was riding out on our behalf in search of help, and found them in the village. Édouard and François had come as soon as they could, gathering a force from the nearby garrison as they rode hard to the Chateau.

I saw François scan the bodies trussed up in the back of the carriage, instantly assessing their wounds and our armaments. Only the tiniest smile of satisfaction at what he saw and his slightly raised eyebrow at my hopeful glance indicated his feelings. I found myself broadly grinning back at his restrained but, to me, marked approval. The soldiers took charge of the ruffians, both living and dead, as the Major gave his concise report to Édouard. François proceeded to marshal the staff and orphans in order, sending the maids to prepare food and quarters for the Contessa. Édouard handed her down from the carriage, saying he would receive her and her message as soon as she was refreshed and rested.

Much to my chagrin, she was escorted into the Chateau by one of the younger boys. François hooked me by the arm and marched me down the path through the gardens, almost having to drag me as I tried to watch the Contessa over my shoulder. Once in the garden, François grilled me about the rescue fight. He demanded every detail. What was my tactical evaluation of the ruffian's combat skills? What techniques did I use? How did I deliver the coup de grâce to the man I killed? How had the Major and Petan managed to hold them off? And so on.

I gave him a rough version, but I was annoyed by his persistent demand for more details. I was eager to pursue this marvelous female I had met. When my tone became curt after yet another request for particulars, François raised an eyebrow.

"Perhaps you have some other duties to attend to, Étienne?" he asked slyly. "I would not wish to keep you from something more important."

I had enough sense to recognize the steely faux-sincerity in his tone. I attempted to cover for my distraction.

"I'm just unsettled by all that has happened, François," I responded.

"Indeed, you are." He said, "and by the Contessa herself."

He stated it as a simple fact. I was about to deny that I was affected by her, but I realized it would have been foolish to do so to François. He knew me too well.

My shoulders slumped as I forced myself to confess.

"It is true, François," I admitted. "I am struck dumb by her. She is wondrous! Would I be permitted, do you think, to speak with her?"

François shook his head. "I think it's best if you were to follow the lead set for us by the Maestro. It seems to me that there is more here than meets the eye. Do you not think it strange, Étienne, that a Count should use his dearest daughter as a mere messenger? Certainly, such could be carried with far greater safety and less fanfare by an armed rider, could it not?"

It had not occurred to me, as rational thought was the farthest thing from my mind until now.

"Well, it has occurred to our Maestro, I can assure you," François said. "Let us see what develops before you put your foot in it, my friend.

"Now, if I might distract your attention from matters of the heart with matters of the blade, let us review what occurred. Show me your moves, Étienne. I will act as the ruffians, and you will tell me how I should position myself and what my attack should be."

With this, François finally broke the spell of my bewitchment by involving me in the elements of our Art. He complimented me on my moves, showing me refinements and correcting errors in my approach. Although these were not apparent to the kind of fighters I had challenged, they would have left me vulnerable to those with a higher degree of skill. We worked diligently to address challenging areas in my practice and enhance my Art. An hour passed before he released me, sweating and spent, with my feet now firmly on the ground, to wash up before dinner.

François's counsel was well advised. While I was bathing, Édouard received certain dispatches from Contessa. Although I did not find this out until much later, they consisted of a plea from the Count for the Maestro to take his daughter under his care. The Count feared greatly that her considerable psychic and worldly gifts would be wasted by the flaws in her character, confessing that his failings as a father caused him not to address them adequately. These documents were under seal, and the Contessa was unaware of the request, believing she carried only scholarly papers. The Count had doted upon his daughter; consequently, she had grown up haughty, proud, and self-centered. She focused her considerable native intelligence, beauty, and unconscious psychic talents solely on manipulating the social world, much as she had learned to manipulate her father. In this way, she could maintain a position of control, always being the *recipient* of attention and largesse, never the grantor. In short, she was manipulative, aloof, selfish, and self-centered.

This attitude would have been unremarkable if she had been only a creature of the nobility. She would have been married off to another noble of a similar selfish character, purely to cement the family's power lines. Unfortunately, as far as the Count and Édouard were concerned, the Contessa had latent but considerable psychic gifts meant to aid the Order in its work. Imagine, if you will, a prize-hunting dog left to wallow in the stable yard merely to dominate the pack, never to be trained and disciplined to bring out the more profound expression of its nature in the keen senses of the field.

Once, I'd have objected to likening people to hunting dogs, but now I understand that our most authentic gifts seek to find their most perfect and Sacred expression. If the Contessa had been raised with sensitivity to her gifts but without indulgence, she might have been left to choose her path, whether to use her gifts for the Order or some other path her heart was called to. But for such gifts to be available to one so egotistical and self-serving was something too dangerous to be contemplated.

The Order could not leave her unguided, just as her psychic gifts were to flower. This flowering had been delayed by those concerned about such things in the Order, but this delay was growing steadily more precipitous. It would not hold much longer. It became incumbent on the Count to salvage the damage he had wrought by spoiling his daughter. Otherwise, the Order would have to permanently stifle her power growth to prevent her magical potential from wreaking havoc in human society.

Some circles believed it was too late, but the Magister Primo of the Order thought otherwise. Édouard had earned quite a reputation for miracles in the Order for what he had accomplished with his orphan army. Might Édouard induce the required Alchemical transformation with the Contessa he had with us?

Édouard saw it as a worthy challenge. He had learned much from observing us and applying his mastery of alchemical principles to the human sphere. Having transformed the base, unrefined matter of us orphan boys to gold, could he not take such rarefied and overly refined metal and make of her a stronger alloy? Immersing the Contessa in life at the Chateau might be just the thing to bring her down to earth. She must come to discover her common humanity for her own sake, even if she chooses not to serve the Order and its larger mission for humanity.

All of this Édouard disclosed to no one except François. Certainly not to the Contessa. We, the orphan residents and staff, knew nothing. Word was passed that we were required to use the strictest manners concerning her. No conversation would pass between us and the Contessa; we were to avert our gaze and bow our heads should we see her, and never to speak in her presence. She was too highborn to be sullied with us; we were to act as mere servants; only the most tremendous respect was to be shown to her. We were forbidden to talk, play, sup, or engage with her in any form, or François would have an accounting with us.

We might have taken such orders from Édouard as challenges worthy of outwitting, all in the game. With François invoked, we understood these to be incontrovertible rules of law. We'd all felt the literal sting of his correction more than once. The Contessa was thus effectively isolated from all within the Chateau but the Maestro and her servant.

And what was his plan? What better heat to boil the Alchemical vessel than that created by its latent fires? Alchemically, the Contessa was a substance formed too singularly. Refined only in worldly manners, she had never had to refine her flaws and impurities through life challenges due to her father's overprotection. Now, as the internal fire of sexual maturity heated the vessel, her base impurities sought an outlet but could be released only through the narrowest channel of selfishness.

Alchemy requires the raw ore of human nature to be *putrified*, broken down into its constituents, and purified of its crudeness.

Then, finally, distilled to its most rarified nature. Without these steps, one's essential gold could not shine with its innate power.

She demanded admiration and manipulated everyone to achieve this end, caring not a whit for those she drew to her. What did all this cover? It remained to be seen. The Maestro believed nothing was to be wasted, even impurities. To him, everything was an ingredient to be used as fuel for the transformation. The Maestro also saw an opportunity to exercise his devotion to Drama, and none of that priceless substance would be wasted!

So, he made quite a great show of it: she must be treated "worthy of her station;" he solicitously worried that such a crude country manor could not give her the comfort she deserved. She must have the best of everything. She absolutely must not be distressed by contact with common riff-raff, namely, we orphans whom he had pledged to protect as charity.

And so, the Contessa became bound within a cage made up of her conceit. It was a prison of splendor where her very existence was worshipped, but a prison nonetheless. It had everything she could have wished for except, of course, human company. The Maestro even saw that her lady-in-waiting was kept busy on many errands "to ensure her mistress's comfort," so even this familiarity was denied her. Everyone around her treated her grandly and with proper royal distance.

At first, I did not have the wit to see the impact of this treatment upon her. I was smitten and, so, blinded to facts as are all who are smitten. As some of my compatriots described to me later, she preened herself before the deference and admiration heaped upon her by Édouard and by, at his direction, the rest of our company.

Then, without anyone with whom she could boast about how deserved all our fawning was, she appeared disconcerted. No matter, she simply redoubled her efforts, becoming even more vivacious, bossy, demanding, and imperious in tone and manner. All of this was met with instant assent under Édouard's watchful and guiding eye. The more demanding she became, the more she was given. The more charming and coquettish she became, to better reap our attention and admiration, the more she was showered with compliments, admiration, and displays of affection. But no genuine warmth was derived thereby. It was all very extravagant, fulsome, and, like her, utterly empty.

And the Maestro was having a field day. He gloried in his role; the drama whetted his tremendous appetite for High Theatre. He bowed and entreated; he lavished praise upon her; he flew into magnificent rages at imagined slights to her on her behalf. He attended to her every need, though he was always, regretfully, called away to some necessary duty whenever she looked to have a real conversation. He was her father, doubled, yeah, tripled. Nothing was too good for her, but in the end, it was indeed nothing, after all.

Familiar as we were by now with the Master's manner and purposes, it began to be clear, even to me, that all of this was due to a higher purpose than merely coddling a spoiled noblewoman. In response, I became disillusioned. I felt sour on her, seeing what before I had thought was nobility now as merely tyrannical and aloof. I began to see beneath her beauty and superficial charisma. I did not like what I saw — or, more accurately, I began to dislike her — for my own superficiality and naiveté, which had led me to be so attracted to her. The lifting of the gauzy curtain of infatuation left me feeling somehow betrayed, as if she had done something personally to me, rather than acknowledge that the error in judgment was my own.

After many weeks, a change had come over the Contessa. Her rigid back began to slump. Her arched eyebrows began to fall. She became withdrawn, issuing fewer orders and demands, followed by fits of desperate and increasingly childlike tantrums. Back and forth until even this last gasp of pettiness was spent, she began to look beseechingly to us, imploring us with her eyes to approach her, to release her from this cage of isolation she now found herself in. François, on orders from the Master, made doubly sure we were schooled to respond only with mandatory obsequiousness.

It pained us to do so. Though we found her unpleasant, we collectively felt the game had gone far enough. To continue seemed little more than cruel.

But the Maestro had spoken. The nut had not been subjected to this much pressure, only to be released before its shell cracked and revealed the seed it might contain. So we all tried to avoid her altogether, going out of our way to avoid passing by the wing where she was housed.

It was often my wont to take a shortcut through the flower garden as I did my daily duties. It made for an easy entrance through the back door of the great hall and afforded me a moment to feast my eyes on the flowers and herbs tended therein. Crossing through it one day, I rounded the hedge and came face-to-face with Contessa Marcella. I immediately swept off my cap and bowed deeply to her, as we had been ordered to do should anyone encounter her. I immediately apologized for disturbing her meditations, sullying her view, and exposing her refined sensibilities to one as low as I...all while subtly backing away so I could turn and escape.

To my dismay, she flung herself at me, grabbing my arms in an iron grip while falling to her knees in the dirt before me, wracked with sobs.

"Oh, please," she cried as she clutched at me. She leaned her brow upon my forearms. "You mustn't bow. You do not disturb me in the slightest; I am most grateful to have come upon you."

I tried to pull away from her, continuing to voice effusive apologies. She would not let go of my arms! Her desperation made her grip shockingly strong! She did, however, allow me to pull her to her feet while her sobs continued, her face downcast as if she feared to look at me and see judgment on my face. There was no haughtiness to her posture. Her shoulders were bent, rounding over her previously proud chest, and her eyes looked red and pained. She eventually braved herself enough, as her sobs abated, to look up and catch my eyes.

"You are Étienne, yes? The Chevalier who came to our aid on the road?"

I nodded, though I was certainly no knight, but feared digging myself into more trouble than I was already in by risking speaking.

"I had not the chance, or the wit really," she said, dropping her eyes with shame at this admission, "to truly thank you for what you did for us."

"It is my honor to have served you, milady Contessa," I sputtered. "I am your humble servant. It would have been my honor to have given my pathetic life to rescue someone as worthy and important as you."

Excessive, but precisely as we had been instructed to act toward her.

"Oh, please don't, Étienne! I cannot bear to be treated with such formal distance anymore," tears welled up in her eyes. "Though I know I deserve it, as I haven't been very kind. I've never felt so lonely in my life. Please, don't treat me this way, Étienne, or I'll simply be shattered if there's no one to help me fix my mistakes."

With this, Marcella broke down completely, hardly able to stand as her sobs wracked her body. She was deeply and genuinely distraught. As far as I could discern, this was not an act designed to elicit concern from me. For perhaps the first time, she recognized she was missing something and could not find a way through without another's help. I led her to a small bench along the garden path and sat her down. Casting caution to the winds, I sat awkwardly next to her. I couldn't do otherwise, really, as she would not release my hands as she cried.

Bees buzzed over the flowers and about us in the warm sunshine. Sobs rolled out of her periodically in waves. I freed one hand to woodenly pat her shoulder in a reluctant attempt to provide some comfort. She eventually calmed and quieted. I sat dumbly beside her and wondered what ire Édouard would display for my having ruined his alchemical procedures. Whatever credit I had built up from the rescue must now have become pure debt.

Looking at her now, she no longer appeared beautiful, seeming instead to be piteous. Despite her privilege and riches, she was only now realizing her ignorance about what was inside her skin, just as it was inside others. Looking at her, I felt a swell of gratitude for my friends and companions at the Chateau, as it was apparent that she could have had no real friends or comrades to share things with. For her, people would be either competitors or servants. There could be no in-between. The discovery that her need to be the center of attention had rendered her empty and alone must be nothing short of horror for her.

She spoke now, haltingly, her voice thick from crying. "I had been thinking here in the garden when you came down the path, Étienne."

Her red-rimmed eyes stared past me into the foliage.

"When I first came here, I felt exiled by my father to some country pigsty, and I was so *very* furious."

I stiffened at her description of my beloved home and almost took to my feet.

"No, wait, Étienne. Please hear me out before you misunderstand me," she pleaded. "I see now how ignorant I was and how arrogant."

I settled back stiffly onto the bench.

"I could not believe then that I had been thrust amongst such a raggle-taggle bunch of commoners, orphans all. I, who had been to the Italian Court and felt, only there, among those worthy of me, was outraged to have been left to fend for myself amidst such a rough crowd."

She shifted her gaze to catch my eyes.

"But then, I began to notice something. I watched you all from my balcony window, bantering, playing games, and doing your duties. You all seemed so vibrant, so full of life. I tried to make myself even more vivacious in an attempt to outshine you all, but to no avail. Mine was all an act. You…you all were filled with something… so real. I could not reproduce it! Whatever it was, it was not subject to my will. And the more I tried to mimic it, the further it receded from me. I was not just lonely; I was *false*. None of my acts or poses were more than the thinnest paper next to this vibrancy and fullness of life I could see so clearly in you all. I longed to join you all to wrest this secret from you. What filled you all? I still could not fathom it."

She paused as if a little breathless from the telling. There was a hint of color in her face now, almost a passion. Her eyes glistened, and a smile came to her lips. I realized it was the first genuine one I'd seen, with none of that calculated artifice. It truly lit up her face. She continued.

"I watched, consumed in my growing loneliness, and even I had to recognize what it was for all of you. It was so simple, in a way; I don't know how anyone could have missed it, except I did because of how deeply mistaken I have been. You know what it is, Étienne, don't you? What is it that fills you all?"

I shook my head. "I don't understand, Mistress."

She looked forlorn momentarily at my use of the formal honorific, but her fervor carried her on despite this.

"Of course, you don't. It is natural to you, Étienne, but not to me."

She briefly shook the hand she had been grasping to get my attention and make me listen to her more deeply. I was startled as I had forgotten she was still holding my hands.

"Étienne, what do you feel when you wake in the morning and rush down to see your friends at the table?"

"Why, I guess I feel pleased," I said. "Leastwise, I do unless Joucain has placed toads in my stockings again," I laughed.

"Yes, that's it," she said. "It is so natural to you that you don't need to name it. You love."

She nodded at me as if to assert that I had confirmed her theorem by my admission.

"So simple. It's not that you are loved. Well, this too, of course, but that you *love*. It fills you with joy to see each other. It is in your voices when you call out to each other, even when arguing. You are not trying to hurt each other with your tempers. It is because you care. I had missed out on this and thought to make up for it by gaining more self-regard, only to come up empty-handed because I did not know how to love. I knew not how to; I even feared that to give to another in such a way would leave me lessened."

I knew what she meant as she said it. It was true, but I had never thought much about it before. The Maestro and François had shown us all how. They could be stern and angry sometimes, but there was always love. They took pleasure in us always. We naturally passed this back and forth. No greater pleasure was mine than to ride in the gate and have my friend Louis run up to grab my reins and clap me on the shoulder. Petan, Joucain, Tonton, and Bora were my world, and I loved them deeply. My heart swelled with my feelings for them.

"Is what I say foolish?" she asked.

"No, milady," I answered. "I understand. You are right, although I have not thought much about it before. I'd rather be an orphan here than come to any royal court."

"Please, you must call me Marcella. It is my name, and I have not gotten much value from my titles lately."

I nodded but said nothing, not wishing to commit further until I confessed my complete transgression of the rules to the Maestro.

"So," she continued, "I have realized that you know something I must understand and am compelled to understand. I am the orphan in this way, and you all are *en famille*. You know how to love. Will you teach me about it? Will you talk to me about your world and your friends so I can learn what you're caring about? I promise not to be a bother, Étienne, but I can see no other way."

I told her I would think about it, but I could barely stand to sit there with her any longer. I was already in hot water and felt it was about to boil over. She noticed my restlessness and spoke further before she completely lost my attention.

"Before you go, Étienne, could you tell me why you fought the ruffians for us? What possessed you to risk yourself so? Was it nobility? Did you expect a reward or compliments for your bravery?"

"It wasn't any of those things," I said. "The Major was in trouble. I could not do otherwise than go to his assistance."

I had not thought about it until she asked.

"He is family to us here." I mused on this further, "But in truth, I would have responded to the call even if it were an unknown traveler. So I have been taught, and I could do no less."

She nodded. "It is as I suspected. You did it out of love. Oh, not for me because you did not form your crush until you saw me."

I blushed scarlet at this.

"I scarcely deserved it from you, truth be told, though I expected nothing less. But that is it, Étienne, your risk was not to gain something; it was from your love for the Major, your family here, and perhaps even some loving sense of your place in humankind. I can hardly fathom caring about anything that much. But I must learn. I cannot go on as I have. Tell me, Étienne, were you not afraid for your life?"

"I had no time to be frightened, Mistress," I replied. "But I've had little fear of death in any case since I have been shown that I have come through that passage before. I am afraid only to lose the friends that I have now, my compatriots, and Édouard, François, and Mathilde, of course."

Marcella's eyes widened at this, then she blinked and softly spoke, her eyes downcast. "It is as my father had tried to tell me, though I did not have the wit to listen to him. Perhaps I, too, must be shown this passage you speak of. Perhaps it would enlighten me about Life, as it enlightened you about Death."

Marcella released me then, and I left her sitting, looking quite wrung out, on the bench in the garden. I sought out Édouard immediately, only to find him going over accounts with François. Without pausing, I blurted out what had happened. The Maestro grilled me for a full accounting while François stood sternly with arms folded at the Maestro's side. Édouard's mouth quirked, and his smile grew as I detailed what had occurred.

"Excellent! It is the break we have been waiting for. By all means, my boy," he exclaimed. "You may answer her questions; do not hesitate. Satisfy her curiosity completely. That is your assignment now."

I left, surprised and a bit bewildered. It was not the answer I had expected, but the Maestro was never what I expected him to be.

Thus, initiated many long conversations with Marcella. You must understand that I had moved beyond my infatuation with her. I was curious about her but cautious.

I was willing to humor Marcella because of Édouard's request, and when I wasn't fulfilling my duties about the Chateau or engaged with my fellows, I would meet with her. We would walk through the garden or on the paths in the immediate surroundings of the Chateau, usually followed at a discreet distance by her lady-servant as chaperone, and Marcella would pepper me with one question after another.

To my great surprise, her curiosity about me, my life, and all of the residents of the Chateau was genuine. It seemed she had begun to burn, in her isolation, to know about others, to fathom what drove them and what they had experienced that was different from her. She had watched us from her royal prison, and the alchemy of her loneliness had finally broken through her disdain. Her native perceptiveness had always been bent on finding a point of gain, but she had no reference points for learning about their inner life.

And she was exquisitely intelligent. Her incessant questions were not random; she would pursue a subject, probing until she had as much as she could gain from me in all its ins and outs. Her mind could not rest until she understood what she saw in front of her. Frustrated by the Maestro's turning this considerable intelligence towards its usual target, the manipulation of others, she was now free to give rein to this other problem: to imagine our lives, our loves, our devotion to each other, and the cause. Her forlorn and isolated heart was now driving her profound curiosity. I had become her window into another world, and if she could get me to open the shutters to it, she felt she could glimpse the way, though she could not yet enter. She was desperate to find the path to step into that world herself and experience what her self-centeredness had so precisely denied her.

Her attempt to learn through me was not merely for information. A deep empathic psychic capacity native to her had previously been used solely for her own desires. The Order had dampened it lest its growth be used for worse than simple selfishness. I suspect the Maestro released some of these bindings to help her better understand others. This now growing power, the power to attune to the emotions and inner being of another, was now turned to acquire qualities that mere intellect alone could not. Her heightened physical resonance initially heightened her confusion, as if the ability to sense others' emotional nuances made her see the starkness of her own lack even more clearly. It was this emptiness, this gap in her being, which she became acutely aware of for the first time in her life, but it motivated her craving to transform more than anything. She turned her considerable intellect to this task, and now she possessed a budding psychic ability to sense within another's skin. In this way, she would extend herself to feel inside mine as I spoke to her.

And though Marcella seemed to have a deeper, genuine appreciation for my feelings and viewpoint, she still could not find a way to unlock her own. Is it possible to pry open one's own heart? Intellectual knowledge alone could not provide what she ached for.

Upon hearing my report of our interaction, Édouard had a proposal. No matter how closed off we are in our current lives, we have felt love before in all its many forms in some other lifetime. Much as Édouard used the Egg of the Phoenix to release me from my fear of death, now he used it with Marcella to release her from her selfishness, which he called her fear of Life. As was the rule, I was not privy to her visions, but I witnessed the results of that Alchemy at work in her. I had gone through it before myself.

The soul can stray from its intended path due to misguided conclusions from challenging experiences. We often make secret vows to avoid being hurt in the same way again, which can lead us to adopt rigid beliefs and fixations. These can limit our ability to fulfill our soul's purpose.

With alchemical devices like the Egg, the recipient's soul shapes the prior lives seen, and the lessons to be drawn are revealed. The Egg opens the door to the storeroom of Far Memorie, but the volumes that are taken from the shelves, and the pages perused are determined by the soul's deep needs, not the magical object. This is as true in the Arts Psychic as in everyday life.

Whereas my soul, struggling with the Lessons of Fear and Life and Death, drew on those aspects of the many lives I had lived, these lessons were not the only or even the main point of many of these lives. Indeed, after my denouement in the manure pile, I spent many months reviewing these memories at Édouard's behest, grasping how much the issues of fear, pain, and death had blinded me from seeing the love, the adventure, the great learning, the joy, happiness, and beauty, all as much a part of life as pain and suffering.

For Marcella, the volume her soul pulled from the shelf to review was the book of love; her selfishness and closed heart were not solely due to her indulgent father. It was brought with her from previous times when betrayal and deep hurt provoked vows never again to be subject to another nor desire love herself ever again. Having so vowed and closed the shutters to love, many aspects of her being had become dry, stunted, and distorted, much like a plant denied adequate sunshine for its nurture. Her indulgent father merely affirmed a position already reached, her soul convinced that such indulgence would best serve its commitment to self-protection.

Through the Egg, Marcella did not find stories of death and self-sacrifice, as did I, but rather tales of love and betrayal, yearning, disappointment, isolation, tribe, and so on—all the myriad ways her soul had struggled with human relationships and love, as well as the myriad lives and times she had loved and been beloved.

It wrought a change in her that was moving for me to witness. She could not speak to me about the details, but I could see that everything she had known and believed was being dismantled. At first, she became even more tearful, isolated, and distraught. Though our conversations continued and her curiosity about others grew even more insatiable, she seemed distant, even amid her insistent inquiries. She seemed to be behind glass.

In other instances, I would see her peering from her chamber window, looking down upon the goings-on of the Chateau. From this distance, I could see tears streaming down her cheeks, and her expression was one of deep pain. I recognized in this the formation of the hermetic seal of the *Vas Hermetis*, the alchemical vessel. Within it, the pressure was building, and the raw elements of her nature entered Putrefaction, breaking down and being purified from the action of fire and heat.

Did the Alchemist, our Maestro, build this vessel for her? He would say not and that he only screwed the top on a bit tighter and moved the vessel more directly over the fire. He believed that we create our sealed chamber, forged out of the walls we have built against the pain of Worldly existence. Further, he would note that each act of disregard, each conjuring of hatred or hardening of heart, abandoning one's duty, and so on, merely thickened the walls of our hermetic vessel such that even more heat and pressure were required to render transformation.

To the Maestro, there was no ultimate way to avoid or surmount the true nature of our soul; every attempt only slapped more substance to our vessel, as a clumsy potter might add too much clay to the pot spinning upon his wheel rather than refine his technique. To the Maestro, his art was merely to find how to put the final turn on the lid and stoke the fire hotter.

As for me, I could only watch, offering her my earnest conversation, hoping she would find her way out of this gilded cage. Marcella had sealed herself away from the life of her soul, which she had now come to crave so desperately. Now that I saw her as a dear friend, I fervently wished she would find her heart's desire.

The first crack that showed itself to me was when I walked through the rose garden one morning and saw Marcella standing before a bush of the Master's rare and beloved yellow roses. She held one fragrant bloom in her hands and gazed at it with such rapt attention that she was unaware of my presence. I paused, not wishing to intrude, yet I could not stop watching her.

She looked like she would drink each petal into her if she could. This was not the arch and haughty expression of old nor the pained and yearning expression I had seen lately. There was wonder, even awe, as if she saw its beauty for the first time. She had found an echoing bud somewhere within her that, like the one in her hand, was similarly clamoring to open and bloom in the sun.

As she gazed at the rose, I saw that glistening tears trailed down her cheeks and dripped from her chin. As if taken by impulse, she clasped the bloom to her heart in an embrace like the dearest and most beloved friend, one who had long been on a journey and who had finally returned home.

The change of angle of her head brought her eyes suddenly upon me, where I stood watching her. She was momentarily startled but recovered, giving me a smile and nod. To my surprise, with the flower clasped to her heart, she bowed to me as if to honor me for sharing this intimate moment with her. Marcella then turned and continued her meditations down the garden path. I stood there for some moments longer, thinking to give her privacy and space, but to contemplate the hidden yet palpable light I'd seen emerging from her. Roses have always been incredibly precious to me, and their blooms are wondrous creations, but the blooming of a soul outshines them in ways that cannot be reckoned with.

From her, I learned an even more jaundiced view of the Church than I had from Édouard's irreligiousness, and her scathing rendition of the foibles of the aristocracy removed any penchant I might have had to see them as my betters. Marcella had no such illusions, and her keen intelligence, perceptive eye, and cleverly outrageous stories exposed me to the ruling classes in all their presumption and naked stupidity. And now that her bitterness and sarcasm were finally being distilled out of her, she seemed to want to illuminate this world to me —not to show off her independence from it, but to educate me about the broader world, just as I had helped educate her about the inner one.

Indeed, both François and Édouard had taught us about such things: manners, the structure of court and government, and a realistic view of the Church and society. But neither of them was genuinely interested in these topics. They presented them as lands one must traverse during one's true mission in life, but neither cared for the scenery.

François only knew what allowed him to be flexible and to blend in while pursuing his life's mission—a path that was clear to him and which he followed without deviation or detours, no matter where he was. Édouard saw it, like everything else, as theater and could take on any role needed.

On the other hand, Marcella had engaged fully in this world from birth. She applied herself to mastering it from the most intense of human motivations: complete and unfettered self-interest. In this way, she had no illusions and focused only on learning what would work to further her advantage and what would not. A purist, she had played the game with as thorough a sense of purpose as François but with an even greater interest in bending the outcome to serve her ends as opposed to the utter detachment François gave to serve a higher purpose. From Marcella, I began to understand why someone could hunger for power even as she had started to reformulate her relationship with it. This served me well at times in my life, particularly when I needed to negotiate in the fields of power on behalf of the Order's aims and the Chateau's continued existence when it was in my charge.

As the roles of teacher and student reversed, I was wide-eyed at the world she shared with me. I accepted this switch without question and was grateful she would share it with me. I was too young and provincial to fully appreciate the value and power of the gift I had given her—to have bared my heart openly so hers could open and nourish the parched places.

Also, I did not have the wit to recognize the intimacy growing between us; the hungry and needful places in myself were also opening now in the presence of one trusted and beloved. Not the puppy love of infatuation I first had. I was long past this, thankfully, and in truth, I did not view her as an object of passion. It was more the resonance of two hearts unfolding for the first time. We were like two plants that grow next to one another, such that their tendrils and leaves intertwine and interlock so naturally; it is only later that they are recognized to have become one: perhaps only noticed when they must, as happens, be pulled apart and transplanted afar.

As Marcella was released from her inner prison, I saw an inner light growing within her —a radiance that had not been there before. Supplanting her steely strength was a quality of loving kindness as she walked about a world she saw for the first time, interacting with others in the Chateau. Was it that flame shining from her that, unbeknownst to me, lighted the tinder gathering in my heart? I considered myself only a companion on her journey. Our friendship was such that we could fall into silence and be comfortable in each other's presence, gazing at the landscape in wonderment or simply resting thoughtfully after lengthy discussions.

There came a time when, engaged in one of our deep discussions by the river, we simultaneously fell into one of those companionable silences, this time merely gazing at one another. Feeling my inner radiance aglow from my time with her, I looked into her eyes and, for the first time, recognized an answering radiance shining back to me. A hand quickly sought a meeting hand. So complete was our rapture in each other at that moment that neither of us moved to kiss or embrace.

But young passion is a power all its own, and it flared as does smoldering tinder when but gently breathed upon. The fire burst forth from us, flushing her face with color and surging with sudden heat in my chest.

Then, we were wrapped in each other's arms, our breaths and lips pressed together. When we finally broke our kiss, I held her and looked into her shining eyes, gently brushing a strand of hair from her temple, breathless and hearts racing.

"Étienne, *mon cheri*..." she whispered, "my cherished one."

I kissed her again, falling into her mouth and scent.

We kissed more, first longingly and then lingeringly. Eventually, we came up for air and laughed together in mutual delight.

Marcella had truly learned to love, indeed. *Mia, Marcella!* And, in her dive into love's deep waters, she'd caught me like a fish and swept me up in the vast net of her heart.

CHAPTER V:

To Love

Where before we were oftentimes companions, now, whenever our duties gave us leave, we were inseparable. We were compelled to seek each other out, if only to cross paths between tasks. We were each other's first true and deep love, a love born from having opened unknown places together.

Our first weeks in love were entirely innocent. The mere fact of falling in love was so new for us both that we were preoccupied with its overpowering sensation of intimacy and closeness. We would walk through the garden, arms laced, reveling in the simple warmth of the other. When we paused to embrace and kiss, the scent and presence of each other absorbed us as our lips and breath mingled and our hands tightly clasped.

The change between us was not unnoticed, as I was called to present myself to François shortly after that first kiss. I did so at my earliest opportunity, catching him as he walked out to the stables. He paused to face me and, without preamble, made it clear that he was aware of what had occurred with Marcella. François then succinctly laid out the rules, responsibilities, and expectations he had for me regarding her.

To wit, that it was my foremost and *sacred* duty to protect *The Contessa* Marcella, underlining her title and position with his most authoritative voice, especially from even the *hint* of scandal or any slight to her reputation. This included, most specifically, my duty to protect her from the loss of her virginity or, worse, from the risk of pregnancy.

Further, François elaborated, it was my duty to ensure that *the Maestro*, acting as her foster parent, was not seen as failing to guard the Contessa's virtue under his protection. Such would wreak havoc on the Maestro's ability to fulfill his mission for the Order.

"And should you throw caution to the winds and disobey these limits," François said with a voice of steel, "I will befall you like a mighty wind."

I stood calmly in the face of his admonitions.

"I understand completely, François," I said. "Please know that Marcella and I have already spoken of this and set limits to expressions of love consistent with these same concerns."

François looked at me blandly but sternly, as if he expected no less, but it was evident in his look that his points superseded anything Marcella and I had discussed. He dismissed me and continued on his way to the stables.

I reported this to Marcella, which led us to discuss how we fell in love. I believed that Marcella, far more worldly and experienced than I, must have some inkling of the feelings building between us. I'd understood from things she'd said that the play of love had been a tool for her since she first discovered the effect of her charms on men and women alike. I was sure that I was alone in my surprise at the turn our friendship had taken. Marcella shook her head ruefully and spoke with frank self-honesty.

"As skilled as I was in flirtation, Étienne," she confessed. "I have been as profoundly ignorant of love as a fish of air. My skill was in portraying love precisely because it risked me nothing."

A sudden sob caught her in the stark impact of this truth. I drew her into my embrace to comfort her. When she had recovered and calmed, she elaborated further.

"I was not enamored with the other but with myself and my power over them. I thought it my genius, you see." She shuddered with horror at the realization of how misguided she had been. "What a piddling genius it was, serving only to keep my heart stunted and in the dark."

Tears welled up as she mourned all she'd lost living as she had.

She confessed to me that even her love for her father now appeared as a kind of fierce loyalty coupled with essential animal fondness. She had always felt an arrogant disdain for what she saw as his weakness, but now could see it as his deep paternal love.

The Maestro's alchemy sealed her in a hermetic vessel, where she dissolved the barriers she had erected to love. Cooked in the chymical solution of devotion, camaraderie, and love that was the Chateau, her true heart finally opened.

Dissolved and rendered to her most basic and essential elements, the gods added me into the mixture to serve as the simple catalyst to coagulate the solute into a truer form. It was clear that I was merely a tuning device, a vibrating string from which she could discover her innate inner tone. With her budding magical skill, she could use me as a template to discover herself, but my friendship only assisted her in finding the trail to her innate heart.

Then, when she looked within to dwell in her newly discovered heart, she found that I was there, too —a flame already lit inside her. Likewise, the blaze of her heart's burning flame had sparked a fire in my own without my realizing it. We both recognized that this new, vulnerable state required us to proceed with care. It was new to us both, and we did not want lust to take us over and bring unanticipated harm because of our naiveté.

I felt like a complete dunce for not noticing the love that had grown between us. Evidently, I was immature and naive in matters of the heart. I'd known dalliance before, but *love* was of another order entirely and quite took me by surprise. By the time I realized we were in love, it was already an accomplished fact.

Struggling to clarify what had happened, I sought Eton, my friend and confidante in life's puzzles, to confess my surprise at the events. I shared my insights with him, discussing my immaturity and admiration for Marcella's great intuitive powers, seeking his affirmation after outlining my conclusions.

He stared at me cooly as I confessed, then raised an eyebrow at my summation as he gazed at me down the length of his elegant and patrician nose.

"So, my foolish friend, what did you think would happen?" he asked dryly. "By what distorted logic do you conclude that Marcella's magic initiated falling in love and not yours? Her powers were not even allowed to surface until *after* her alchemical transformation, yes? And in that transformation, *you* were an essential element, no mere catalyst!"

I demurred, saying I was well aware of the service I provided her by conversing freely with her.

Eton rolled his eyes at me. "The things you leave out of your story, Étienne, take up more pages than the story itself!"

He raised his hand to halt my budding protest. Leaving his hand in front of my face to indicate I should withhold comment, he raised only his pointer finger and began listing his points individually.

"First," said Eton, "You willingly opened yourself to the most intelligent, perceptive, and psychically gifted woman you or I are ever likely to meet."

I could only agree with this glowing description of my precious darling and admitted my great good fortune to him.

Adding a second finger, he continued his list.

"Then," he said, "you committed yourself, heart and soul, to her deep inquiry into your heart and blithely ignored the inherent power of such a gesture."

Well, I thought, I only wished to do the best job of it possible once I'd agreed to help her. Why did he call it a gesture of power?

Eton then raised a third finger to join the others and continued his dissertation. "Thirdly, you conclude that your responsibility for missing the import of all this is due to your 'simple lack of maturity' as to the nature of love, yes?"

I nodded, as this was, indeed, how I saw it. It was lovely that he understood my position so well. I shrugged my shoulders to convey that it was simply obvious, hoping to counter the touch of sarcasm I'd heard in his tone.

Eton ignored me. He'd not finished, and the bastard was nothing if not thorough. A fourth finger was added. Perhaps, I thought, his leftover fingers felt lonely and wanted to join the others.

"And, thereby," he opined, "Marcella utilized the inner magical resonance of *your heart's pattern* and, with its resonance, allowed her heart to be alchemically transformed, yes?"

I suppose it was true as far as it went. Except that what he had wrong was that *Marcella's* magical power was operating here. To ascribe it to a mystical power of *my* heart was ridiculous!

But I was beginning to glimpse where Eton was heading with all this, and I was sure I did not like it.

The scholar Eton raised his thumb to join the spread of the previous four fingers, waving them in front of my nose to affirm the principle of etheric wholeness contained in the magical number five, or something, and made his final point.

"And finally, due to the magical power that has been cultivated in you through your *years* of training with a master alchemist, refined further by a holy abbess, and greatly amplified through your studies with the last High Druid, to boot, the pattern of your loving heart became engraved within her, so that she discovered her own heart!"

I protested that he was making more of it than it was. I would agree with him only if he granted that I was merely sharing my story with her, simply a narrative, don't you see? Besides, I complied with the Maestro's express instructions and intended nothing beyond serving the Maestro's request.

"Nothing *intended?* But of course!" Eton exclaimed. He threw up his arms theatrically as if in capitulation, rolling his eyes to convey his sarcasm. It appeared that he had gleaned too much of our Maestro's theatricality. I was convinced that it did not suit him.

"Nothing of *your* magical power, you say?" Eton said. "Oh, oh! You did not *intend* to practice magic, so there must be no such power at work? Of course, you believe your part was only your simple, *natural* actions? No wonder you conclude it's due to 'immaturity,' as that is the only explanation you have. Truly, you are ignorant of the magical power you have acquired!"

He guffawed loudly and slapped his thigh, laughing at my reasoned argument as if it were the punch line to a great joke.

I slumped against the wall. I had an all-too-familiar feeling that Eton had outwitted me at the game even before I'd begun playing it. Eton was the acknowledged genius amongst us. All of us orphans were outclassed before we entered into an argument with him.

"Étienne, *mon amis,* you are always clueless when it comes to yourself," he pronounced bluntly, "always, always, *always.* And especially clueless concerning the extent of your magical power."

I tried to interrupt him, but he wouldn't let me and continued with his soliloquy.

"Please hear me, dear friend, when I say that your blitheness at how the two of you fell in love is *not* due to your immaturity about love. It's due to a far more important blind spot you have. It is your blindness regarding your understanding of *yourself.*"

Accustomed to Eton's bluntness, I only raised an eyebrow, challenging him to make his case. I'm sure he didn't consider it much of a challenge.

"*Mon Amis*, you have a considerable aura of magic, whether you intend to do anything magical or not. All of us know this about you, except you, of course! Collectively, we love you despite our frustration with your profound cluelessness." He smiled at me, shaking his head as if in wonder. "Everyone at the Château knows of this quirk of yours, even the kitchen maids!

"Étienne, it is a ridiculous belief that only when you intend to do magic do you have magical power and effect. It all feels 'natural' to you. Therefore, it is 'simply' you being yourself.

"And your magical power has only increased since your sojourn to Brittany. You credit it only when you commit an intentional act, as you did when you moon traveled for the rescue. Why do you think everyone, especially Matilde, was so heartened and *relieved* when you arrived home unexpectedly after Eustace's kidnapping?"

I protested still that he was giving me way too much credit for Marcella's transformation, especially with this surprising result of our falling in love.

"You have your moments, Étienne," Eton stated dispassionately, and for a short moment, I almost believed my argument was getting through to him. Alas no.

"But about this, my friend, you are an imbecile."

Eton spoke this plainly, like reciting a basic fact of nature. You know, like "The air is cold today," or "Water is wet," or that "Étienne is an imbecile."

Eton blew a breath out between his pursed lips to give dramatic emphasis to the heroic effort required to explain his argument to such a simpleton.

"Don't you know, Étienne, that when your heart is engaged, and you tell us all a story, you provoke in us such a vivid picture of the scene, with all its accompanying sensations, that we feel it's occurring as you speak?"

His question seemed rhetorical, so I decided to be silent for its sheer novelty.

"And when you recall to us an important memory, Étienne, do you not know how powerfully you evoke it, so much so that we feel all your accompanying emotions along with your story?"

He watched my eyes, pausing to let this sink in. He looked dissatisfied, perhaps concluding that my thick skull was not sufficiently soft and warranted a soaking in additional facts.

"And further, when you demonstrate to us a martial technique, you impart to us the body's *feeling* of movement so we may learn it more easily?"

I wouldn't have put it like this, only that I had a knack for teaching others.

"This is magical power in action, is it not? To transmit something with means beyond those of the everyday world?

"Yes, I know," Eton interjected before I could protest. "You were about to say that you do no spells or incantations, that you gather no power from Nature, nor pronounce any formal prayers. It's a given that your only 'intention' is to communicate and help.

"Yet *every act of your committed heart,*" Eton continued, "*everything that comes from your true nature carries unintended magical power…* naturally!" He dropped his hands to his lap. "It is so natural that you don't even think about it."

"Stay with me here, Étienne. Why do you think Édouard sent you to the Old Man? I can tell you why, my friend, as I heard it from his lips. The Maestro believed that you were the *only* one of us with enough *natural* magical power and presence to stand up to that kind of teacher and benefit *despite* his difficulties. Édouard knew sending an apprentice with sufficient power was necessary, or nothing could be learned. He also knew the Druid would see this as a sign of respect. The Old Man would see that his time was not to be wasted.

"It tortured the Maestro to realize, after the fact, that he had unwittingly put you in the hands of a teacher unworthy of your gifts. He confessed this to me in confidence, seeking my honest opinion because he believed he had failed you by not finding out more about this teacher. I told him that his assessment of *you* was correct and that he should instead be rightfully proud that you proved to be more than up to the challenge. And you would be up to every challenge thereafter. Of course, I already knew how proud he was of you, so the cure was already present."

I was stunned to hear this from Eton. I had never held the Maestro responsible for the Old Man's manipulations and was surprised to hear of Édouard's remorse. Equally surprising was what Eton revealed about Édouard and his assessment of my magical power to deal with the Old Man.

Eton stood and squared himself in front of me. I recognized his posture as that of presenting his conclusions.

"So," he proclaimed, "I agree that you indeed face a crisis of immaturity, Étienne, but not immaturity concerning love. Your task is to recognize and claim the *fact* of your magical power and that you marshal this power on behalf of *everyone* you love.

"Your coming to care for Marcella as your friend meant you would summon all your magical power to make your heart's pattern available to her. You couldn't help but do that. It took little of her nascent empathic magic to tap into what you radiated so powerfully! Marcella's magic only emerged because of what your generous act made available to her."

I had nothing to say in response and glared stubbornly at him. Eton turned and walked away, leaving me to stew on his lecture.

While it was always wise to take Eton's analysis of anything seriously, I still believed he overestimated my "magical power," as he kept putting it. There is nothing magical about just conversing with someone, is there? I would speak with Marcella about this, confident that my beloved would appreciate my viewpoint and support my reasoning. Heartened by my decision, I hurried off to find her.

We were cuddling when I brought it up. Marcella sat in my lap and nestled into me; her head tucked warmly between my chin and collarbone. I loved to rest my nose into her hair to breathe in her fragrance. Her breath was soft upon my neck, and I could feel her nodding under my chin as I summarized Eton's points. To my great dismay, Marcella agreed with Eton completely!

"He is correct, my dearest," she murmured into my blouse. "There's no need to reject his astute observations. Of course, it is true, as nothing *but* your natural magical power *and* unselfconsciousness could have gotten through to me."

Feeling my muscles tighten at this, Marcella lifted her head from my chest and sat up to look me directly in the eye before continuing.

"Mon cheri, Étienne, kindly do not dismiss this most important truth."

She put on her most seductive and coquettish expression, knowing I'd be charmed and disarmed, even as I saw through such a transparent gambit. It made me laugh, easing the tension in my body. She smiled, pleased that she had achieved her intended result. My dearest didn't believe in fighting fair, something François admired and appreciated during their martial training sessions.

She slipped off my lap to stand directly in front of me. Resting her hands on my shoulders, she leaned enough weight on me that I had to brace myself to support her and engage my physical strength to meet her. Such a clever woman!

"You are a grown man, Étienne, with considerable magical and personal power. I would have nothing less for my true love," she said, firmly squeezing my shoulder muscles for emphasis.

She then added, "Therefore, it's essential to confront honestly and fully what you are. You asked no less of me, *oui*?"

I nodded, taken by the fierceness in her eyes as she listened to my agreement.

"Étienne, if you don't face the truth about who you are, you won't understand why I sensed that you, *and only you,* could give me what I desperately needed. Even back then, when I was so arrogant and pitifully ignorant, even I could see that you radiated your power to those around you."

She gazed into the distance as if lost in remembrance before shaking her head, her raven locks swirling around her face. I was so captivated by her shimmering beauty that she had plenty of time to wander through the halls of memory. I was still so caught up in admiring her beauty that I was startled when Marcella continued talking, unaware of how she affected me.

"You had no idea how infuriating it was to see this. It was simply maddening that you didn't realize the power you possessed! To acknowledge that you had such power yet chose *not to* use it for selfish reasons was beyond me. I thought it a waste knowing that many in my world would kill to be thus empowered."

"Such an irony," she continued, "that it was only *because* you were oblivious to your power that I felt safe enough to learn from you. As I got to know you, Étienne, I realized that you could never use your power to take advantage of me, that it would never even cross your mind to manipulate me. Never! Even *I* could see that. As I grew eager to understand what had been hidden from me, I trusted that you would give yourself to me fully without expecting anything in return.

"I could intuit your heart's pattern and let it resonate within me. Left to my own devices, I'd have taken years to discover what the loving template of your heart demonstrated to me directly! It was as if you loaned me your beating heart, so I could find my own, from the inside, as it were.

"And all of this because you gave to me so fully, freely, and guilelessly, because I was your friend." Her eyes glistened with tears of gratitude as she said this.

I pulled her close, pressing my cheek to hers. I was overwhelmed to hear her talk about this part of her journey and by the incredible act of trust she had shown me. Marcella's tears streamed down, moistening the skin we shared. I was glad I hadn't known then what she and Eton had been telling me about myself, as I was able to give more than I would have if I'd been self-conscious about it.

Marcella separated from my embrace and dried her eyes with a handkerchief. She resumed her fierce expression and gathered herself to give me everything she could.

"The Maestro," she said, "created the alchemical vessel where my impurities were sloughed off, and I cracked open to my hidden depths. But it was *you*, my love, who immersed me in the magical power of your heart so that I could find mine."

Her fierce expression softened, and she smiled. "I'm still amazed that you asked nothing from me in return for this service!" Her eyes widened with wonder. "I could hardly believe that you wanted it for me *simply* because you had come to care for me as your friend.

"What a pearl without price, *mon chéri*. And, what a conundrum! You offered me the treasure of my heart, wishing only that I should have it for myself *alone!* No one in the world I'd come from would ever conceive of such a selfless act."

Though tears streamed down her face again, she maintained a steadfast gaze as she held my eyes.

"The very act of your wanting this for me, with such purity and magical power, showed me more of the true nature of the heart than could have all the words in the world."

Marcella smiled broadly, pulling me into a palpable blanket of her love. We leaned our heads together, briefly resting our foreheads and sharing a breath of gratitude.

Marcella pulled back and straightened her back, her posture firming into what François once called "the steel whipcord of the Contessa's spine." She stepped back enough to place both palms on my chest and formally addressed me, summoning every ounce of the considerable authority available from her breeding.

"And now Étienne, it is necessary that you claim *everything* you are. You must understand the magic and power you carry, completely— its effect on others and its nature and limits. I will not have you diminish the man I love, nor will I allow you to be less than full in your power to serve our purpose together."

From that moment on, Marcella made it her mission for me to be the man in truth that she knew me to be and would accept nothing short of it.

CHAPTER VI:

The Alchemy of Ingredients

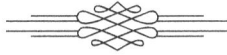

Marcella met me as the man I was becoming, giving me the confidence to enter my full magical power. I met Marcella as the woman of heart she was becoming, and this gave her the confidence to open to broader realms than she had ever imagined.

Freed from the prison of her self-conception, Marcella was a bird a-wing. Her considerable innate psychism, suppressed by the Order lest her selfishness misuse it, now bloomed and had to be discovered and mastered. Marcella would bring her sophisticated education and vast intelligence to bear as she became acquainted with its nature.

Then, there was a natural alchemy between us. It added another dimension, a higher order that even I could recognize. Though our talents and natures were quite different, alchemically we complemented each other, rather than opposing, where plus and minus might cancel each other out; our different natures, even magnetized to the other. We naturally tended to amplify and draw out each other's power. Much like the Maestro's amber rod, when rubbed with wool and held overhead, it pulled hair toward it. Are not lovers drawn to each other as hair to the amber rod?

The Maestro taught that the first step in an alchemical operation was to gather and purify the ingredients. He taught that it was *all* ingredients —good, bad, and otherwise —nothing left out or wasted, our faults as much as our virtues. What were ours?

Marcella's insistence that I claim my magical power necessitated thoroughly re-evaluating my education in magic and natural energy since my arrival at the Chateau. Why this? Marcella intuited that I might be so oblivious to the magic I carried because of Édouard's excessive cleverness as a teacher!

"*Mon cher,*" she explained, "your Maestro invariably taught you in ways that kept you from recognizing you were being instructed. Édouard is the Great Trickster, is he not? He delights in deceiving all of you into learning despite yourselves. It is his special joy and his unique mastery. He delights in this even when a thing could be more easily learned by being direct!"

I loved to listen to her when her face was alight with such enthusiasm. She entranced me. I had to bring myself up short to register what she was saying. Focus, lad, focus!

"You told me once, Étienne," she continued, "how Édouard so cleverly tricked you into learning to read?"

Indeed, he had. Early in my residency at the Chateau, when Édouard was learning what made me tick, he noted how desperate I was to earn my keep. I feared being abandoned again and hungered for Édouard's approval. I felt guilty for surviving when my family had not and, therefore, unworthy of that which I so desired. And, I was too ashamed to admit I couldn't do what he assigned, so I would struggle along rather than ask for help.

Of course, the Maestro did not see these things as impediments; instead, they were simply the "ingredients" in his alchemical solution to tricking me into learning to read.

My earliest task was to attend to him in his study, where I would sit at his desk and see to any requests he had, such as for refreshments. Periodically, Édouard would ask me to fetch a title from his precious library. I had only the basic rudiments of letters, but would run to the adjacent library, repeating the word he'd given for the title in a breathy whisper, even if I didn't understand what it was. I'd search feverishly through the shelves until I found a volume that appeared to have the appropriate letters, and then I'd return at a run to deliver it. Édouard would examine it, usually pronouncing that it was the wrong one. He would then patiently explain the letters that spelled the word and send me to search again.

At first, I would repeat this charade many times for each title until I'd found the correct one, whereupon he'd issue glowing praise for my success. Gradually, my mastery of letters and my vocabulary expanded. I also became intimately familiar with his library, and reading began to open new worlds to me. Once he'd proven to himself that his alchemical methods worked with a 9-year-old boy, he gave me over to François for a systematic and stringent study of languages. By then, I'd already been captured by the spider's web of the written word.

I nodded to Marcella, letting her know I understood her reference and that she should continue with her thesis.

"The Maestro resorted to similar indirection and trickery as he taught you all magic, the energies in nature, and revealed everyone's native intuitive skills, did he not?" I could only agree.

"To me," Marcella said, smiling in delight, "his most amazing trick was getting all you boys to meditate, correct? No one but the Maestro could get distracted boys to *compete* at sitting still!" she exclaimed. "And on and on: he made it a game to match the energy of rocks so you'd learn magical camouflage, an advanced skill even adepts of the Order find challenging. He bamboozled you, Étienne, into recalling a prior life with the Order, taking advantage of your vulnerable state after the exorcism and leaving you with an ancient missive about a tragedy that *you, yourself,* had written during life in Roman times serving the Order!"

She shook her head from side to side in wonder at the Maestro's cheek.

"What craftiness! What skillful misdirection!" she marveled. "Yet such cleverness comes at a cost. By intention, your learning was so seamless that acquiring your remarkable, magical powers seemed… unremarkable! It left you believing that the Maestro was remarkable, Étienne, but it was your remarkable ingredients, your native talent, that he leveraged with his tricks."

As always, I felt uncomfortable with her giving me too much credit, but I was beginning to see her point. What boy would see anything that was so much fun to be the result of his ability?

She looked excited to see that I was on board with her thesis and drew her conclusions. "And this is why you've come to believe, mistakenly, that what you do is only 'natural', as if anyone could do it when it is nothing of the kind! You do a disservice to all he's taught you if you do not claim the remarkable magical power you now carry."

Over the ensuing weeks, Marcella required me to recount every magical skill I'd learned, one by one, no matter how simple they seemed or how easily acquired. There was tracking my fellows and learning to track evil into the other realms. There was how I'd learned to sense others from a distance and merge hearts and minds with my fellows to join our magic in missions. And there was how Édouard tricked us into following him to his "University" of Nature and the energies of water, earth, and air.

Then there was the Old Man, who gave me access to his lineage, including the immense powers of the earth and the forces of life. He'd tricked me from pure selfishness, using my loyalty to Édouard to manipulate me into agreeing to be initiated by the Moon Goddess and all her inconceivable power. She had dismantled and reassembled my physical and spiritual bodies to handle her colossal power without destroying or driving me to madness.

Marcella threw up her hands in dismay.

"Étienne, you must listen to yourself!" she huffed. "You tell me that a goddess disassembled and reassembled you! Can there be anything *less than extraordinary* about that, let alone 'natural?'

"Add to this what you've revealed to me, that before your journey to Brittany, your spiritual body was healed in an ancient ritual by two high priestesses who drew from the very power of creation to remake you whole?"

I looked sheepishly at her. I'd never put it all together before. These were the things that made up our life at the Chateau. My mentors advised me to practice, and I trusted their guidance. It was simply what we all did together.

As I collected it all to recount to Marcella, I was coming to see it differently, just as she hoped I would. I realized I was oriented to this as a child, unconsciously and without perspective. My beautiful and oh-so-clever beloved had made me reflect, re-evaluate, and see myself more distinctly for who I was. In short, to grow up.

Marcella laughed at my abashed pose and gleefully poked me with her finger. Her gorgeous brown eyes glimmered with mischief and love as she continued. "It is little wonder that I felt that you carried something exceptional, even before my talents were in evidence?"

As the recitation progressed, it became evident how the Maestro imparted his teachings while making it seem like a game. At the same time, I understood that the ingredients he was working with — within me and my fellow students — possessed immense potential for transformation. After all, he had summoned us to his side to become his soldiers of light. While the Maestro might not have expected children to show up, he trusted that we were suited to his call, or we would not have found him. The latent talents we brought from prior times serving the Order simply had to be cultivated and honed.

As my reexamination, prompted by Marcella, brought me new understanding, I shared these insights with my confidants, Eton, Bora, and Louis, encouraging them to reexamine the Maestro's trickster tutelage. This way, the Alchemy of Ingredients worked its magic upon us all.

Concurrent with Marcella's project, I had mine for her—to fill the gaps in her magical education. Her first gift to come to the surface had been a rather powerful empathic ability, which she had utilized to discover and take on the pattern of my heart, opening her own. While her more profound gifts were still unknown, I knew I could teach her the mystical powers and energies of nature, which I was so practiced in. These were things about which Marcella knew little. She was intrigued that she might surprise the Maestro by displaying unexpected magical skills, so she asked me to keep it to ourselves. She had displayed similar mischief by concealing training with François in martial skills from me, so I thought it only fair that, this time, I join her in the ruse.

As it turned out, our mutual projects were complementary. As I taught her about nature's energies, she would point out how I used my magic to teach her, and the more her skill grew with energy, the more she could perceive and tell me. Her empathic gifts were now used to observe the unintended use of my magical power and to reveal my "natural magic," making it more available for conscious use.

"You realize, *mon cher*, that as you teach me about the rocks' energy, you wrap me in your magical aura so I may connect to their vibrancy?"

Well, no, I did not realize this. I gave her my most cogent and thoughtful response.

"What?" I said.

My aristocratic beauty rolled her eyes at me.

I knew I was following the steps of this attunement process as I walked her through them, but I wanted to ensure my description clearly conveyed what she should do and what she should sense. I hadn't thought to harness the rocks' energy within myself or to envelop her in their resonance through my aura or something similar. I wasn't trying to extend the energies to her, or not intentionally. My intention did not matter; I simply did these things, for which she was grateful.

I had to reflect on how this came about. Indeed, the practice had become effortless for me; I had to attune to the rock's resonance before my bones vibrated with it. I also realized that there was a deep desire in my heart for Marcella to know these things I thought were so marvelous. I *wanted her to be included in this kinship with the rocks and* see the earth's power.

What made the description I gave Marcella more than just words was that I was recreating and generating the material I was teaching her to guide her through the steps.

"My love, what you give me is more than telling me a series of steps. As you describe these practices, *you are full of the magic you teach.* How can I *not* be vibrated by this energy? Your heart's enthusiasm causes you to do everything you can because you care so much that I know this precious thing."

I hated to admit Eton was right, but as he had told me, "*...every act of your committed heart, everything that comes from your true nature, carries your unintended magical power....*"

After this, I found it impossible *not* to notice that I had immersed her in what I was teaching and evoked it. As I began to claim this as a skill in and of itself, it became even more effective. I'd thought it a simple extension of my wish to help her better grasp the thing. I realized it was foolish of me to have separated desire from intention. Any magician worth their salt knows these are identical. Marcella rapidly gained facility in perceiving and working with the energies in Nature, a testament to both our gifts.

As the moon approached fullness, I sensed I was to introduce her to the Moon Mother's potency. I took Marcella to the hilltop where I had prayed to Mother to transport me to the rescue. I did my devotions aloud, imploring the goddess to grant Marcella an experience of her power. After receiving assent, I opened my connection to the Mother. I was about to describe this to Marcella when she gasped aloud.

"Oh, Étienne, *c'est très fantastique!*" she said. She shook her head back and forth as she stared at the moon's rising presence, breathless and gasping from what she was feeling. "Never have I felt power like this. You are her intercessor on my behalf, and I am under your auspices as her priest. I can only imagine what it took to become so much a part of her that she comes through you without thought." I only glanced at her face to see that Marcella was utterly entranced by receiving the moon mother's blessing.

At one time, I would have reckoned that I was only directing Marcella's *attention* to the Moon's power. But now, I could see that intention was not required for me to include Marcella directly in my connection to the Mother. Once I intuitively understood that I was supposed to do this, forming an intention was unnecessary. I opened up to the Mother, with Marcella included, because it was my utmost *desire* for her to receive what I'd been told to give her.

I'd been playing a shell game with myself, distracting myself from seeing what I did by calling it something else. I'd thought that magic required formulas, ritual, and willful intention, but once granted access to power, we call it up as much through our desire as through conscious intention, for good or ill.

Marcella continued, detailing all she could about this experience. "You loan me her glow already inside you; it is clear it is at her behest! She pours her blessing upon me as her gift through your intercession…."

She paused to reflect and shook her head in frustration: "No… that's not quite correct… I make it too complicated. Grant me a moment, my love, to do better for you; it's hard to put into words."

Marcella closed her eyes and focused her intelligence inward, working to clarify what she felt on my behalf. I was happy to give her all the time she needed, as it allowed me to gaze at her beauty while I waited. Eventually, she opened her eyes to speak again, and I had to bring myself out of my besotted entrancement to be capable of listening.

"Étienne, it's more than that. Through you, she rings me," she ventured. "You are her vibrating bell, and you resonate me without being directly struck."

Marcella's poetic metaphor was lovely, but I must have looked puzzled. What she said made sense, but there was something I still didn't grasp. Marcella gazed downward for a moment as if listening to an inner voice. Then, she caught her breath and stared at me wide-eyed.

"*Mago del mio cuore*," she said, lapsing into her native tongue as she did when surprised. She looked at me as if she had solved something that had long puzzled her. "Magician of my heart, I understand better now. You simply don't see it, do you? The Mother just showed me that her blessing rings continually inside you as a result of your initiation. But you only seem to notice your connection to her when you've performed your familiar ritual. You don't realize that when you serve at her direction, it is an act of power, ritual or not!"

Of course, I thought, it had to be so. When I brought the Mother to mind, I never felt that I was bringing anything through me or drawing something from the goddess. I simply opened it, and there it was. But I'd always performed the ritual steps first and thought that was responsible.

It was through Marcella that the Moon Mother instructed me on what it meant to be her intercessor. The Old Man had taught me nothing about this role, despite his hidden agenda to make me his priestly successor. He was desperate to do so before he succumbed to disease, fearing to fail his vows. His former High Priestess visited me in a dream, revealing his hidden agenda and affirming that his misguided, coercive effort was not my task.

Though I was not her priest, I was her initiate. I was pledged to her nonetheless. Having been granted her power —call it what you will —I would be her intercessor or do anything else required when called to do so by her. So it was that Marcella taught me the role that my mentor, the Old Man, had never instructed me in—the art of serving as an intercessor.

So we continued in this way, instructing each other. I would teach Marcella about the magical forces I knew, and she would teach me how to use my magical power to do so. Oh, how the Moon loves her circularity! Marcella, the student, teaches the teacher how to serve as an intercessor so that he can better instruct her. In turn, she, as the teacher, will better prepare him to teach! And so on, without beginning or end, indeed. And who, exactly, is the teacher here? And who is the student? Me? Marcella? The goddess? Is there a difference here, really? Exactly!

As we walked around the Chateau, I would attune her to the energies of nature all around us. I would harness these energies into a cloud around us, enveloping Marcella until she grasped its template. Her aura grew brighter and larger as she gained access to these energies, and we both gained greater and greater facility with our tasks.

CHAPTER VII:

Distillation

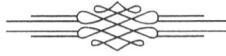

While Marcella and I worked on fostering each other's abilities, the Maestro and François conspired to keep us as busy as possible. Having both received lectures on the importance of confining our physical affections only to above the neck, Marcella and I had enough discipline to keep our promise. Disciplined or not, our mentors were not foolish enough to leave us time with which to get into trouble.

I already had so many duties that finding time to squeeze in our walks was a challenge. As our primary focus was cultivating each other's talents, there was hardly any time for *amore*.

Similarly, Marcella was here to receive what only the Maestro could give her. And, now that her native ability had been released, her days were crowded with all forms of study for her to master. She spent many hours discussing and assimilating her memories from the Egg with the Maestro to ensure that her alchemical transformation continued. Though my love was no wilting flower, serving the Order could be a dangerous business, and a member needed training to handle it. She was taught to use codes for secret communication and practiced them in her letters to her father. She was also required to train with François in self-defense.

François assessed her temperament and selected the stiletto as the weapon of choice, especially for a woman of her station. The "little steel" was a needle-like dagger, appropriately of Italian origin. Made to different lengths, it could be fashioned for concealment within a lady's abundant skirts or made smaller for more fitted riding clothes. Primarily a stabbing weapon, François thought it just the thing for a woman whose most likely need would be in close-quarters fighting. He also perceived that her intelligence fitted the requirement for precision in its use, and her temperament was suited to piercing.

I knew she was training with Francois, but they conspired to hide her level of proficiency from me. Then, François sought my assistance, stating that he needed "a suitable fighting partner who'd challenge, but not damage a novice."

I arrived at the scheduled time, determined to be careful with her. Marcella, however, did not mirror my gentle intentions with her own.

At François' nod, I approached with my weapon concealed at my side. I intended to control the skirmish from the start to limit any chance I'd hurt her. She deftly distracted me by flicking her skirts to show her ankles, adroitly parried my weapon hand to the side, and stepped gracefully inside my guard to press her body against mine. All this caused me to overlook that she had the point of her blade beneath my chin until it pricked my skin! I could do naught but yield.

I openly praised her for her clever tactics and impressive skill! Unaccustomed to genuine appreciation instead of flattery, Marcella blushed with pride. Not the pride born of her former haughtiness, but that earned through hard work. She had hoped to impress me, she said, and had worried she'd be defeated, given my years of training.

François said only, "Well done, Contessa!" Reserving his lengthy critique for me, he dressed me down for underestimating my opponent, making assumptions based on sex, and for being distracted by such simplistic maneuvers as ruffling skirts and female ankles! He noted, on the other hand, that Contessa's use of such simplistic tactics was an *intelligent* response to his training. He'd drilled her to take *every* advantage of the opponent's weaknesses and to fight dirty, relying on deception rather than strength. This was the only time I underestimated her in combat, and I would never make that mistake again.

As her mastery of nature's powers deepened, Marcella announced that a crucial perspective was missing, as all her teachers were distinctly masculine. She stated that she needed a feminine perspective on magic to address this missing element. She declined to explain her reasoning to me, asserting that my inability to grasp it readily validated her argument.

Her selection of a mentor showcased her remarkable transformation and was genuinely admirable. Before the Maestro's influence, she would have undoubtedly deemed this choice as beneath her—none other than the resident Wise Woman, the heir to an ancient feminine lineage of magic and healing, and the Empress of the house and hearth—Matilde.

Her heart transformed, Marcella could now see beyond the social judgments of her class, recognizing genuine qualities in others unlike her. She rightly intuited that only Matilde had the deep, hidden knowledge of the feminine side of magical energies she needed, and she sought Matilde's help without hesitation.

Thereafter, Marcella always referred to Matilde as *Magistra*, an Italian honorific equivalent to Maestro, the feminine form. When they would pass each other about the Chateau, Marcella would curtsy with eyes downcast, acknowledging *"Magistra."* Matilde accepted the honor with a broad smile and nod.

I once ventured to ask my love what exactly Matilde was teaching her. Marcella would demure, saying only, "Woman's mysteries."

Teacher and acolyte were now often together, leading the younger boys to refer to them collectively as "the M's." This was due to the boy's tendency to nickname every curious phenomenon, their fondness for the two, and their need for the feminine in their lives.

Marcella was drawn to the younger boys in our group. They had been under her eye as she had watched from her too-distant window in her alchemical isolation, and had become of great interest to her now open heart. Matilde assigned Marcella to instruct them in manners and comportment, saying Marcella was a "native speaker" of such things, in a way that François, who had been responsible for this kind of training, was not. I'm sure Matilde believed it would be a vehicle for Marcella to cultivate her heart further.

As you could imagine, they became passionately competitive, hoping to impress their lovely teacher with their mastery of civilized ways! We older boys became envious of the warmth this beautiful governess lavished on her charges. Truthfully, I was mainly jealous of the time she gave them, as we had so little for each other left over.

I, too, had my responsibilities: guiding the younger boys, teaching martial skills to my fellows, leading all in exercises and practices assigned by the Maestro, and performing numerous duties on behalf of the estate. I also continued training with François in fighting and languages.

In addition, I had pledged time to assist the Abbess in specific tasks before Marcella arrived at the Chateau. These typically require a half-day's journey to the Abbey, time to complete the task—which may involve waiting for suitable conditions—and then another half-day riding back to the Chateau. Learning that the Maestro had involved me in his work on behalf of Marcella, the Abbess informed me that she would temporarily defer my responsibilities to her. I was relieved, as my time was now so packed that I couldn't afford such time away.

Shortly after this, the Abbess sent word that she would come to the Chateau in a few weeks for a formal visit to meet the Contessa. She also intended to meet with the honored Matilde and determine how she might assist her in supporting Marcella's studies.

CHAPTER VIII:

The Alchemy of
the Sun & Moon

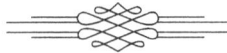

I've said before that I've had no talent for alchemy myself, but one cannot live with a master such as Édouard without absorbing some principles of the Art. A title from one of Édouard's folios in his precious library kept coming to my mind regarding Marcella and me: *"The alchemy of the Sun and the Moon."* Édouard referred to this as the principle of "necessary opposites," saying these opposites did not negate but enhanced and amplified the qualities of the other. What might this mean for us?

It was undoubtedly true that she was the Moon to my Sun, not only for her feminine, lunar nature but also because she so generously reflected to me what I was doing to help me learn.

Then, how was I the Sun for her? True, I did my best to radiate the powers I was teaching about so she could sense them directly. But I realized I wasn't as generous in my role as she was with me. As the Sun, I'd only shone the barest light on her, like giving a plant only small flashes of sunlight, enough to sensitize it but not enough to grow.

Marcella had told me I was "full of the magic" I was teaching her. In this light, I should infuse her with as much of this magic as possible instead of only attuning her to it. Then, I decided, I would be the true alchemical Sun to her Moon.

She required no convincing to participate in my experiment, as what we had already done had yielded significant benefits for both of us. I needed to discern how I could bring these forces directly to her.

"My dear heart," I said, "I think it would help us if we sat face to face, and I could keep both of your hands in mine."

It was a quiet time in the garden to stroll when others were about their duties, and we wouldn't be interrupted. It was, however, overlooked by a window on high where her handmaiden could chaperone our conduct without overhearing us.

I gathered two stools from where they stood at the garden wall and placed them where we could sit knee to knee, and I took her hands in mine. As she was already familiar with the collective force of living things, I thought it would be one to experiment with.

"Let us start with something you've felt before, the force of living things."

She nodded, and I could sense her attune herself to this immediately—what an excellent partner to our endeavor she was!

"That's it, *mia amore!* Now, I'll do my best to bring its power to you."

I reached out to the force that radiated from the mass of living things around us and gathered it to myself. My eyes closed in concentration, and instead of merely resonating its signature to Marcella, I did my best to direct it to her through our joined hands. I found myself sweating from the effort, yet I felt no different from before, and I was sure the experiment was unsuccessful. Marcella would typically be narrating what she was experiencing by now, but was silent. Finally, I gave up the effort, and I opened my eyes.

What I saw fully explained her silence. Marcella's jaw hung open in an astounded expression; her eyes were open, and her eyeballs rolled up, showing much of the white. Her face and neck, the skin left visible by the coverage of her courtly dress, were flushed to a bright red hue, looking as if she'd been sunburned!

I was worried our experiment had failed, but now I'm afraid it has worked too well! I released her hands and leaned away a bit.

"Marcella, my love," I insisted, "look at me, my dear."

She shook briefly as if I had startled her, and I noticed the flush start to diminish. Though it looked like a struggle, she brought her eyes into focus, but still seemed preoccupied with her inner vision.

"*Mon Dieu, mon cheri!*" she exclaimed, her voice choked with emotion. "What you did opened up a realm I had never imagined possible! The power that flooded into me cleared the avenues of my perception, throwing everything wide open."

She shook her head back and forth in amazement, blinking to try to clear her vision.

"At first, my eyes were open," Marcella said, "and I thought that I was seeing the energies of the garden plants, invisible to me before this."

"Then I no longer saw the garden around me, but it seemed underwater, watching currents flowing in a vast ocean. Within these waters were people, the collective mass of common folk, moving together like shoals of fish. Then, some were the leviathans of this ocean, casting waves and currents all around them that rippled through the mass of humanity. And some appeared more like groups of predators at the hunt, striking at anything they could devour. So much, Étienne, it's too much!"

She clutched my hands like a drowning woman, lost in this ocean of human affairs. I was desperate to help her find her way back to me. I reflected that only the rocks could withstand the roiling, changing ocean waves. Accordingly, I drew on the resonance of the rock below us and directed it as a steadying force into Marcella through her gripping hands. I pushed it into her bones, the rocks' natural counterparts in the body.

Her panic soon subsided, and she looked less overwhelmed by oceanic forces. Her tight grip on my hands loosened, and I could see her back ease from its bracing. Her expression softened, and her eyes came into sharp focus as she finally saw me.

"Oh my God, thank you, my love, you saved me from drowning in power," she said with relief.

She suddenly threw herself into my arms, pulling my face to the crook of her neck to feel my physical presence firmly against her skin. I was so relieved not to have harmed her that I lingered there to breathe in her fragrance.

We stayed that way to support each other with the warmth and presence of our bodies. She explained more when she straightened up from our embrace to look at me again.

"You are bringing me back to solid ground. I was overwhelmed with power, more than I could handle. I never imagined such power existed! All the barriers, remnants of the limits the Order had placed on me, were thrown aside. But without them, I was thrown into a vast sea and feared I would drown in an ocean of human turmoil!"

Thinking a walk would help us settle more, we ambled through the garden until our legs were well under us. We discussed our experiment in more detail. I told her what I had done to infuse her with power, and Marcella tried to articulate her perception of this ocean of human affairs into which she had been tossed.

As we walked and talked, Marcella discovered that she could tap into her perception of this again, but now she was more distant rather than immersed in it.

"From where I see it from now," she said as she contemplated her inner vision, "it is more like having a bird's view from above, so I can begin to discern patterns and currents I know I am to understand. I must remember to continue alternating with the resonance of the rocks in my bones, though, or I shall fall into it again."

She clutched my arm firmly, holding my bicep in her grip as she noted this last caution. Ignorant of the realm she was privy to, I had nothing to add, but I did nod encouragingly to affirm the importance of the practice with the bones.

Our walk took us out of the garden and out a back gate to circle the Chateau. We arrived back at the entry gate to the Chateau proper and, by now, felt we had a grasp of the impact of our experiment. I pledged a more bridled enthusiasm with the fuel I had supplied. Marcella promised to seek advice from Matilde and Édouard on how to study these new perceptions safely.

After we parted, I reflected on the difference between our psychic gifts. My talents were specific and focused, well-suited to the mission of spiritual battle Édouard had called us to. Marcella's perception broadened.

I liken myself to an expert sailor who knows how to work the sails to take advantage of wind and currents. Marcella's skill was of a different order: more like a master navigator who could intuit the not-yet charted map, even discerning the lay of invisible continents by their distant reflection on weather and currents.

The sea she navigated was the collective waters of humankind. Her talent was charting the social and political currents shaped by the landscape of power and the winds of human emotion and desire. She later called this the "emanations of all our turning and churning fates." But first, she must learn to perceive them without losing her footing.

I could better appreciate her rare and precious gift and why she had been sent here. Other psychic powers seemed much more local in scope by comparison. The Maestro's alchemy was crucial to make her worthy of her gift, whether she made this available to the Order or not.

Marcella's value was more significant than mine in specific ways, not just because of my love for her, but also because of my upbringing. I had been raised to participate in a collective effort where everyone understood that we served a cause greater than ourselves. Every soldier, including a soldier of light, knows what is worth sacrificing for, and a worthy sacrifice enhances one's value rather than diminishes it.

It occurred to me that I might be called on to sacrifice something so that she could serve her mission. As an aristocrat, she had duties and responsibilities and would likely have to return to Italy. It was the first time such a thought had pierced the bubble of young love, making me shudder. I endeavored to push it out of my mind.

Marcella and I sought counsel from our mentors on what had occurred. While Édouard hoped Marcella would dissolve these barriers and reveal the gifts the Order had anticipated, he had not expected us to be so expedient.

"Ah, Étienne," he said, "I knew that you were teaching the Contessa about magical energies as I could sense their vibration in her, of course, but I underestimated how ambitious the two of you are!"

He shook his head ruefully, pretending disapproval, but I could see the glimmer in his eyes and hear the humor in his tone.

"By god," the Maestro continued, "you filled her with so much magic that you blew away any barriers remaining! I see you have too little comprehension of the power you'd acquired with the Old Man. It is a lack that we must remedy, and soon."

"The Contessa also confessed her project for you to claim your magic, but, like you, she does not appreciate the true extent. It is the blind leading the blind!"

The Maestro paused. His eyes looked far away, and he stroked his beard as he often did when gazing into the ethers. Then he focused his eyes on me again and clapped his hands on my shoulders.

"You may continue as the Sun to her Moon once Matilde has helped Marcella put some protections in place, but gently, lad, gently! You both must learn to amplify her skills and carefully unfold her talents. Matilde and I will counsel her on this."

Matilde understood the urgency of bringing Marcella's talents along. She thought it best that Marcella learn how to utilize my energy safely. Matilde guided us in practices designed to instill Marcella's self-direction in our experiment and develop her self-protection against magical power. In one exercise, she asked Marcella to resist my energy actively, likening it to building muscle by lifting weights. We did this by gradually increasing what I was sending until Marcella could control it, determine how much she wanted to use, or even block it entirely. Matilde insisted that Marcella would need to defend herself from the harmful magic cast at her just as much as she needed to have sources of energy from which to draw.

Beyond adding magical energy to enhance her native ability, I had little else to offer. The realm in which her talent operated was beyond my skills and understanding; I could only listen to her discoveries and offer my support.

Serving as her Sun helped Marcella develop her native psychic talent, but we again underestimated its cumulative impact. "The alchemy of the Sun and the Moon" was not just a metaphor for one person serving the other; it was explicitly an alchemical one and, therefore, in service of transformation. Having called on alchemical energies, we did not realize that deeper forces were being activated, bringing things to a boil.

CHAPTER VIX:

Desire's Incitement

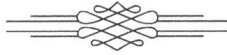

Preoccupied with the fun and excitement of our discoveries, we were oblivious to how all this magical energy was also fueling our desire. We drank a highly fortified wine as if it were *vin ordinaire*. Then, convinced that our drunkenness signified success, we imbibed glass after glass until utterly besotted.

Playful kisses gave way to explorations of lips, tongues, and taste. My journey along the enchanting curve of her jawline veered toward another, beckoning my lips to an impossibly soft earlobe. Only her sudden gasp snapped me from entrancement.

Oh, those curious and impulsive lips! They could hardly be blamed for their wandering! They were simply following the allure that drew them and couldn't help themselves! They could have easily strayed from earlobe to throat, and throat to bosom if they'd not been halted by an act of will.

Magic waylaid us, too, when we only meant to greet each other with a kiss. It stretched ordinary seconds into eternity, giving Marcella all the time she needed to rest her forehead on my shoulder, her warm breath teasing the skin beneath my blouse. She inhaled deeply to savored my scent, sending a shiver racing down my spine and igniting sparks throughout my body. Only a gust of wind pulled us back to reality, and we separated, pretending it hadn't happened. But the sparks lingered in me for hours.

Perhaps our stubborn wills alone might have sufficed to contain our youthful desire, even with the magical energies at play. However, the alchemical nature of our pairing was far more complex than anyone had anticipated. What we believed to be mutually beneficial instruction had unleashed far more potent archetypal principles drawing on powers beyond the human sphere.

At its most essential, what is alchemy? Transmuting earthly lead into spiritual gold by refining select ingredients, purifying and distilling them, infusing the mix with archetypal principles, and heating in a hermetically sealed vessel to unify and achieve the quintessence—divine gold.

And are not Marcella and I such select, refined ingredients? There is no doubt that we each had been purified and distilled by the Maestro's alchemy to bring out our essential spirits. And, in our work together, we'd become infused with the primordial energies of nature, then the higher feminine and masculine principles by the goddess herself?

In response to our mentors' demands for chastity, Marcella and I steeled our resolve against natural yet forbidden impulses. We forged a hermetic vessel sealed by our restraint, and then, fueled by a magical fire, the ingredients were cooked under tremendous pressure. Either our vessel would burst, or the ingredients would transform and unite in the Alchemical Marriage.

Said this way, we were fortunate that the buildup became unbearable before either of these scenarios unfolded. Similar to an overstretched rope, something painfully broke between us, snapping like a whip and driving us apart.

"What on earth?" I exclaimed.

We stared wide-eyed at each other.

"That was painful, Étienne," responded Marcella, "I've never felt the like before!"

Though physically shaken, still, the fire smoldered between us.

"Whatever it was, Étienne, I shall not let it divert me from your kisses!"

I decided that I should not make my beloved out to be a liar, so I smiled heroically and brought my lips to hers. We closed the distance between us to continue our lips' discourse with each other.

It was only a few kisses when something burst painfully between us once again. We had reached a juncture beyond our capacity to control or understand. It was time to ask for counsel.

I happened first upon Francois and gave him a summary of what had occurred. He listened to my description, nodding thoughtfully.

"Both of you contribute more than it appears at first. However, this is not my area of expertise," he said. "You must consult the Maestro on this matter."

I bowed my thanks and went to look for Édouard, who was in the Great Hall, having just given the traditional monthly audience for the estate's tenants. He asked me to sit with him and present my concerns, so I described what had happened.

Édouard was aware that Marcella and I were instructing each other, despite our supposed secrecy, but he had not realized the extent of our efforts, nor our outsized success. He thoroughly questioned me on all the details of our self-assigned studies and the complete sequence of events leading up to them.

"Well, Étienne," he said, arching an eyebrow at me. "I suppose that I should have expected this of two such magical creatures, but I thought you would be so preoccupied with *amore* for a while and would have little head for studies! My compliments on your initiative with each other. It appears we need to instruct you on how to circulate the energies so they do not build up and can be put to some use."

Édouard invited me to join him in the library, where he consulted various volumes and spoke of the many ways to circulate, disperse, or transform sexual energies. He showed me diagrams and breathing practices, described visualizations, and elaborated on the theme until I was dizzy.

It seemed he aimed to teach us how to "transmute" our sexual energies into a more spiritual form. He warned that this wouldn't be easy, especially considering our youth. It seemed to me that what Édouard was planning required more from us than we had. Love and desire were so very new to us. I had little enough understanding of how my sexual desires worked. To manage its energy seemed well beyond me.

I remained silent about my doubts regarding his plan, as the Maestro seemed quite enthusiastic about the project. Even as he sent me away, he was grabbing more books from the shelves, saying he needed to research before deciding on a plan. Sometimes Edouard's excitement overshadowed practical concerns for a little while.

I shared this with Marcella at the first opportunity, confessing my confusion. She was just as uncertain after speaking with her mentor. Matilde only said she would talk to the Maestro, but thought that we should avoid touching each other or stirring our passions for now.

Neither of us liked that solution. It turned out to be moot. One of the boys interrupted us to tell me that I was to see François immediately.

"We received a missive from the Abbess," François told me. "She has summoned you to the Abbey; you will leave without delay. She has requested that you join the Major as an escort for her travel to the Chateau."

I arched an eyebrow in wordless query.

"Yes, I know," he said. "The Maestro wonders also at this unusual request. Not only is her visit at least a week earlier than we had planned, but there is no reason for the Major to need your assistance as an escort."

It was clear to me that the Abbess had a hidden agenda in her "request." It was also clear that I'd learn what that was only by complying without delay. François arranged with Matilde for food I could eat on the road and had the groom ready my horse, while I gathered my travel gear and arms. It was only a morning's ride, but the puzzling request left me wanting to be prepared for whatever might come.

Marcella was in her studies with the Maestro and could not be interrupted, so I could only leave a regretful note with her handmaid. Swinging my saddlebags over my horse's rump and myself into the saddle, I mounted up. From long habit, I checked that my knives were readily available and not entangled in clothing.

Since Marcella's arrival at the Chateau, I'd not been further than the village. Only a few hours' ride at a good pace, and it was no journey to Brittany; yet I felt a rush of excitement to be on the road again. I admitted to myself that I'd missed the spirit of adventure, and I was sure my horse did as well, so I gave him his head and left the Chateau behind.

The weather was mild, and the road was in good condition, so I approached the Abbey walls by mid-afternoon. The Major greeted me at the gatehouse, where he had his quarters; men were not admitted into the cloister proper, except for the priest who came to give communion. He was not surprised to see me but shook his head when I asked if he knew what this was about, saying only that he was glad to have my company. I was to share a room with him, and we'd leave early in the morning for the Chateau. I took care of my horse, found him a place in the stables, and then rested by doing a few exercises and blade drills. The Major and I shared a meal, reminiscing about our travels together, and I went to bed shortly after dark.

When I awoke, the Major pushed some bread and a mug of tea into my hands and told me to meet him at the gate. The Abbess's carriage was waiting outside the gate, my horse already saddled and waiting, with his reins tied to the back. The Major, in full campaign style, was already mounted, circling in guard and always looking towards the road. Suddenly, the doors to the Abbey compound opened, and two nuns stalked briskly through them. One gestured to me, indicating that I should attend to the Abbess, who herself stepped through the door and stood waiting for my assistance.

I bowed to her, sweeping off my cap and holding it long enough to indicate the depth of my respect. It was too early for all this! "Enough with the formalities, Étienne! We have much to talk about," said the Abbess. I straightened, offered my arm, and escorted her to her carriage. After helping her in, she announced, "You'll sit with me until we've talked."

This was unusual; I had never been in the carriage with her before, let alone sat with her on a journey. I hauled myself up to sit as far from her as the bench seat allowed. The two nuns easily muscled a few bags of clothing into the back and then positioned themselves next to them. The stable boy was acting as the driver, and at a tilt of the Major's chin, he shook the reins, and we rolled noisily off.

We had hardly left the grounds when the Abbess seized my arm and drew me closer to her.

"We can't talk over the noise with you sitting in the next county, Étienne, come closer." She held onto my upper arm after I did so, keeping me closer to her side than I was comfortable with.

"So, lad. What happened with the Contessa yesterday morning?"

I must have gaped like a fish in surprise. How could she have known something had happened then? How? Because she's the Abbess, and I had ample experience that she always kept her finger on the pulse of things over the years.

She smiled as she watched me reason it through. "Of course, I've been attending the events at the Chateau. I've been feeling things build up between you two for weeks now, and it was clear that they had reached a peak. Why do you think I'd moved up the plans to visit? When it became clear two days ago that there was no time to lose, I summoned you here before your master's cluelessness would leave you two lovers to damage yourselves! The man is the greatest magician of our age, but he has no idea how to handle gifted young people with their burgeoning desires.

"Now tell me everything!"

So, of course, I did.

For the most part, the Abbess remained silent as I recounted as best I could. She shook her head, looking dismayed, now and then, and catching the eye of the senior nun seated behind us on the cart's floor, who was also listening to my tale. I described the experience when something had discharged painfully between us, causing the Abbess to exclaim, "What? Describe that again, and do not omit a single detail of what it felt like!" I added what I could, but had little more to say, so the Abbess took a different tack.

"Tell me everything from the very beginning," she said, "every detail. This time, starting with the Contessa's first arrival at the Chateau."

I composed myself and shared the story of my ride to aid in the fight against the robbers, my infatuation with the beautiful Contessa, and the entire narrative of Marcella's dissolution and transformation via the Maestro's alchemical intervention. I told of how, with the Maestro's encouragement, I'd come to see her as a friend, and opened myself to her inquiries about my life with my fellows, inadvertently giving her, an empath, my heart as a template on which to form her own. And I told her how we realized we'd fallen in love, highlighting the limits we'd imposed on ourselves in expressing that love, as well as the even more stringent ones imposed by Édouard.

When I spoke about how we came to teach each other, I was instructing Marcella on the energies of nature and the moon, and how she took it upon herself to ensure I embraced my magical power and authority.

At this, the Abbess looked to the heavens and exclaimed, "That man may be the greatest magician of our age, but he has no idea how far such gifted young people will take things!"

Then, the Abbess questioned me in detail for the first time. What practices did I share with Marcella? Why did I introduce her to the moon's power? What did Marcella reveal to me about the nature of my power under the moon? Did I have any idea how granting a *female* of such a caliber access to a *feminine* power would do?

When I told the Abbess about my conclusion — that if I were to be the Sun to Marcella's Moon, I should radiate *more* power to her, rather than just teach her about it — I heard the nun behind me blurt out, "Oh no, he didn't!"

I confessed, sheepishly because of that comment, that our first attempt had worked altogether *too* well, flooding Marcella with more than she could handle. However, it had also fully awakened her oracular talent. The Abbess arched an eyebrow at this.

"I take it that your experiments were not part of the Maestro's program, but an outcome of a decision made by you and the Contessa, yes?" the Abbess asked slyly.

"Oh yes. It was all on us," I reassured her.

"And the Maestro never noticed the flares of power from the two of you?" she continued.

"Not to my knowledge, your reverence," I responded.

"Don't try to butter my bread, young man. Just finish your story."

Lastly, I recounted how it had become increasingly challenging for us to control our desire for each other and how we had to renew our deliberate effort to restrain ourselves. The final episode, when mere kisses caused an intense discharge of magic between us, prompted us to seek help from our mentors.

The Abbess nodded at this. "It is precisely what I'd been noticing when I attuned to you two. Something was building that was about to burst, and I seemed to be the only one noticing how serious this was! You say the Maestro was searching his tomes for ways to control all this sexual energy?"

I agreed.

"Such foolishness!" the Abbess exclaimed, sitting back with a huff. "I'd sooner ask you to control a storm! Not possible, Étienne.

It's a waste of everyone's time and energy. Neither you nor Marcella is cloistered religious, and Édouard is no Abbott, experienced in shepherding young people through their ripening impulses. I must think about how to help you."

With this, the Abbess released my arm and, relieved, I moved to make space between us. The Abbess held her rosary, praying with her eyes closed as she fingered its beads. I looked behind me to where the two nuns were sitting on the floor with the luggage. The elder nub was staring intently at me. During my visit to the Abbey for special studies, I recalled my brief interactions with her and her profound healing gifts. I don't know what she was seeing, but as she continued to gaze at me, I felt naked and exposed.

Perhaps my staring back, or the defensive expression on my face, got her attention, for she finally broke her gaze and looked away, before turning back to me with her apology.

"I'm sorry, Étienne, I didn't mean to be intrusive, but you have changed so much since I last saw you. Power gleams from you, like the sun contained in a burlap sack with the light leaking through the weave. We must teach you to hide it better so that you don't give that fact away to every sorcerer you encounter."

She turned away to lean her head against a clothes bag, closed her eyes, and it looked like she fell asleep. What is it with these women? She must have learned her manners and tact from the Abbess! Her declaration as well as her dismissal had taken me aback, and I decided I had had enough of nuns' machinations for the moment.

I told the stable boy to bring us to a walk, and I jumped off when we had slowed enough. Letting the carriage pass, I ran beside my horse until I could unfasten his reins from where they'd been tied and led him to the side of the road to mount up. It didn't take me long to catch up to the carriage and assume the rear-guard position, freeing the Major to scout ahead. The Abbess had interrogated me for almost two hours, and we only had about an hour left of our journey to the Chateau. Unsure what the Abbess's visit would bring, I decided to enjoy the freedom of the road while it lasted.

When we arrived at the Chateau, Matilde and François had gathered everyone in the courtyard to greet her, as if she were royalty. While others assisted the nuns in getting out of the back and unloading the luggage, the Abbess sat regally, then allowed me to help her down.

Although I could sense her eagerness to speak with the Contessa, the Abbess took the time to greet every child and house servant, asking warmly about their spiritual and material well-being. She was quite beloved by all, even though she could be intimidating when exercising her full authority.

Finally, Édouard presented the Contessa Marcella, who curtsied deeply to the Abbess.

"I am honored to meet you at last, *Madre Superiora*," Marcella said in her charming Italian accent. "I humbly request your guidance and wisdom, your Reverence. Étienne and I require your counsel for our studies together."

The Abbess was smiling at my beloved's respectful request.

"My dear, I apologize for not being able to come sooner, and I am at your disposal. My entire visit here is dedicated to furthering your studies and growth.

"Come," said the Abbess, taking Marcella's arm. "Let us retire to your rooms, where we may explore your needs together in privacy."

She turned to Matilde, who was standing to the side.

"Respected Matilde, could your kitchen girls provide us with refreshments? Then, kindly join us, as we would value your wise counsel."

Matilde smiled, "Already seen to, Abbess. I will join you when I have made sure that all is in accordance with your wishes."

The Abbess ignored Édouard, who had been looking eager to meet her and give his report. She sent a piercing glance my way before being guided by Marcella towards the stairs to her suite. I took it as a sign that I was to keep silent about our conversation on the journey to the Chateau.

The two nuns attending her closed ranks behind the Abbess and Marcella, cutting off any notion Édouard or anyone uninvited, for that matter, might have had to join the pair. I was not at all surprised to see two kitchen maids toting trays of food, which Matilde had obviously anticipated well before the Abbess's request.

Louis, François, and I walked up to the Maestro, who was looking a bit dismayed, and stood with him a moment in silent commiseration.

Louis was the first to speak.

"Looks like *La Révérende Mère* has the situation in hand, *oui?*" he said. "So good to know who's in charge around here."

Even Édouard had to laugh at Louis' characterization, and we slapped him on the back in the spirit of camaraderie.

"Well, Maestro," said François, "As you have now been spared the burden of leadership for the afternoon, perhaps a little recreation is in order?"

We all knew well what François meant by "a little recreation." He found working up a sweat during sword-and-knife drills to be terribly relaxing… for him. Édouard and I exchanged eager smiles.

The two of us had turned Francois's grueling workouts into a more recreational affair by challenging each other to increasingly hilarious versions of martial competition. Matilde had nearly burst a blood vessel during our last bout, chastising us resoundingly for the "criminal abuse and misuse of food." We'd ended that day's workout by taking two long loaves of bread as our swords.

Our rules stated that we could only touch the opponent's weapon with our own or with a specific body part. The goal was to eliminate the other person's sword, with the mouth being the only other allowed body part, meaning the opponent's sword could only be eliminated by eating it!

François, adroitly snagging Louis, who was trying to make his escape, said, "I have plans for you, too, lad. I think it's time for you to learn to study the staff in fighting. I know our little Petan would be happy to help you spar, he's gotten quite good with it!"

Louis let out a loud groan. There was nothing "Little" about Petain; he was the largest boy in our group. His greater reach made practicing with weapons against him quite risky. Despite Petain's kind heart, he approached his training with utmost seriousness. Sparring with him often left significant bruises. Louis had no time to prepare or escape as Petain, having heard his name, came over to us, wrapped his massive arm around a grumbling Louis's shoulders, and cheerfully escorted him to the practice area.

I glanced at Édouard and said, "So, Maestro. What weapons should we select today for our closing bout?"

Édouard glanced toward the kitchen, where pasta hung to dry in the sun.

"What do you say, Étienne, to noodles at 10 paces?" said the Maestro, just loud enough for Matilde to overhear.

"Never!" she shouted, scurrying to guard the fruits of her labors in case we were serious.

"Hmm," I mused thoughtfully. "And what would our rules be for such a weapon?"

As Édouard and I linked arms and followed François to the training ground, we heard Matilde's peremptory tone calling out.

"Don't even *think* about it, you two... scoundrels!"

The Abbess remained in virtual seclusion with Marcella for several days. They reportedly dined either in Marcella's rooms or in the garden, where the kitchen maids set a table for them. Whether in the garden or strolling around the Chateau for exercise, the two stern nuns closely guarded them, signaling to everyone that they should not be disturbed. The only other person invited to join this gathering was Matilde. Wise Women's work, indeed.

I was glad that Marcella received much-needed feminine support, but the mystery behind closed doors created an odd tension between me and the Maestro. We could only wait until the Abbess finished her work, hoping for answers. I was less concerned about the unknown and more preoccupied with missing my daily intimacy with Marcella and our magical work. The forced hiatus did seem to ease the sexual tension between us, but my fantasies and dreams of her persisted, reminding me it was still there underground.

If I hadn't known Édouard so well, I might not have noticed that he seemed a bit off balance from being ignored by the Abbess, although he hid it well. I surmised that his being off balance was likely her goal. As we traveled from the Abbey, I noticed she was displeased with the Maestro, feeling he had not kept her adequately informed about the Contessa and had failed to consult her regarding what had transpired between Marcella and me. Perhaps she was only making up for lost time by concentrating her focus so intensely on Marcella, but maybe she was also giving the Maestro a dose of his own medicine by letting him languish for a day or so.

It wasn't until early on the fourth day of the Abbess's visit that one of her assistants told Édouard and me that she had requested a meeting in her rooms to discuss her findings shortly after breakfast. Édouard and I approached the door to the suite of rooms reserved for the Abbess at the Chateau and were ushered in by the two nuns who attended her.

My eyes immediately went to Marcella, of course, and I hurried to where she sat, glad to be in her presence again. As was proper in a public setting, she offered her hand for me to kiss, which I gently took while bringing my lips to her soft skin. Even from this brief touch, I felt an immediate surge of desire that seemed to be returned in kind. Though we hadn't seen each other for three days, a lesser version of that painful spark shot between us the moment our desire flared, and I had to release Marcella's hand and jump away from her.

No longer preoccupied with each other, Marcella and I realized that the room had gone silent, and everyone in it was staring at us. Everyone, including the Abbess and the Maestro, both of the Abbess's attendant nuns, Matilde, and, much to my surprise, François. They all looked quite wide-eyed at the phenomenon they'd just witnessed. All except for the Abbess, who instead looked smug, as if what had just occurred confirmed the rightness of her opinion. She looked at Édouard and, to his dismay, shook her head almost imperceptibly, with an expression on her face that wordlessly conveyed, "And you hadn't noticed *this?*"

It was Matilde who broke the uncomfortable silence.

"I would invite everyone to sit so that the Abbess can tell us her findings," she said.

I sat on a stool across from Marcella, drinking her in with my eyes. She was beautiful, as always, and it seemed that her time with the Abbess had been beneficial. She looked free of strain and was glowing with energy. She smiled happily at me, conveying that all would be well.

"Let us begin," said the Abbess. "The Contessa and I have discussed quite a bit these past few days, and I hope I've helped her start sorting out the oracular visions that have come about recently." The Contessa Marcella nodded her agreement, and they shared a moment of understanding that the rest of us were not privy to. "I have also worked with her to utilize better the energies which Étienne has introduced her to, so she can use these to foster her work rather than leave her overwhelmed."

The Abbess next turned to address the Maestro.

"The Contessa and Étienne have spoken to me in detail of the alchemy you performed, Édouard, I think that is the proper term in this instance, *oui*?"

The Maestro, unusually non-committal, shrugged and said simply, "It will do for now."

The Abbess's placid demeanor changed swiftly to one of glowing pride.

"I must say, my friend, that what you accomplished was an astounding performance of alchemy and magic," the Abbess expressed earnestly. "I will spend much of the next months, with your help, puzzling out exactly how you grasped the nature of the Contessa's ingredients so readily, and, even more, how this led to the formula that uncovered her true nature."

Édouard's face showed relief as the tension he'd been holding eased, but it was more than this. Her recognition and approval were clearly of great importance to him. All at once, I understood the two of them in an entirely different way than ever before.

I knew that Édouard carried some worry that the Abbess was unhappy with his efforts with Marcella, but it seemed to me that the proof is in the pudding—his success proved the correctness of his formulation. However, Marcella's influence had matured me, allowing me to understand that there was more to these two remarkable figures in my life.

Indeed, they were spiritual peers and collaborators. Indeed, they had few other equals and none more trusted. But I could now see that Édouard and the Abbess were more than mere compatriots; there was a deep *fraternal* bond between them. The Abbess was as a sister to him, in truth, though not by blood, and Édouard was to her a brother in kind. Recognizing this relationship for the first time shed light on their behavior toward each other during recent exchanges.

The Abbess expected, as "Grande sœur," to be more involved in his work with Marcella. As "elder," she would be naturally entitled to such consideration from him, the "younger brother," and was irritated that he hadn't sufficiently sought her counsel. From her view, Édouard would seem to be showing off by insisting he do it all himself!

And I could see that Édouard had not been showing off at all, but was simply working within the realm of his mastery. His understanding of Marcella's ingredients and his ability to craft the alchemy needed to remove the impurities and reveal her true nature were instinctual genius. A similar instinct drove his spontaneous, creative improvisation when Marcella sought me out. In this, he was more like a brilliant artist working with his medium, something not available to collaboration.

As the master artist and the *petite frère* in the relationship, he displayed his finished painting to her and, like every little brother, wished for her admiration of his accomplishment. He hoped for her recognition of his magnificent art, but her sternness made him fear her disregard.

Thankfully, the Abbess had figured this out on her own over the past few days. I was sure that my beloved Contessa played a role in shifting the Abbess's view. Marcella's empathy and social sophistication would have made their *frère et sœur,* brother and sister, relationship obvious to her from the first moment she saw them together. She would see that the Abbess's disgruntlement was likely based on a misperception of Édouard's intent. Woman to woman, Marcella would have been in a position to present an alternative motive— his wish to win the approval of his *grande sœur*.

"My deepest thanks, my dear Abbess, for your high praise," Édouard gratefully acknowledged. He gestured grandly toward Marcella. "My efforts helped to crack her false shell, but for discovering the seed of her true self and nurturing it into the flower we see before us, Étienne deserves much credit."

The Abbess paused to let this sink in, which I appreciated, as there must be some dust in the room, making my eyes tear up.

"We now have an entirely different problem to solve," the Abbess continued, "Which is that Marcella and Étienne are being asked to do the impossible here."

She paused a beat to let her starting point sink in.

"They've been asked to restrain their physical desires for each other. To their credit, they had asked this of themselves even before more stringent requirements regarding this were imposed."

She had a neutral expression, but I knew she was addressing François with her comment about imposition. Not to be outdone, François wore an even more neutral look, if such a thing were possible, in response.

"All this might have been enough," the Abbess continued, "except that the magical forces they've tapped into have only intensified their desire for each other. As you've all just witnessed, it has caused an unusual and potentially dangerous magical phenomenon."

There were nods of agreement all around. Judging by the expressions on their faces, which ranged from concerned to dismayed, I got the impression that the phenomenon that occurred between Marcella and me was not something anyone was familiar with.

"The solution considered thus far is to teach them to transmute the energy of desire somehow. However, this kind of thing is only accessible to those who are familiar with and have a basic mastery of their desires.

"This certainly does not apply to these two virgins," she said. Then, casting a questioning glance at me, added, "Well, near enough to virgins!"

Everyone except the Abbess's two assistants laughed at this.

"Having little experience with their desires, expecting them to contain and transmute them has too little basis. And now, the magic they've accumulated has become attached to their desire, complicating things further."

Her analysis seemed accurate, but were there other options for us? I hoped that the Abbess had something in mind, but my imagination failed me. As Mother Superior, she was accustomed to guiding young novices in chastity, but I assumed she was as much a virgin as Marcella, so I wondered what she had in mind.

"So, the most essential consideration is that the Contessa must keep her virginity intact, yes?" she queried.

I looked to Édouard, François, and Matilde for answers to this. They looked to each other, and each shrugged, agreeing that this was indeed the fundamental requirement.

"Good, we agree," she acknowledged. "If you all would humor me for a bit, I wish to consult the expert here on Nature's principles. Maestro, you have shown me in your laboratory how an amber rod, when rubbed with a woolen cloth, builds up a kind of invisible lightning and will discharge that energy in a spark when the rod is brought into proximity of another person. Tell me, if that person is touching the rod or your hand that holds it, will they still be shocked if you bring the rod close to their body?"

The Maestro stroked his mustache, as he did when deeply reflecting on something. A gleam grew in his eye as he was working out where the Abbess was going with this. Well, at least one of us was getting the picture, not me, as I was utterly confused.

Édouard stood up and made for the door, saying, "Let us find out! I will obtain some equipment from my laboratory and shall be right back."

He was gone for only a few minutes, returning with a small wooden case, from which he extracted a beautiful rod made of the purest amber and a woolen cloth. He commenced to rub the rod vigorously with the cloth, and walked up to me. "Hold out your hand, Étienne," he ordered.

I did so, while he slowly brought the rod toward my fingers. When it was nearly touching me, there was a "snap," and a blue spark shot from the rod to my fingers.

"Ouch! What the devil, Édouard!" I said, shaking my fingers to dispel the pain.

"Don't worry, Étienne, it won't damage you!" Édouard insisted. "Now, touch the amber rod with your other hand, and we'll repeat the experiment. We will both maintain contact while I charge it with the cloth again.

We managed to find a position to hold the thing together while he rubbed it with the cloth.

"Now, Étienne, keep holding it with me and slowly bring the finger of your free hand towards the rod."

I did so reluctantly and waited for the painful snap, but to my relief, nothing happened this time.

"Aha!" the Maestro announced with enthusiasm. "The answer, my dear Abbess, is that the person will not be sparked if the charge is built up in both partners at the same time."

The Abbess looked pleased at the support for her surmise.

"So, I'm sure you'll be surprised that this proposal is coming from me, but it's the safest option we have. I will be straightforward. If the goal is to preserve the Contessa's virginity, and so understanding that intercourse is expressly forbidden to them, they must be free to quench their desire for each other safely!"

There was a brief hubbub of reaction to this suggestion, coming as it did from a chaste Mother Superior of the Church.

"What!" "You can't be serious." "But Abbess…"

The Abbess raised her hand until everyone again fell silent.

I have thought it through very carefully and cannot find another way to defuse the buildup between them so they can continue working together for the benefit of the Order. Anything else would waste time we cannot spare and energy they lack, for nothing. Much like amber, an invisible charge grows that, according to Natural Law, must jump the gap. If their desire has an outlet, they can learn to disentangle their magic from it. Please take a moment to consider this before raising your objections.

Marcella seemed to be trying to suppress a twinkle in her eye by avoiding looking directly at me. I was almost overwhelmed by excitement at the thought that we'd be permitted to do more than such utter restraint. I thought the sparks between us might jump across the room if aroused any further.

Édouard stroked his chin as he parsed what she was saying.

"So, dear Abbess. I believe I am following your argument. Would you permit me to review your points?" he queried, to her agreeable nod. "You believe that the two of them have already demonstrated that they are capable of restraint and decorum, given their natural desire. Yes?"

The Abbess nodded her agreement, which Matilde added to, saying, "And admirably so!" leading Marcella and me to smile with pride.

"I can certainly agree with you," the Maestro went on, "that they do not have the experience to use methods of transmuting desire to other purposes. You believe that desire fueled by magic, or magic fueled by desire, has become untenable."

The Abbess agreed he was laying out her case accurately so far, gesturing with a rolling motion of her hand for him to get on with it.

"So, if a way can be found to defuse this dangerous mix of magic and desire safely, their desire could be given an acceptable outlet, and they can then learn to work with the magical energies separately from it.

He looked to the Abbess for confirmation, then to the rest of us to ensure we had followed his rendition, and confirmed that everyone clearly understood what she was proposing.

"I daresay that you, Abbess, are not the one to be instructing them in sexual expression, am I correct?" Édouard said, almost as an aside.

If anything might make the Abbess blanch, I would think it would be his question, but she demonstrated much aplomb and acceptance of the earthy side of human life, simply agreeing this was so without a hint of discomfort.

Little did I know just how practical and earthy she could be.

CHAPTER X:

Uncoupling Desire

One might think that being given license to act on our desires with each other, within the proscribed limits, would be a joyous outcome. But, before the joyous part could be gotten to, we faced having specific instructions on sex. Must I add how mortifying it was for people of our tender age to have others, particularly adult others, giving us detailed instructions about the practice of sex?

Our mentors, Matilde and Édouard, advised us, separately and together, giving only a few suggestions. They seemed to recognize how embarrassing it was for us to talk about, especially for me, as it seemed women were more used to discussing these things with each other than men.

The first necessity was to defuse our magic-laden desire, allowing for touch without risking the dangerous build-up and discharge. Edouard, master of the most complex arcane arts, for once had a straightforward solution in mind: to exhaust desire beforehand through acts of self-pleasure! Certainly, the practice was familiar to me, having grown up in a household of boys. It had been a necessity for quite some time, really. He left it to Matilde to inquire whether Marcella was familiar with such things, as neither Édouard nor I dared pose the question.

The Maestro felt, in any case, that I was likely the main problem! I wasn't shocked by this conclusion, as I had come to the same conclusion myself. I'd recalled what the nun said to me in the carriage on the way to the Chateau, and how it might have contributed to my interactions with Marcella. The nun told me that I had gained a lot of magical energy in Brittany, which was insufficiently contained. If I inadvertently radiated it to Marcella in our ardor, I might indeed be fueling our problem. I explained this to Édouard.

"Exactly!" he said. "It makes sense that the initiations from the Old Man would only make this more powerful. I admit that I had not realized how unaware you were of how you loan your magic to assist others. I have neglected your training in self-containment!"

As Marcella's access to the magical energy of this nature was still developing, he thought that what entangled our desire mostly came through me. By the principle of simplicity, we would start with me and see what that did.

His first instruction to me was that, before I met with Marcella, I was to "manually release" my built-up desire and see if that allowed us to touch without the magical discharge. I did so. More than once! This helped somewhat, but was insufficient on its own.

Whether self-pleasure was part of the "Woman's Mysteries" acquired with Matilde or had been something Marcella knew before, Marcella was prepared to contribute her part. We each prepared through "manual release" before our next meeting. Again, this further lessened, but did not prevent, the uncomfortable magical discharge. However, by temporarily reducing our physical hunger for each other, my perceptive Marcella noticed something that had not been apparent before.

"Mon cheri," she noted, "You taught me too well! Having learned to draw on magical energy, I can see that I draw it from *you* when we are together without realizing it. And, I thought this was simply my feeling of longing for you!

"Generous magician that you are, you give no thought to granting me the energy I call for. The two of us have colluded in this coupling of desire and magic."

I understood immediately that she was right. It was but a small leap for us to realize that Matilde had already taught us techniques to modulate the magical energy I radiated and for Marcella to control what she absorbed as the alchemical Moon. Édouard worked with me to better contain the magical energy I'd acquired with the Old Man to bring it more thoroughly into my intentional control.

It was a tremendous relief for both of us to sort out the magical energy from the sexual chemistry stemming from our youthful attraction. These two forces had so strongly amplified each other that everything between us became overwhelming. At last, we could kiss and touch again without sparking the previous surge of energy, and we were no longer so consumed by our lust that we couldn't resist it. We were now free to act on what our bodies were feeling.

I grew up mostly around men, so I was unaware of women in general and knew little about the female body. I had two past experiences with young women, both of which were awkward because everything was new and uncertain. How do you flirt and charm? How can I get a kiss? How do you kiss, and what do you do with your lips and tongue? When do I use my hands?

The two girls I had been with were equally unaware of their own bodies as of mine, but their enthusiasm gave me some confidence that I was wanted, even though I didn't fully understand what their responses meant. I could not manage my urges long enough to interpret what their bodies communicated to me.

With Marcella, it was a whole different matter. We had come to know and trust each other so profoundly. To our surprise, even if it was obvious to others, this had led to love, and we were committed to the best for each other, first and foremost, before even ourselves. Now we were allowed pleasure, so long as it protected her virtue.

Édouard and Matilde recognized that young men often acted selfishly, with little attention to their partners› needs. Therefore, they wisely decided that I should focus exclusively on Marcella at first. They required this of both of us. This was not as impossible as it might sound, because the Maestro had weighed my "ingredients," and knew that my need to serve others, my commitment to discipline, and my role as the eldest, all meant I would undertake temporary self-denial to give to my beloved.

And I was in love, and my primary concern was to discover what gave her pleasure, rather than seeking my own. Her ecstasy in response to my acquired skill was my greatest reward. Well, my equally great reward.

I discovered that my intuitive sense, developed for our fight against evil, could be redirected to the skirmishes of love! And what a marvelous battle is love, where any side's surrender leaves both victorious!

Tracking her reactions from within, I could sense which touches pleased her most. I learn how the intimate touch of my lips, tongue, and kisses could send energy flowing through her, and chase it into an even deeper gasp. I discovered the wondrous architecture of feminine pleasure, a spiral staircase on which to coax her, turn by turn, ever higher, until a last step would launch her soaring into the sky. Thence, to fall safely into the cushion of my loving arms, to luxuriate and ascend again. What intoxicating stuff!

Marcella's challenge was uniquely hers. All her life, her beauty and charms served only her ego's goals. Her heart had been sealed away, guarded even from herself. Her body was a tool, primed and polished to manipulate others, but never included in her deeper self. Then, her heart opened, and I was within. Now, she wished to claim her body and its language of pleasure and desire as the natural expression of her heart's love.

At the behest of our mentors, she accepted, for the moment, my unilateral efforts to serve only her pleasure. I knew that my Contessa's competitive nature and her love for me meant that this imbalance would not stand for long, and that eventually Marcella would be intent on learning to elevate my pleasure above what I did for her!

Yet, her magic was impossible to deny. No matter that my focus was on her, with the fullness of her power and her generous heart, she found she could include me in her pleasure, and so turned the tables on me. And though she couldn't yet explore my body, she could use the naturally produced magical energies of her pleasure to envelop me. Wrapping me in this energy, she saturated me with her rapture, until I was carried into flight along with hers.

She was pretty proud of her discovery. She looked down at me and reveled in her newfound power. My head had fallen onto the cushion of her hip's soft flesh, and my eyes were glazed from the unexpected ecstasy she had brought me to.

"You have no idea what you have unleashed," she told me, "my dear and reckless man." Her eyes smoldered with ardor. "For I shall melt you in my fire like candle wax, until you are boneless, and captive in my bower."

And, yes.

Oh, yes.

Melt me, she did.

Chapter XI:

To Love & Serve

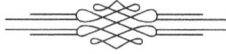

The Maestro wisely required little of Marcella and me until our pent-up passion eased. When he judged this was so, he gave us new assignments to continue developing Marcella's facility with magical energies. Of course, we discerned that the speedy completion of our assignment meant that the leftover time could be used for... other things!

After showing she would please me, even if through the energy of her own ecstasy, Marcella insisted it was time for her to explore more direct ways of doing so. As I am naturally unselfish and devoted to helping her, I agreed to sacrifice myself on behalf of her discovery of my body. Marcella quickly navigated and mastered the ways she could bring me to pleasure.

All this was delicious, but we discussed that something felt to be missing. We surmised that the natural and mutual movements of intercourse, what we understood of them anyway, would more easily let one build and achieve a peak together. While intercourse itself was forbidden to us, we set about discovering ways we could concurrently pleasure each other without conjoining organs, to arrive at a simultaneous peak.

On one occasion, we were practicing this discovery of mutual pleasuring. Perhaps we became less disciplined about separating the magical and sexual energies from each other, or maybe the Maestro's assignment had already built up more magical energy than we realized. Still, this time brought a completely unexpected result.

We had become adept at the building of pleasure, especially so at the expeditious route to this, as we often had little time to act in privacy. We moved each other speedily up that mountain path of pleasure, expecting to be flung off the top into the peak of physical ecstasy. Instead, our peak tossed us higher still, all into Marcella's sea of visions.

I floated as if in deep waters. I had no idea what had happened, and didn't understand what I was witnessing. Faces, buildings, and landscapes swirled by, as if carried by currents or waves, with no order or reason to it. I was hardly fit for much thinking anyway, being aswim in the aftermath of my own orgasmic pleasure. For a while, it simply *was*.

Then, it faded from sight, and I became aware of the sensation of my lips upon my lover's neck and her sweat-damp hair pressing against my cheek. Our arms were still between us, my fingers wet from her moisture, and her hand still gripping my manhood, sticky with my discharge.

I lifted my face from her neck to stare wide-eyed at her. Her eyes remained closed, and her lips parted as she panted for air. She appeared absorbed in her thoughts, but gradually surfaced and opened her eyes. When she could focus them, she smiled at my astonished expression.

"*Mio Dio!* We were tossed so high that we burst through into what the Abbess had called the Greater Sea of possibilities. *Oh*, m*ia amore*," Marcella said breathlessly, "I could see so much more than I could before!"

I nodded, pretending I understood her, which was false, but I was very confused. Her greater skill must discern patterns where I had only randomness.

Shortly, Marcella appeared to descend from the heights enough to better focus her eyes on me. She arched an eyebrow, indicating that she had discerned my transparent dissembling.

"You don't need to humor me, Étienne," she said with a smile. "It's obvious that you were as overwhelmed by my vision as I was at first, when your magic threw me headlong into it."

"But, but…," I sputtered, trying to form words and thoughts. "But, I don't belong in such a realm! I have no talent for envisioning things, and it was a mess!"

"I beg to differ, my clueless man," Marcella responded. "You have your own visionary talents… no, no, don't deny it… just because you call it 'tracking' doesn't mean it isn't visionary. After all, you say that you can find your loved ones in your mind's eye. Is that not vision? This is another aspect of your magic that I require you to claim!"

It seems that I have a habit of keeping things in different compartments, and I miss their connections. To me, my tracking was always like following a *feeling* about things; the images were simply a product of that.

"And," she continued, "if I can enfold you to bring you along with me into physical ecstasy, it should not be surprising that can I carry you into my visionary ecstasy as well! I only intended to bring you into the heights of pleasure, but our extra magical energy boosted beyond mere physical peaks!"

Curses, I thought. Another detail of my intimate life that I must, no doubt, discuss with Édouard! As plainspoken as we French are about sex, typically, I preferred at my young age to keep some parts of my life reserved from my elders. Alas, it was not to be. I didn't wish to risk the license for our newly found pleasures by concealing something so crucial from the master alchemist!

When I told the Maestro what had occurred, he was unsurprised. He said that he had expected this kind of thing to happen eventually and would consider it for a bit. A couple of days later, he took my arm, saying cryptically, "It's the moon," and that we would confer about it as we walked.

"Your initiation into this lunar tradition introduces powers that there are no guides for in the alchemical texts. Perhaps why the alchemical procedures yielded so little fruit!" the Maestro opined.

"All the texts view the lunar qualities as passive, receptive, and feminine in nature. None attributes the kind of magical force to her that your tradition gives you access to. Then, we have Marcella too. I surmise that the Moon's energy is somehow compatible with her, and she has learned to pull it from you with hardly a thought."

He believed that my initiation into the Moon's mysteries had played a key part in the energies between Marcella and me. He suspected that this had strengthened the alchemical connection between us. Édouard wanted to understand it more deeply than he had, and we discussed it.

Our discussion was notable because it was the first time he treated me as an expert with something to teach him. It was not that

I was no longer his student in many things, but rather that, during our discussion, the Maestro was also willing to learn from me.

"I must admit to you that I was surprised on your return from Brittany to find that the Old Man had made you a full-fledged initiate in a lunar tradition," the Maestro opined. "Based on my prior studies of historical magical traditions, I'd thought that lunar veneration was believed to be reserved solely for female initiates."

I was ignorant of any such precedents. The Old Man's empowerment by the goddess was so self-evident that it never occurred to me to question anything concerning our role as men in any of it.

Of course, I understood that the Moon goddess was a feminine power. After all, she was always referred to as "she" or "Mother," making it clear that she was viewed this way from ancient times. She was also associated with feminine things, such as women's monthly cycles, the ebb and flow of feminine emotions, and her control over the daily tides of the 'mother ocean.'

Though I referred to her as Moon Mother from respect, as the old Druid did, there was nothing warm or maternal about being in her regard. Her attention was more like that of a dangerously powerful aunt than a mother. Even so, as her initiate and devotee, there was *something* I could identify almost as a quality of love from her. But it was distant, nearly unrecognizable as such, especially compared to the maternal love I felt from Matilde, the closest thing to a mother in my life.

Still, describing her in human terms, like male or female, would be foolish. My glimpses into her mind made it clear that she was a vast being, *not at all human*. Fitting her into our human categories was a childish attempt to feel a false sense of understanding. Her concerns went far beyond any human matters.

I discussed all this with Édouard, who questioned me further and added it to his existing knowledge. His alchemical work required timing procedures according to the lunar phases, so he studied ancient lunar traditions to deepen his understanding.

"During my studies years ago," the Maestro revealed, "I learned that female initiates could more readily allow the goddess to *inhabit* them. Their own bodies made them familiar with her watery nature—her cycles, her different faces, and her dark, hidden aspects. On the other hand, men have little of this in our own bodies and would be driven mad if inhabited by her.

"I wanted to review my records on this, as I vaguely recalled finding, in some Roman manuscripts, a few mentions of Druid priests who served a Lunar deity, much as you've described with the Old Man. Male initiates appeared to be rare, and my research led me to believe that certain conditions had to be met for a man even to be considered for initiation."

Édouard knew from my account that the Old Man's nature was quite masculine, and Édouard wondered how he could have tolerated initiation and regular exposure to her power without becoming deranged. I came to a halt, holding up a finger to let him know I needed a moment, and opened myself to my connection with the moon, especially with her priestess. It took but a moment to confirm what I had guessed, and I came back to Édouard, and we retook our walk.

"Ah, Maestro, you must not assume that initiation means the same thing for men as for women. For a man, initiation does not occur through inhabitation by her. What I saw in the Old Man and with myself is that, for the permanent pledge of devotion and service, she grants the regard of her mind, and permits the use in her name of her immense force and power."

I told him how the moon mother had dismantled and reconstructed my spirit body so it could withstand her great power without being destroyed.

"The Old Man submitted himself to her *authority*, but she did not subsume him. His masculine nature was not twisted or diluted by that which his body was not fitted for, nor was mine."

As the Maestro and I discussed this further, I began to see that, for the Old Man, serving a feminine power as a priest actually reinforced his masculine nature rather than detracted from it. I thought of my friend, the Major, who, similarly, found meaningful service to his military nature in guarding and protecting the Abbess. For the Major and the Old Man, the masculine principle of serving and protecting that which is worthy affirms the highest of masculine spiritual principles. I noted my thoughts aloud to the Maestro.

Édouard considered this as we walked, then said that my upbringing at the Château had formed the archetypes I brought to my initiation by the moon.

"You were raised by two distinctly masculine figures, myself and, of course, François, and acquired a solid foundation in masculine principles from us. I daresay that the discipline you learned under François served you especially well in Brittany, giving you the strength and fortitude to withstand the Old Man's severe disciplines, schemes, and challenges."

Édouard smiled at this, expressing his fatherly pride in me. We embraced for a moment before he slapped me on both shoulders, approvingly. We turned to continue our walk, and he kept going with his commentary.

"You also had two women in positions of high authority for the role of maternal figures—Matilde, the earth mother, disciplined, nurtured, and nourished you. The more austere Abbess was the one who healed your physical and psychic wounds and guided you as you developed your psychic talents. Two strong women, each powerful in different ways, fundamentally shaped your understanding of feminine authority and, I believe, your relationship to feminine energy in general."

He paused long enough for me to consider the implications of these figures in my life. I understood completely what he was telling me. Beyond the personal and familial ties between us, he said, I carried them as templates, guiding my conduct towards these principles within myself and in life.

I realized that, as I grew into a man, my understanding of masculine energy—reflecting Édouard, François, and the Major—was based on serving higher principles, especially that of defending those in need. This included the sacred feminine, symbolized by the Abbess and Matilde. The dedication and service of these men to the highest feminine principle, whose knowledge and authority could only exist secretly under the corrupt suppression by the Church, was evident to all of us at the Chateau, even though it was unspoken.

"Most importantly, Étienne," the Maestro reflected, "you faced this lunar initiation without the 'will to power,' which drives most men in such matters. From your description, I can conclude that the Old Man is an unfortunate example of this, as he sought power to counter a profound sense of unworthiness.

"You, however, Étienne, went to her, not for power itself, nor to prove your worth, but as an affirmation of the faith placed in you by all of us at home. I believe you intuitively understood that the moon represented a greater feminine power you already felt you served, through Matilde and the Abbess. The Old Man manipulated you into that initiation, but the decision to serve the feminine had already been made within you. You recognized that this goddess was in harmony with the template you carried, and opened yourself to her simply, honestly, and without hesitation."

He'd put something into words for me that I'd not articulated, or even thought about, really, but was instantly recognizable, and I made an enthusiastic agreement.

"By all that's holy," Édouard exclaimed, "it never occurred to me that you would be forced to make the commitment of initiation without forethought! By his reputation, he was highly principled. No one realized that the press of impending death could create in him such unhinged desperation.

"But you showed that you were equipped to make this choice! The Moon goddess responded in kind, without hesitation, and with the same fullness with which you pledged yourself to her. Your lack of pretension and absence of any personal desire for power protected you from being distorted by her presence."

I hadn't thought deeply about my initiation in Brittany since I'd returned. It was simply an accomplished fact, and I had been busy stepping into new challenges and responsibilities once I was back home. I did my best to be worthy of the moon goddess by continuing my devotions. Edouard's comments made me reflect on how the Old Man had challenged my seriousness and the value of my teachers. I would step up to prove my mettle, or die trying. My mentors believed in me; otherwise, they wouldn't have sent me to the Old Man. I had tacit faith that they had prepared me sufficiently.

And Édouard was correct that I understood the goddess represented something familiar, as if I had a template to recognize her nature. Saying 'yes' to what she offered was, in this way, only an expansion of my service to the feminine, just in a higher form. In this light, it was also evident that the Abbess's rituals assigned to me to prepare me for Brittany had already placed me under the moon's aegis. Had the Abbess foreseen the initiation I would face with the Old Man? Perhaps. I'd ask her... maybe... someday. She was often cryptic in her responses to such questions.

In any case, I realized I'd surrendered to the moon's mystery even before I arrived with the Old Man, whether the Abbess had foreseen this. I recalled how he challenged me that first night, declaring, *'Offer yourself, without hesitation, or I will send you packing back to your Maestro.'* Fortunately, offering myself to her as supplicant completed what I'd begun months before under the Abbess's direction, though I had only understood that now.

"And now, with Marcella," the Maestro continued, "you give of yourself in that same way, unstintingly, that the feminine power she contains may rise to its fullness and authority. As with the Moon goddess, what you give to Marcella will be returned in ways beyond measure."

He shook his head at this. He looked somewhat humored, like he could hardly believe my good fortune, and all gained without a shred of intention on my part. I had benefited from the higher principle known as the blithe luck of fools. I grinned back at him with raised eyebrows to let him know I was just as astonished at everything I'd been granted as he was.

Then, the Maestro's tone grew serious, ensuring my attention for what he said next. "You will be given back much more than you realize, Étienne, for Marcella is a power all to herself, surpassing any of us in this aspect, most assuredly. The Abbess and I hope that her power will exceed that of the Order itself, which hangs on the brink of its downfall. We, including you, will do everything possible to guarantee her success."

There were so many implications in what he said that I was astonished. I tried to get him to explain at greater length what he'd only hinted at by these dark portents. He said this was not the time and would say no more about it. He would say only that my sole focus was to provide whatever Marcella needed to prepare *her* for the enormous challenges and difficulties she would face.

I would do this no matter what, whether or not the Maestro's instructions were given, but his dark tone added motivation to support her empowerment.

In any case, our discussion had not solved the problem I brought to him but only provided it with a greater context. No matter what we did, when we practiced mutual, simultaneous pleasures, we were automatically thrown into Marcella's oracular ocean. Marcella was launched into even more profound visions, which made her master the language of her visionary state more and more, leaving me even more confused.

This result led Marcella to desire our dalliance even more, as she could only reach this extraordinary level of vision with me, and I wanted to avoid them because of my overwhelming confusion. But I would not say no to her. Édouard had said we must do everything in our power to help her, as her task was far more daunting than our own. And I loved her.

I could already sense that supporting her in expanding her capabilities might eventually conflict with my greatest desire. But I could not refuse something she felt necessary for her advancement. It was not in me to be so selfish, but I hated that this was so.

It was not without pleasure for me, of course, pleasure I didn't know was even possible. In our favorite way, we yielded to our rhythm of pleasuring, each building upon the other's. We climbed that wondrous spiral staircase together, gazing deeply into each other's eyes. Somehow, as she always did, despite the urge to let go into abandon, our crest brought us higher, into the place of her visions. For an indeterminate moment, tossed in the waves of the sea of human affairs, I had an image of Marcella. I stared at her across a chasm, where she stood looking back at me. Behind her stretched a narrow way, crowded on either side by disasters. That narrow path glowed, as it called to her, and she was the only one who could traverse it. She could not yet see it; she hadn't turned to put it in front of her. She could only see me.

It was the briefest flash, yet vivid and indelible.

As always, eventually we fell out of our rapture, but, for the first time, I could not rest in the languor of my satisfied desire. I knew I must tell her what I had seen, and my heart sank. I was looking at her as she opened her eyes. She smiled broadly at me, still engaged in her vision and the fullness of her ecstasy.

"Oh my Étienne, that was simply transporting!" she said.

My face must not have reflected what she was expecting to see, and her smile faltered.

"What is wrong, my love? Tell me, tell me! Did I do something to displease you?"

I closed my eyes against my tears and shook my head vigorously.

"No, Mia Marcella, oh no, that is not it. I saw something unexpected in your sea of vision, that's all."

At her insistence, I then shared my vision with her. She listened, her perceptive eyes searching my face as I spoke, her expression concerned.

"You may no longer deny your visionary skill, my love," she said when I'd finished. Her concern to help me was greater than any concern for herself. "As your vision describes, I have not yet turned away from you to see it for myself. But I understand what has struck you so hard, my love. It is the chasm you saw between us, is it not?"

I nodded as my words escaped me.

"I don't know if I can reach the heights I need to see without our 'special' exercises, Étienne, but I must learn to do so on my own. I'm too distracted by your luscious presence otherwise, and I cannot turn away from you in the vision state to look for what you have described. I will talk to Matilde about this."

I smiled for the first time at her last comment. Her teasing me reassured me that we were okay for now.

"As I cannot do it by myself, and I cannot do it with your help either," Marcella said to me, "Matilde and I have decided that I must visit the Abbess, and with her help learn to see with a more elevated vision, including to look for signs of the one you have told me about, Étienne."

There was nothing for it but to escort her there. The Abbess herself met us at the gate and told me I would be called on in some weeks' time to collect the Contessa. I was dismissed to return to the Chateau.

When François told me to escort Marcella back to the Chateau, I was so eager to see her that I must have broken my record for speedy travel to the Abbey. Marcella looked haggard and strained. She threw herself into my arms, despite the lack of decorum, in front of the two familiar senior nuns.

When we pulled back enough for my questioning look, Marcella said, "Once on the road, I will tell you everything."

I sorted out her horse and a bag with her belongings, and we set off. We rode in silence until the Abbey was well behind us before we slowed enough for her to speak. It was to be as I had feared.

"I must return to Italy," she said, and broke into sobs.

CHAPTER XII:

Drink Fully the Cup

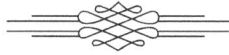

The Maestro's alchemical efforts for my maturation showed themselves in that critical time after Marcella left the Chateau and returned to Italy. From the very start, we had always acknowledged that she would be required to return to Italy when her training was complete. Knowing made no difference when it was finally a reality. It left us both devastated.

When she first arrived at the Chateau, it was understood by everyone, except her, of course, that she'd been sent for a purpose. Whether Édouard could transform her through his alchemy or not, she would eventually return to Italy and serve the family lineage and estate. If the Maestro succeeded, she would remain at the Chateau as long as necessary for training. If not, her stay would be brief, and the Order would implement plans to permanently shut down her gifts, leaving her as a marriageable means to cement the family lines of power.

Then, the unexpected happened— the Maestro's human alchemy worked, in part because of the love that grew between us.

Marcella continued her stay at the Chateau in France, where its unique resources could offer her many of the things she needed. When her training was complete, she would be required to take up both her rightful role for her family and her service to the Order.

Of course, Marcella and I always understood that our parting was only delayed, but it had not seemed imminent. There was so much for her to learn and study that our inevitable parting felt far enough away not to be entirely real. An atmosphere of grand adventure suffused the Chateau, and it was easy to imagine that she would be part of it forever. Neither of us wished to think about what would happen when that time arrived.

Ironically, her urgent return to Italy was not due to her father or the Order, as expected, but from her oracular talent. It was inconceivable to us that her gift—the reason the Order sent her here and why our paths crossed and we fell in love—would lead to our parting.

After her vision was awakened by the magical energy I provided, Marcella turned her attention to mastering this perspective within the realm of human affairs. The inner eye perceives as much through symbols, signs, and portents as through literal images, and it is a language all its own. It must be studied and mastered to interpret the visions. The Abbess understood this gift best, and I recently escorted Marcella to the Abbey, leaving her there to spend several weeks in intensive study and practice.

During her studies there, one of her visions revealed patterns that would later take on major significance for the Order. This became the focus of her attention at the Abbey, and weeks were given over to discerning what this vision was communicating. Marcella was not permitted to speak to me about what this entailed, but revealed that there was only one foreseeable path that would produce a positive outcome for the future of the Order. That singular path, without any question, required her to return to Italy. And to do so with haste.

"I see no other way, my love," she said through her tears, which streamed down her face and dripped off her chin. "The Abbess has confirmed that I am seeing truly; through her own methods, there can be no doubt."

I had seen how much in pain she was as she brought me this news, and was more worried about her than myself. When she told me why, I became numb from shock, a numbness that would fade all too soon, as it was followed by abject misery. I'll spare myself the burden of detailing those last, tortured days together and our even more wrenching farewell.

All too soon, she was gone, and I was left devastated and heartsick. Something had been ripped from my very soul, and it was inconceivable that I could ever be whole again. Marcella was my first, and I truly felt that she would be the greatest love of my life. We were connected in ways beyond ordinary imagination—linked by magical energies and forces that defy mortal understanding, as well as hearts and bodies. All of this felt with a sharpness that only those with young and unblemished hearts can know. As they say with good reason, *"La douleur exquise d'amour,"* love's exquisite suffering.

I'd learned the true nature of love from her—that the well-being of the beloved is more important than one's own—and therefore I could not oppose her decision. It was precisely *because* I loved her that it was an imperative that she fulfill her purpose. To do otherwise would be to stunt her soul, and, because I loved her, would also stunt mine. I would rather tear my heart from my body than stand in her way. While many consider this the greatest act of love one could perform, it was shattering all the same. I'd found much higher wisdom in love, but higher wisdom does not preclude the pain in acquiring it.

I have little memory of the months after she returned to her home. I was young and, like all youth, felt that fate had singled me out for a unique and special suffering. I would guess that I had been declaring myself finished with love for the rest of my life, and likely included all future incarnations and beyond. Or some such equally dramatic and absolute pronouncements.

Ever the alchemist, Édouard usually preferred to let the fires of youth burn away its own impurities, in its own timing. He must have decided that I was turning cold from bitterness, and to wait longer risked my metal warping before he could pound it into shape. Instead, he found a moment while I was still hot and tortured to strike with his hammer while I was still malleable.

It is one of those tricks of far memory that, despite having little recollection of this time generally, the Maestro's conversational blacksmithing strikes through that fog, and I recall his words with exactitude, to this very day. Not the least because he called me a magician, and likened me to *Christ*, almost in the same breath. Suffice it to say, these were not intended as compliments.

Somehow, despite my moping, Édouard had cajoled me into joining him for a long and excessively vigorous walk. The Maestro had learned well that to get young men unstuck, you *must* get them *moving*. He also understood that for stubborn and fixated young men to talk or listen, one must *never* do so face-to-face.

Young men lack real substance but feel they must show it, so they focus on the *appearance* of substance, which means they are focused on pride. Having an honest face-to-face conversation is unbearable because it risks *losing face.* It is too risky to their pride, leading to prideful posturing and arguments. Face-to-face leaves no room to reflect and even less space in which to change one's mind.

So, any side-by-side activity can give a young man a sense of support from the listeners' non-threatening presence. At the same time, they are free to think their independent thoughts, without someone's gaze provoking their pride.

And so, we walked.

And walked and walked.

Then we walked some more.

The Maestro must have been waiting for some sign that I had burned off enough of my mood through exertion, and that he decided it was enough for him to speak.

"My dearest Étienne. I know how much you are hurting from Marcella's return to Italy to take up her duties."

I probably grunted at this. I'm sure that I was unable to summon words, but perhaps the Maestro did not require a response.

"She is an extraordinary young woman, and what you had together while she was here was beyond extraordinary."

His frank acknowledgment of the extraordinary nature of Marcella and of our love might have softened me a little. By this, he indirectly confirmed that my sense of loss was especially acute— more so than any others wounded by love in human history! I was still *so* young, and my *feelings* were genuine, if not objective. There was no point in arguing, so Édouard chose to accept my emotional truth and discuss other matters.

"Of course, my friend, your different missions and stations prevent you from making your partnership permanent in society's way. But know this: your time together is not over. You two have been woven together in ways that will thread you in and out of each other's lives, no matter how you feel or what you believe right now. And no matter the vows you make now in your extremity."

This was at least a glimmer of comfort for me. I hoped that he would leave it there, but the Maestro was not done with his oration, having given the preamble but not yet made his point. After all, his was an alchemical process, and he hadn't yet cooked me up properly.

We continued walking.

"Such a love is given rarely in life," said the Maestro, musing on the Fates, "when given at all."

We kept walking for a while longer, and eventually, I couldn't hold back my feelings about the tragedy that had been forced upon us. I voiced the obvious conclusion—at least, it seemed apparent to me—that I'd been given something extraordinary, without knowing that it was doomed to end before it even truly began. This showed me that there really was no point from the outset. So, I decided that I was done with love, now and forever.

True to form, the Maestro saw my outburst as a crack into which he might tap a wedge, loosening me from my fixed position.

"So," Édouard responded. "Do I understand you correctly here? You must restrain yourself from love because, inevitably, it will end. As you say, what is the point, after all? And, you believe that this protects you from further grief in life?"

I agreed with a nod, affirming that he had thoroughly grasped this obvious truth.

"Therefore, love," he went on, "is something you must now protect yourself from. I understand. It is much like how pious men must be protected from their own impure thoughts by requiring women to be excessively modest, yes?"

I'm sure I tried to correct him. He had gone off track in his understanding of my position. My correction did not seem to dissuade him in the slightest from his argument.

"I see now, Étienne, it's *not* that you need to protect yourself from love, but from love's hurt? Furthermore, you feel your position of guarded and resentful safety is an *improvement* over your feelings of loss, yes?"

Bastard! I hated it when he used my logic against me. It was unfair that he followed my arguments so well and took them to their unwelcome yet inevitable conclusions.

"Ah, Étienne," he continued, the sarcasm in his tone was evident. "Such an improvement this is for your life! You have set yourself to experience life in a wondrously flat and mediocre way, *and* spare yourself from even the merest potential of negative feelings, well into the future. True, I suppose, as you spare yourself from *all* feelings to accomplish this, the good ones along with the bad. I must apply the logic of this magical formula you've found to apprehend its larger truth better."

He waved his hands about in the air as if it would assist him in following the logical sequence of this new philosophy.

"Ergo, perhaps there is no sense in my eating Matilde's wondrous cooking now, for what if I do not have it tomorrow? One would not want to long for it if one cannot have it, eh? Better to destroy all such goodness before it's lost."

"*Certainement,* you *are* spared from hurt, and from life's rich experience— love, wonder, beauty, excitement, and so on. You have a profound and wondrous ability, Étienne, to engrave upon your soul that the feeling of loss is the most essential thing about life!

"And, thinking it through, I see that you are doubly clever! Why, you gain *two* losses for the price of only one! You are a veritable magician, Étienne, for you have transformed the ephemeral wonder of love into solid and permanent misery, becoming a master alchemist in the art of transforming *gold into lead!*"

I blanched at his sarcasm, yet even so, I had to restrain myself from smiling at his clever turn of phrase. I managed to maintain my serious and intent expression, though the familiar gleam in his eye told me he had seen through my mask. He continued, seeing this as a license for even more drama than before.

"Étienne, what a miracle worker you are!" Édouard boomed loudly, "This marvelous talent you have for multiplying your misery. Why, you are just like Christ with the bounty of loaves and fishes, except the obverse!"

I could no longer restrain myself and laughed aloud at these humorous accolades. Édouard on a roll, like this, was too good not to enjoy.

"Oh, Étienne, don't you remember that I once taught you not to insult the gods when they bestow upon you a gift? When they give you the gift of love, at all, you must not complain that its eventual outcome ruined its value. Surely you will be punished for such hubris!

"Think about it, *mon amis*. Would you cast aside everything you gained with Marcella from your mutual love? And that love is still between you, despite the lack of proximity. The Fates grant us only temporary custody of such gifts, so we may learn to appreciate their preciousness. This is not meant to punish us, but rather to encourage gratitude for what we have received. I urge you to recognize how rare and wonderful it is to experience true love, especially of the most magical and sublime variety."

I hadn't thought of that. Yes, what Marcella and I shared was a precious and unexpected gift for both of us. I'd been so miserable, precisely because I'd believed I had lost something beyond value. But Édouard was correct; I should not disdain it so.

He continued, no doubt sensing that the tide had turned and I might better appreciate the wisdom he was to bestow.

"What a pity you don't turn your talent for magical multiplication to *increasing* love rather than its opposite? Your life could be, no, *should* be, completely saturated with Love!"

He had my attention. Unwilling to wait for me to find my line in the Playwright's script, he read it himself so he could follow with his character's oration.

"What love should your life be saturated with, you ask? Why, *all* love! There are so many wonderful kinds—love for your work, love for your loved ones, love for your life, why… love for life itself. Your cup runneth over!"

The Maestro, sure that he had shifted me from my stuck position, thought it was time to emboss his seal upon the lesson.

He brought us to a standstill, turning so that we were face-to-face. He stroked his beard momentarily as he considered how to formulate his thoughts.

"For myself," he said, gazing for a moment in the distance before bringing his piercing eyes back to mine. "*I* would rather drink the cup fully and have its whole nourishment in my belly than worry that the cup will then be empty.

"*All* cups that nourish us will become empty if we drink what they offer," he said. "The vessel of love seems to become a vacuum. All love appears, ultimately, destined to be lost.

"But you must ask yourself, Étienne, where does it go?"

Our walk had brought us back to the Chateau, and Édouard turned to continue through the gate, leaving me to my thoughts. I wandered for hours, letting his words reshuffle my mind and my feelings.

Writing this, six hundred years later, Édouard's deep love for me remains alive in my heart, as does he. And, while I remember little else about this specific period after Marcella's return to Italy, Édouard's passionate exhortation to me indelibly remains. My feeling of hopeless loss, so intense at the time, seems like a mere shadow now, by comparison.

I am still working on the lessons he shared about love and its magical multiplication. Since I seem to have challenges with spiritual learning, I may require a remedial class in this lesson. Sometimes, I believe this is the entire reason for writing these books.

Maybe that misses the point. I've realized, through all this retelling, that Édouard's challenge to me was only partly to help me deal with my feelings of loss. The more important effect, as always with the Maestro, was to trigger an *alchemical* process whose transformative power is *still* working inside me. The puzzle he left me that day, at the gate of the Chateau, keeps circulating inside me.

And if now, after six hundred years, I can feel that Édouard's great love for me is alive, even as I write this, *then where does love go, indeed?*

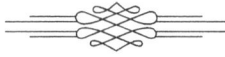

PART II:

The Robere Cycle

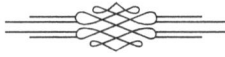

CHAPTER XIII:

The Curious Painting

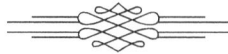

My teacher, Rose, was a remarkable healer, and she, therefore, attracted to her orbit some quite remarkable people, ranging from remarkably talented to remarkably psychic, all the way to remarkably odd. Perhaps I count as one of those last. Judy Marz qualified in more than a few categories of remarkable. She was exceptionally talented, psychic, weird, quirky, and a remarkable artist.

Our initial bonding was over far more prosaic matters: we were attracted to women of a similar nature.

I met Judy at the start of my first residential retreat with Rose, and I liked her immediately. She was smart and had a sly, raunchy sense of humor. She was an art teacher at a public high school and loved her students. The next day, as I was new to the community, I looked across the sea of about seventy people for a familiar face, and there was Judy, with an empty seat beside her. I asked if the seat was free. She readily welcomed me to sit next to her, which I did.

Our seats were located next to the central entry aisle, allowing us to people-watch as they passed by on their way to find seats. Judy entertained me with funny stories about her psychic experiences, interspersed with witty comments about friends as they entered the big room and walked by. Our conversation stopped when a woman walked through the double doors, a stunner, both fair and voluptuous, with a "notice me" attitude shining from her like a lighthouse. She paused briefly, pretending to look around for a seat to make sure all eyes were on her, then she strolled down the aisle.

As the woman walked past us, Judy and I turned our gaze to follow her saunter down the aisle. Our heads swiveled in unison like target-locked radar dishes, following raptly until she found her seat.

Judy and I exchanged a look and smiled, recognizing our shared mindset. Judy flapped her collar in a classic "need to cool down" gesture, and I responded by pretending to wipe sweat from my brow and shaking it off my fingers. We had bonded over our shared and quite politically incorrect lust.

Judy's ribald sense of humor was a breath of fresh air for me. I was often a jokester, but I had learned to hide my risqué side to maintain strict professional boundaries. Judy's humor was hilarious and biting, full of insight. Her comments included everyone, not least of all herself. She often had me in stitches, and I had to work hard to hold back from laughing out loud, especially when she whispered something in my ear while Rose was teaching. After that first morning, we seemed like a couple of middle schoolers who would tease each other into mischief.

She was a generous teacher of energy work to newcomers like me, and was one of the most psychic individuals I had met in a community rich with such talents. Clairvoyant since childhood, Judy generously shared her insights about Rose's teachings, which were extremely helpful to me, as I often felt adrift in this unfamiliar territory.

Growing up in poverty in the backwoods, Judy deeply empathized with the children in need. During her first visit to the Tibetan Bon Menri Monastery in India, she encountered another group of children in need—boys aged 5 to 18—who had been sent by their parents from Nepal, India, and Tibet to receive an education that would preserve their cultural and religious heritage. In her photos, you can see that despite the monastery's primitive living conditions, the boys' smiling faces were filled with light. Judy and many of those she recruited adopted them, and together they took on a mission to raise funds, build a proper dormitory, and improve the water supply.

Judy attracted spiritual phenomena the way some of us attract stray pets. Rose thought it was because Judy's spiritual light acted as a beacon. A case in point: driving past a fatal car accident while on her way to work, Judy finds herself having to deal with the deceased and confused spirit of the car's driver. Sudden fatalities like this can result in discorporate beings wandering about, not understanding that they are dead. I imagine that the shining light of Judy's auric field must have looked like a lighthouse to the deceased man.

By the time she arrived at work, Judy was struggling to calm the shocked and disoriented being who was clinging to her like a drowning sailor. Fortunately, the principal of her school was a dear friend and a New Age compatriot, and they could sit together for a few minutes before classes started, helping the confused spirit to "cross over."

Judy shared this story with a few of us in a tone that conveyed, "Can you believe the stuff that happens to me?" It illustrated why she had learned the art of psychic self-defense early in her life, out of stark necessity. It was eye-opening for me. She taught us these practices, providing us with a brief, practical course in dealing with wandering spirits and "hungry ghosts," as the Tibetans called them.

Over the next year or so, we became good friends. I learned that, aside from helping the Bon children, Judy's most earnest goal was to quit her day job and paint full-time someday.

After attending several retreat sessions, I arrived early one spring day before a startup to find Judy helping set up the meeting room. We hugged, happy to see each other before the rush of other attendees arriving. She asked me to take a walk with her so she could run an idea past me.

It was a beautiful spring day in the Berkshire Mountains, and we strolled through the grounds of the Catholic retreat center. Her idea was to combine her clairvoyance with her painting skills to create portraits that depict people's spirit guides. What did I think? Would there be a demand for this kind of thing in our community?

What did I think? I told her that I thought this would be a precious treasure, and that's exactly what I thought. Sign me up immediately! Some of us have visual impressions of our spirit guides—I'm one of them—but most do not. And even though I had *mental* pictures of my guiding spirits, we can't take photos of them! It would be an incredible gift to have an image of our inner guides and teachers.

And while I knew little about painting, I recognized the significant challenge that Judy was undertaking. It would not only require her to be clairvoyant enough to envision non-material beings in detail but also to maintain psychic concentration during long sessions, all while possessing the fine motor control needed for painting. I was well aware that whenever I entered into any altered state, my ability to sustain it was limited, and I struggled with gross motor skills, let alone fine motor coordination!

The idea completely galvanized me, and I had no hesitation in telling her so.

"Judy, you have to do this!" I said, "And I'll be your first commission!"

She was taken aback by my enthusiasm and presented her customary list of self-doubts and uncertainties about the project. I brushed them off as predictable and told her that I had absolute confidence in her.

I asked, "What amount should I write the check for?"

"Wait a minute, Jim. You've never even seen any of my work, what makes you believe I can do this?"

"That doesn't matter," I responded, "It has 'Yes' written all over it!"

Judy was looking excited about it herself.

"I'll write you a check as soon as I get back to my room. So, how much?"

Judy hesitantly told me her fee, and I shook my head in disbelief.

"No way, Judy, that's too little! This is an incredibly precious thing you are doing, a rare and valuable gift. We can't get photos of our guides after all! You need to charge enough to feel it's a fair trade for the time it requires and a good exchange for the energy it takes."

We went back and forth about this for a while. Judy felt anxious about being stressed to perform if she charged too much. We discussed and negotiated, and in the end, I bargained the price up enough to reflect how much I valued this project, but within a range that didn't make her feel pressured.

"I'll leave it to you, Judy, however long it takes," I concluded. "I won't even ask about it when we talk. Whatever updates you give or not are completely up to you."

When I returned to my room, I wrote the check, gave it to her when we all gathered, and put it out of my mind. Combining her clairvoyance with the complex craft of portraiture would be a delicate process, and I didn't want to interfere with finding her way through it.

When we spoke on the phone between retreats, she occasionally mentioned creating these paintings, but not frequently. A few others had commissioned paintings after she spread the word in our community.

Her agreement with the purchaser was simply, "To do a painting of your spirit guide," but it was left open who would come to the sitting to be painted, and it might not be the guide you expected. She once described to me the fascinating process of seeing who would come forward to "sit" for the paintings and learning to extend her concentration for longer periods during formal sittings. She was finding her way in something no one else could teach her. Other than those glimpses, I set it aside and almost forgot about it.

In the meantime, I had plenty to work on and learn on my own. I was teaching energy work with my friend Carol, and psychic phenomena had become more common. Subtle energy work enhanced and complemented the body-oriented work I'd been doing for years, but it also introduced its own challenges. Since I was new to psychic perception, these impressions, especially from those dealing with early trauma, could leave me with intense emotions, images, and body sensations. Strange energies emerged with several clients processing early abuse experiences. Rose's training gave me the tools to stay grounded, and Judy's practices helped me disentangle from these energy forms. Gradually, I felt better equipped to deal with the strange phenomenon of this paradoxical energy realm.

So, it didn't surprise me during an energy session for a colleague to notice a spirit hovering in the room. This type of occurrence had happened before. Nothing about this spirit's presence was threatening. My inner vision only offered an impression of a man in a rough-spun brown robe, his face shadowed by the hood, yet I felt unsettled by this uninvited presence.

I had learned there were rules about this kind of thing. So, like every New Age rookie, I fell back on a formula to feel more in control. What were the steps again? Ah, yes, I am allowed to challenge the uninvited.

"Why are you here?" I queried silently, my inner voice echoing like a castle guard in an old movie.

It sounded melodramatic, even to me. But I have the right to challenge, so I've been told, anyway.

"Watching," came the singular reply from the shadowed figure.

Okay, I thought, asked, and answered.

Crap. What am I supposed to do now?

I didn't know, so I continued with the energy work to buy time to think it through. My friend was relaxed and seemed oblivious to my ongoing psychic drama. I was not at all happy about this "watching" stuff.

I recalled being taught that, as the healer in charge, it was my right to protect the space in which I worked. I welcomed the spiritual helpers I had some working relationship with, but this hooded figure was unfamiliar, and I did not understand why he was here.

"You must declare your purpose here!" I announced to the presence. The intensity of my statement surprised me. I opened one eye to make sure I hadn't spoken this challenge out loud, and fortunately, my client on the table was unperturbed. Phew!

Again, the only reply from the hooded interloper was, "Watching."

I had had enough of that, I decided. According to the rules, I was in charge and could change them if I didn't like the conditions.

There's a spiritual rule in there: beware of rookies with rule books, for they can smack you in the head with it as they wave the darn thing around in panic.

I summoned as much energy as I could muster, and I directed it like a firehose to push the hooded figure out of the room.

"Not here," I thought proudly, "not on my watch!"

I reveled for a moment in feeling like a spiritual "tough guy," inordinately proud of my declaration of forthrightness and power.

Much later, on reflection, I had to ask myself, what on earth did I think was the problem? Couldn't I have politely asked him to leave? Oh well, too late.

Then, the same hooded figure reappeared during an energy work session. As they say in cowboy movies, this time, I was even "quicker on the draw" and promptly banished the hooded, faceless figure.

As before, I had second thoughts only afterward. Rose had recently chided me about my "fear-to-anger fixation." She meant that when I felt fear, I would quickly jump to anger and avoid the vulnerability of fear.

Was I being too reactive with this hooded figure? After all, I argued, he wasn't doing anything threatening; maybe I acted too rashly.

Well, I countered, maybe there wasn't anything threatening about him, but I hadn't invited him, either. Here I am, working hard, and I don't need some unknown, silent, 'watching' presence creeping me out. Besides, what's up with that dark, hooded robe?

"Really, Jim?" I counter-counter-argued. "You're creeped out by a costume choice? Besides, spirit beings don't really wear clothes, anyway, they're light beings; it's *you* who adds form to clairvoyant vision, into the look of dark robes and a shadowed face!"

I felt somewhat embarrassed after this inner dialogue about how reactive I had been. As it turned out, I didn't need to worry about feeling creeped out or embarrassing myself, because the shadowy figure didn't show up in a session again.

Meanwhile, the demands of my life diverted my attention elsewhere. Having recently separated from my wife, I had more to worry about than spiritual etiquette. I faced the practical challenges of becoming a single parent, settling into a new house and office, and navigating alternating custody of my two children, all of which took precedence over spiritual puzzles for a time.

After several months, my life settled into a rhythm. One afternoon, I returned from the grocery store to find a large, flat box on my front porch, leaning against the front door. Curious since I hadn't ordered anything, I picked it up and glanced at the return address. It was from Judy Marz! I had completely forgotten about the painting.

I carefully cut the tape to avoid damaging anything, then pulled out the well-padded, wrapped painting, which was sandwiched between heavy cardboard. I removed the protective layer of plastic film to reveal a large watercolor painting measuring sixteen by twenty-two inches. I hadn't expected watercolor to be the medium for the portrait, but even at first glance, I could see that the level of detail was remarkable. It looked magnificent.

The outer border of the painting is enclosed and defined by a Gothic-style design painted in metallic gold. The ornateness of the border evokes the decorative stone tracery found around medieval cathedral windows. This border divided the painting into two main sections: a dominant upper three-quarters panel and a lower triptych comprising three small panels along the bottom edge. The main upper panel depicted a man in the flowing white robes of a monk's habit, standing on a grassy verge at the edge of a tranquil pool, facing the viewer.

The monk stands in front of a carved stone bench, with dark pines and the lush greens of deciduous trees behind it. Judy's composition is striking: the pond in the foreground features yellow water lilies dotting its surface, and the slightly rippled water reflects the standing monk and the trees behind him. After taking it all in, I looked at the monk in more detail.

I'm first drawn to his eyes, which are a striking blue, then to his sandy blond hair and short beard framing a warm, genial face. His posture conveys a calm welcome, his arms relaxed and open as he presents the objects. His left hand holds a stalk of lily blossoms, while in his right palm, held like an offering, is a glowing quartz crystal cluster. He gazes directly at the viewer, his expression a profound blend of kindness and love.

Looking at the triptych of smaller images along the bottom of the frame, the left panel shows a small falcon perched on a branch. The right panel depicts a lamb standing on a patch of grass, backed by dark pine trees. In the middle panel, a jeweled gold chalice is displayed, with its glowing contents emitting three beams of light.

As a whole, the composition conveys the peacefulness of nature and a tone of profound mysticism, with each scene seeming like a window into another place or time.

Returning to the monk, there is a red Templar cross blazoned on the chest of his surplice, perhaps embroidered there. He wore the hood of his white robe raised to cover his head, but pulled back enough that his whole face was evident to the viewer.

I blinked, drawn to look at that detail again with a growing feeling of dismay.

Ah, yes, of course. A hooded robe…

Hooded.

Oh, my. A sudden wave of embarrassment swept over me as I realized this was the same spirit I had so forcefully, rigorously, and self-righteously expelled from my presence.

Twice.

Well, I justified, it was a *dark* robe when he first showed up, and there was no cross displayed to apprise me of his pious nature. Further, in my defense, the hood of his dark robes cast a shadow over his face. How was I to see his gentle countenance, only now revealed in the portrait?

My defensiveness was so reflexive that another part of me was compelled to point out the flaws of this argument.

So, Mr. Defensiveness, I countered, could it be that the monk came wearing his Sunday best for a *formal* portrait sitting? Perhaps he thought the occasion warranted his lovely white robes instead of the drab, workaday, *dark* homespun ones, don't you think? I mean, grow up! This isn't a cowboy movie from childhood, where the bad guys are in dark hats and the good guys in white ones!

Mr. Defensiveness decided not to argue after this.

Wow, this was pretty embarrassing! I hope I haven't damaged our potential connection by pushing him away. I sent a shy apology out into the universe for my impulsive actions. I sincerely hope I haven't ruined things with… whoever this monk was.

Okay, look at him again. How did I feel about him, aside from being embarrassed about my behavior? I examined him again, but I didn't notice much feeling, one way or the other, which was confusing. It's not that I expected any particular reaction, I guess, but I thought I'd have *some* emotional response. Shouldn't there be at least a 'click' of recognition from seeing his portrait? Or, even better, a moment of insight, a sudden understanding? Or *something*?

I suppose I had the notion, when I'd commissioned the portrait, that Judy would paint a spirit guide who was *recognizable*, you know, someone I was already familiar with. But she'd always said she paints whoever shows up for the sitting. There was no contract for painting a particular spirit guide.

The painting's beauty and precision made Judy's artistic skill evident. She expressed more in a watercolor than I understood the medium was capable of. The monk's kind and peaceful tone came across with clarity and feeling.

Yet my emotional response was… not much. Looking back, this should have been my first clue, but I didn't know how to interpret my lack of response at the time.

Perhaps Judy had painted the wrong spirit guide, I speculated. She'd been working on several commissions at a time in addition to mine. Could the monk have come to sit for someone else's painting, and Judy misunderstood?

You know, like when your package is delivered to your neighbor's house by mistake. The spiritual realm can be pretty confusing, and psychic impressions are precisely that—impressionistic and inexact, even for experienced folks like Judy. It could happen that way, right?

I was working very hard to blame my lack of reaction on external factors, even though I didn't realize it at the time. I admitted I felt somewhat disappointed after anticipating it for so long. Looking back now, it feels like a scene from a TV family sitcom, with the clueless dad who is completely unaware of his own foolishness, even though the audience sees it clearly.

Later, after further reflection, I realized that my *lack* of reaction might seem suspicious, especially since, during my initial encounters with the spirit, I had responded with enough emotion to trigger my psychic defenses.

As the Bard once said, "Thou doth protest too much… Or, too little… Maketh up thy mind!"

I had no answers to this. There's no point trying to make myself feel something that isn't there, so I put aside my puzzlement. Instead, I had the painting professionally framed, as its beauty, at least, deserved, and hung it above my desk in my office. I figured there might be a lengthy getting-acquainted phase; then we'll see.

Whatever.

Time passed, and the "getting acquainted" phase yielded little in terms of acquaintance, nor did it foster a deeper connection with this monk spirit. Instead, the opposite occurred. I began to sense that my problem wasn't really that there was a complete absence of feelings toward him. Like seeing a vague shape moving in deep waters, beneath my supposed indifference, an unease stirred about this monk, occasionally veering into fear. It was entirely at odds with the loving manner portrayed in the portrait. None of it made sense. I had commissioned a painting for this?

Then, he started to appear in person, so to speak—no longer just as a picture to look at but as a presence in the room while I worked. He showed up most often in sessions with clients dealing with childhood trauma. One client was struggling to confront a particularly difficult episode from her childhood. She couldn't bring herself to speak about it, feeling frozen with fear. She was getting frustrated because she thought she was far enough along not to freeze up like this.

She looked at the painting behind me and asked, "Would it be okay if I call on the monk for help?"

I was surprised by her request. Most clients didn't even notice the painting, despite its prominent placement on the wall. This client, in particular, was not at all inclined toward New Age concepts, such as spirit guides. I had to trust her perception of what she needed for support, as trauma work was hard enough as it was, so I told her, "Of course, you can."

She paused to gaze at the painting. Almost immediately, a wave of energy swept through the room, accompanied by a sense of loving calm. There was a noticeable effect on the client, as I could see her relax. She rested in this moment and then found her voice, speaking of the horrible episode for the first time. She was no longer numb and could feel her sadness and anger clearly as she talked about it. Later, she told me that the monk's peaceful energy had allowed her to feel safe enough to break her silence, so she could acknowledge her grief for the terrible harm she had suffered.

Similar instances to this occurred, and my reticence toward him began to soften. If my clients trusted him enough to seek his assistance with their healing, then at least I could follow their lead. Over time, I got the impression that the monk's particular spiritual mission was to heal the wounded child parts within us.

Still, it seemed odd that the monk's warmth was palpable to me when he showed up with clients, but I sensed none of that when I was by myself. Meditating on his image in the painting, I remained detached. Was I *deliberately keeping* him at a distance? I didn't know. Nevertheless, I kept meditating on the painting, guided by Rose's idea that nothing changes unless we invest energy and attention into it.

Eventually, a few things penetrated even *my* dense mind. I learned his name was Robere (pronounced Ro-*bear*, like the animal), an early French form of Robert, which left me wondering if he had a connection to my time with Édouard. My uneasiness lingered, though I did not doubt that his presence and intentions were for the good.

I decided that building my relationship with him was worthwhile for others, if not for myself. How generous of me. His ability to heal others was impressive enough, even if it wasn't exactly what I expected from commissioning a spirit guide portrait.

As these things often seem to go, I had to trust that there *might* be something cultivated beneath the surface. I had no conscious awareness that anything was happening or if it was, what it might be. Still, I had learned from Rose that we can grow spiritually when we connect with teachers who possess a higher level of consciousness and energy than our own. When I'd had this experience before, I was often unaware of any change in me until it had already occurred, like realizing you'd grown because your clothes no longer fit.

Our typical moment-to-moment experience gives us a misleading sense that the one experiencing those moments is the "me"—both the origin of intention and the focal point of the experience. We assume that our subjective awareness encompasses our entire existence, that our conscious intentions are the most significant factor, and that our aware, conscious "self" is the one steering the narrative.

But our consciousness is so much more than what we are conscious *of*. We are more like a house with many rooms. We mostly inhabit just one room —the only one with the light on —thinking it is the whole house. We may not even know there *are* other rooms unless, by chance, we get a glimpse of them.

Modern "rational" mind will insist that there *are* no other rooms, and that any glimpses are merely fantasies or mental aberrations, or solipsistically that there is no house at all! Most won't venture into the dark, choosing instead to remain in their singular room of awareness and call it a life.

In traditions like those Rose had taught me, there are beings for whom the rooms or dimensions that seem dark to us are bright to them. That's why we call them, unironically, "beings of light." They guide us towards more illumination, helping us realize that we are greater than our current awareness can encompass. This can be frightening, though, as our present awareness might lead us to believe that the dark rooms in our house contain something bad simply because they are dark.

Ultimately, my defensiveness and emotional distance from Robere didn't matter. His presence, along with the changes happening within me, in the background, started to unlock the forgotten rooms in my soul's house.

I was in the middle of my busy workweek when two consecutive cancellations left me with some unplanned free time. I saw it as an opportunity to meditate on Robere's painting, so I gazed at his portrait hanging above my desk and took deep breaths to center myself.

After a while, I had a clear sense of Robere standing beside me. Nothing was fleeting or vague about his presence. It was so real and solid that I almost turned my head to see him with my physical eyes. This was a first with him! I calmed myself down so I wouldn't jar myself out of the meditative state. Something changed, and I felt that he was now standing in front of me, between me and the painting, as if my desk wasn't there at all. As in the portrait, Robere was looking at me gently, lovingly, and patiently.

Abruptly, an immense sadness welled up in me, a grief without any story or apparent cause. As tears streamed down my face, images formed vaguely in my mind, emerging from a dense fog. I closed my eyes, falling into a vision of remembrance, and found myself as Étienne in that time, with Édouard in France.

Chapter XIV:

The Merlin and
The Monk

I had only been a resident at the Chateau for a short time, but it was long enough to have been assigned a few minor duties. As a foundling and orphan, I was going about the tasks I'd been assigned quite industriously, intent upon pleasing my benefactor, the Maestro. Like any boy of nine or ten, I was always open to opportunities for food. I had cleverly detoured through the kitchen and "liberated" a honeyed confection from Matilde's baking table. I was smugly enjoying it when I heard François call out.

"Étienne! Where are you, boy?"

"Coming, François," I called out. I was licking the sticky crumbs off my fingers, unbothered by the crumbs littering my shirtfront, as I moved toward his voice.

François waited for me by the fireplace in the Great Hall. He looked me over, shaking his head at how much debris a boy could collect in just a few hours, and told me to go and wash up. I was to return here, clean and shining, to meet a visitor.

"Maintenant *s'il vous plaît*."

His tone and words indicated that I shouldn't delay.

The Maestro occasionally received visitors, but I had never interacted with them before. Being just a foundling, I had no more status than any other servant in the household—probably less, since I was a charity case. I had never been asked to meet a guest before, and the idea made me quite excited!

Ah, the blitheness of childhood.

Eager to see what this new situation might bring, I quickly washed up, brushed off my clothes as best as I could, and ran back to the Hall, water droplets shaking from my still-wet hair.

As I turned the corner into the hall, I saw Édouard and François already talking with our guest. I took a few more steps into the room, but suddenly stopped as if I'd hit an invisible wall. I froze there, panting and breathless, in a state of shock. A small part of my mind insisted that nothing about this visitor warranted my reaction, but it didn't matter. I felt pure terror at the sight of our guest.

The visitor appeared as a gentle, peaceful, and harmless monk dressed in a rough-spun, hooded wool robe. He resembled a Cistercian, part of a large monastic order, and was a familiar sight in these times. His hood was pulled back, revealing smiling blue eyes and raggedly cut sandy brown hair, tonsured to expose a shiny, sun-reddened scalp. His short beard showed signs of gray.

Despite his poverty and plain appearance, he seemed bright in the unlit room, as if an inner light shone from within him. Long after this event, François called it a *beneficence*—a term for performing Christian deeds—suggesting that simply being near the monk was like being granted goodness, without further action needed from the holy man.

To me, Édouard seemed to exude a unique quality, though it contrasted greatly with that of the monk. The Maestro's aura had a robust strength that I could sense even when I wasn't looking at him. In contrast, the monks' presence felt more godly, gentle, and loving, offering comfort without expecting anything in return.

Despite all this, I was inexplicably paralyzed with terror, unable to move and overwhelmed with anguish at just the sight of him. Maybe I wasn't entirely paralyzed, as I had unconsciously been inching back away from him until I bumped into a bench against the wall, as far from the man as I could be while still in the room.

The Maestro and François stood nearby, the Maestro watching my reaction keenly, while François maintained his usual calm and detached attitude.

The monk appeared to focus solely on me. He smiled warmly, his loving eyes brightening as he rose to get a better look. He paused briefly, softly whispering to himself.

Finally... finally," he said, "at last, we meet again."

François' eyes widened when he heard this, not only because it suggested we had met before, which was impossible, but also because, although he'd known the monk for many years, this was the first time he had heard him speak. The monk had been under a vow of silence for thirty years. I knew none of this at the time, and wouldn't have cared anyway.

I only knew that these whispered words made my fear spike even more sharply. I felt strangely divided, most of me overwhelmed with terror, while a small part of me recognized the lack of any real threat to justify this. Nothing made sense. I could not be safer than here with my protectors, François and Édouard, but it didn't matter.

The Maestro finally spoke.

"As I told you, Robere, the boy isn't ready," Édouard said calmly. "It's too soon. He will dissolve into a puddle if we keep him here any longer."

The monk glanced to the side for a moment, perhaps listening to something only he could hear, before turning back to Édouard and nodding his consent. François dismissed me, and I edged sideways, keeping my eyes on the monk until I reached the doorway, whereupon I turned and made my escape.

I sprinted to my secret spot in the hayloft. It was my haven, my cave where I could be undisturbed. Climbing the ladder, I threw myself onto the bed of straw and lay there, struggling to calm my racing heartbeat. Eventually, exhaustion took over, and I drifted into a restless sleep.

I awoke hours later to the dinner bell, having slept through the afternoon, and made my way to the kitchen with caution. The monk had gone, and nothing was said of him for a long time.

CHAPTER XV:

Through A Glass Darkly

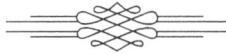

Some weeks after the vision of Étienne's terrifying first encounter with Robere, I sat in my office and looked at his figure in Judy's portrait. Even though the event happened over five hundred years ago, it felt as clear as if it had occurred yesterday. It was the first memory I had of actually meeting Robere in person. While it shouldn't have surprised me, given my time with Édouard, since so many of my past-life memories seemed linked to that period, I was still taken aback. Maybe the painting wasn't wrong after all.

It revealed nothing about who the monk was to me, seeming to be only a cryptic teaser. True, it confirmed that my reactions to the painting were defensive—but any idiot could see that by now, even a PhD. It didn't require four years of postgraduate study and a dissertation to see that.

I still had no idea *what* I was defending against. Why was I, as Étienne, so terrified? I had to accept that Robere was truly significant, even if I didn't fully understand why.

All I could do was keep meditating on him in the painting, hoping to gain more insights through impressions that gradually emerged, while 'looking through a glass darkly'—dim, fragmented, and unpredictable. Sometimes, I experienced vague impressions that stirred my emotions even without any reason. At other times, I saw almost photographic images that, however, lacked narrative, context, or emotional depth.

I couldn't resist trying to turn this chaos into a narrative, seeking meaning in it. It felt unnatural, and I knew I was just making things up to fill in the gaps. Sitting with something so unclear was hard, as I disliked the uncertainty.

I developed a sense —an intuition —rather than mental images or inner dialogue. From this, I knew that the monk Robere had been deeply connected through many lifetimes, yet I had somehow lost him.

Simply acknowledging this evoked an overwhelming flood of shame, guilt, and sadness. "*I'd* lost him." Somehow, I was the cause of it all; I was the one at fault.

But who was he to me? And, what exactly had I done? No answers emerged, but within the fog of vague intuition, some disturbing shadows lurked. I struggled to recall what might explain it, but only glimpsed vague impressions. As they accumulated, these impressions suggested that whatever the story was, it wasn't a good one—I felt that I had done something terrible.

Mon Dieu, what terrible thing could it be? Had I murdered him? No, no, that's not it. Betrayed him? Again, no. Why would I guess at these things?

It had become clear that we had once been close—very close, even. In what way? Were we family? Siblings? Best friends or comrades? Were we lovers? Once again, intuition told me that it was none of these. All my questions led nowhere. I imagined scenarios that might fit my impressions, but they were all false, and I knew it.

Only this feeling, that I had done something terrible, that I'd somehow created a rift between Robere and me. I stopped asking these pointless questions, but I was left to face a relentless feeling of guilt, without knowing why.

That's all I had for a long time, knowing it couldn't be forced. Maybe more would come to me, or not, as the case may be. Not being a paragon of acceptance or patience, I had to resign myself to the situation.

I don't recall precisely how my understanding progressed, but eventually, enough insight accumulated to make a meaningful impact. For some reason, it reached a tipping point.

One morning, as I meditated on Robere's painting, it became clear to me that whatever terrible act I might have committed was only part of the problem. No matter what I actually did, the real damage was, in some way, to my soul. By causing a fracture between us, I had separated myself from the goodness, love, and divinity that Robere represented.

The moment this thought formed in my mind, it struck me like a lightning bolt—powerful and impossible to ignore. Despite the lack of details, I knew it was true, beyond reason, logic, or any spiritual understanding I'd ever had.

I tried to brush it off and rely on the comforting familiarity of denial, telling myself I must be imagining all of this. What was I even talking about? Damage to my soul? What did that even mean? It was way too much fuss to be making over a simple watercolor.

And, I had enough maturity to know how quickly we can jump to conclusions based on intuition. It didn't help that spiritual energies are expansive, and this can evoke powerful emotions. It's tempting to craft stories that match the emotional intensity stirred by intuition, rather than waiting to gather more impressions. In my experience, when I took the time to gather more information, the story often turned out to be less dramatic than my initial, expansive feelings had indicated. Ah, I thought with some relief, that explains it: I'm being overly dramatic. That must be it, I decided.

I wanted to believe that was the case and clung tightly to this explanation. Yet, tucked away in a padded room somewhere deep in my mind, I couldn't shake the feeling that I wasn't being dramatic *enough*.

My conclusion must have let me off the hook enough that I let it be. There was a period when I didn't actively try to work on remembering more, and the painting seemed to lose its glow. It was just another decoration in my office. I stopped working on gathering any more impressions. I'd put the whole thing aside, right? In reality, it was more like sitting on an egg that was incubating.

I don't remember anything about the context now, or what I was doing, when a scene from my youth suddenly came vividly to mind. But it wasn't set in 20th-century America but in 15th-century France, when my name was Étienne.

CHAPTER XVI:

Even The Angels Knew Not

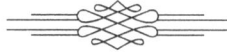

15th Century, Northeast France

The Maestro, François, and I had all agreed it was time for me to take a decisive step to resolve the riddle of the monk, Robere. I was now a man, and it was time to face things head-on. I hadn't seen the monk since that time at the Chateau seven years ago, but I no longer seemed to fear him.

Perhaps I'd borrowed some confidence from François, who had referred to the monk, Robere, as a man of "unquestioned Godliness." I trusted François completely and had never heard him speak so bluntly about *anyone*. And François trusted the monk completely. So, I had to treat it as a simple fact. Thus, there it was. François and I saddled up and journeyed a day or two by horse to find Robere in his forest hermitage.

The scene is vividly etched in my mind, sharply illuminated by the unique early autumn light as we sit in his rustic forest home.

The air carries the crisp, unmistakable scent of Fall, and dust motes shimmer as they dance through beams of sunlight.

Looking at Robere in the shadowed light of his hut, I feel an overpowering need to grasp my connection to this man. Something deep and mysterious pulls me in ways that defy explanation but feel momentous.

The forest hermitage is small and roughly constructed. It has a dirt floor, cool under our feet. A single large window lets in air and sunlight, with its shutters thrown wide to welcome in light and fresh air. A low fire burns in a fieldstone hearth; the light from its flames casts flickering shadows in the thatch above us. Despite the coolness of the dirt floor and the roughly hewn structure, this simple abode feels warm and homey, providing me with a sense of calm.

I no longer feel the irrational terror in his presence that I did during our first meeting years ago. However, I am still somewhat wary, as so much was still unknown. I know very little about him—only his name, that he was a solitary Cistercian monk, which his habit confirmed, and that he had lived under a vow of silence for perhaps thirty years or more.

I knew he was the monk who rescued François when he fled his priestly studies. As François began instructing me, he explained how he learned what he was teaching. As a boy, he had been "given to the church" by his parents to become a cleric. One day, while walking through the woods, he was attacked by thieves. In a fugue state, his hidden warrior nature emerged, and when he regained awareness, he found the men dead at his feet.

Horrified by his actions, he wandered the forest, maddened by his identity crisis. Starving and ashamed, he came upon a hermit monk, Robere, who took him in. The silent monk brought François to Toric, his martial arts teacher. Toric taught him the Way of the Straight and Curved, which François was passing on to me along with its mystical philosophy. The story and François's reverence for the monk made him seem more than human. What can this man have to do with me?

Robere and I sat on a couple of crude three-legged wooden stools, facing each other across a rough-hewn table. François had settled himself on a bench behind me, where, resting his back against the wall, he laid out his equipment and began sharpening his sword with a whetstone. Having studied with François for years, I found the raspy song of metal on stone familiar and comforting, with its rhythm of stroke-and-pause, stroke-and-pause, stroke-and-pause.

I had not only studied with François, but I had also studied the man himself, so I knew that he only sharpened his sword when he was already at ease. He *never* did this to settle his nerves or calm himself. For François, this act was performed only in the right frame of mind, expressing his profoundly centered state. It was *never* a method to create it.

From across the table, Robere gazed at me with a gentle expression. I returned his gaze as calmly as I could, trying to gain a deeper understanding of him from what I saw. He seemed ageless. His sandy hair, crowned with a tonsured pate, had turned silver at the temples, the silver drifting down and spreading like windblown snow into his blond beard, hinting at a maturity that comes with years.

However, the bright blue intensity of his eyes countered this suggestion, conveying instead a sense of youthful spirit. In contrast, the corners of his eyes were lined with crow's feet, the kind acquired from years spent outdoors and squinting in the sun. Yet, his cheeks and neck showed hardly a wrinkle, further giving the impression that he was younger than he appeared. The hut's atmosphere perfectly reflected the softness of his gaze and the tranquility of his spirit, a testament to one who dwells deeply in the sacred.

I shifted my gaze from him to observe my surroundings, turning to watch François sharpening his weapon behind me briefly. The situation struck me as contradictory; here was François, the consummate fighter, calmly honing his tool of war, yet perfectly at ease in the monk's peaceful sanctuary. It made no sense to me that François, a figure of coiled steel and deadly intent, could ever belong here with this gentle monk seated across the table from me.

Looking back at Robere, it was clear to me that this man of faith could never tolerate the presence of someone committed to fighting, which was a clear violation of the path of love and peace that the monk represented. The natures of these two men were, without a doubt, in complete opposition, inherently incompatible.

Yet my certainty regarding their natural contradiction mattered not at all: they were unbothered by my views on their incompatibility and existed in complete harmony. Anywhere else in the world, such men would be at odds, yet here, they displayed total acceptance of each other.

This made the monk even more of a puzzle to me than he had already been. It brought to mind what François told me years ago about how he first met Robere.

The silent monk accepted François and wordlessly recognized that his hidden nature could not be countered or contained by the Church life he had pledged to. Robere understood that it was a spiritual necessity to bring the boy to someone who could instruct him in embracing the warrior within, as his nature had revealed.

It mattered not that Master Toric's martial training contradicted Robere's mission of peace.

François's purpose in sharing his story was to convey a sacred principle essential to his way: one must learn to be in accord with one's nature. This principle was vital for both François and Édouard, who believed that failing to do so causes grievous harm to one's soul. Had François suppressed his hidden warrior nature to become a cleric, it would have been like a wolf trying to live like a rabbit. Yet, the Church would insist that the wolf learn to eat grass and run from danger, highlighting the monk's significance in recognizing François's nature *and* supporting its resolution in this way.

What kind of man could do that? What sort of holy man, especially, because sensing his powerful, peaceful emanations, it was clear that nothing less than holiness empowered him. Most priests or monks would have directed François back to the churchly path from which he had fled in his unworthiness.

Understanding all this did not reassure me about the monk; instead, it provoked a paradoxical reaction. The more I recognized Robere's profound holiness, the worse I felt in his presence. It was as if he shone so brightly that everything flawed and imperfect in me was illuminated, standing out starkly and provoking a frightening feeling of utter shame.

I came to grasp the irrational fear that gripped me during my initial meeting with Robere at the Chateau. Under Robere's singular light, unaware that it revealed every flaw of his soul, a young boy would simply perceive the monk as terrifying. Just as it did then, Robere's radiant presence penetrated my darkest corners, revealing the fundamental defects hidden even from myself.

This insight struck me like an avalanche, and I must have gasped aloud. Every positive belief I held about myself—even the confidence carefully nurtured during my time with Édouard—was stripped away, as if it were no more than a facade. I had to summon all my training to resist fleeing from the monk's presence, as I had done once before at the Chateau.

Robere leaned toward me, reaching across the table to take my hands in his and pulling me from my thoughts. Surely I was unworthy of any solace from him, and fearing I might soil him with my tainted flesh, I recoiled at his touch.

He was unperturbed by my response, and he held my hands firmly so we would not lose contact. With an even gentler smile, he exuded an aura of acceptance that wrapped around me like a comforting cloud, giving me space to pause and collect my thoughts. I'm astonished by the swift shift in my emotions, and I yield to his warm, seasoned hands. We remained like this until all the turmoil inside me seemed to calm.

Reassured that I had found some measure of calm, Robere nodded, closed his eyes, and seemed to drop into a state of deep meditation. Without ceremony, I was drawn into his altered state and lifted by a swirling trance. I felt myself drifting back, away from him, though his hands still held mine, and I faded to another time and place.

I am in a fight in the dark. In the pitch-black night, I struggle to free my knife hand from the tangle of my clothing. The smooth texture of the knife's bone grips is as familiar to my hand as my flesh.

I struggle, blunting the thrust of my attacker's blade in the thick cloth of my cloak, working to gain some advantage. I'm desperate to free my blade entirely for use. Pulling until it is freed, I attack. We grunt from our efforts, he to thrust and cut, I to block and counter with a slash. I miss, and he takes the opening, slashing back to rend my sleeve.

My face flushed with panic for a moment, but it turned to glee as I sensed an opening. I stab, feeling a meaty resistance as my blade cleaves flesh. He gasps in surprise, and I am taken over by battle rage; I stab viciously, again and again. Hot blood drenches my blade, running over my fingers. My opponent falls to the ground, and I stand over his body, chest heaving, heartbeat thunderous in my ears, elated. Victory!

The moment is singular and triumphant, a triumph so great that everything my soul sought had reached its zenith.

Even as the moment of triumphant victory peaked, another aspect of my soul recoiled in utter abhorrence. Identical in proportion and opposition, one aspect of my soul can no longer bear this path of violent victory, while the other cannot bear to forsake it. These counterposed aspects of my soul's conflicting nature may no longer abide.

There is pain beyond imagining, a sense of rending and tearing multiplied through uncountable dimensions of our soul. The very fabric of the soul is breached, and in agony, it separates and divides in twain.

With all its exhilaration, violence, and agony, despite how outlandish it seemed, I knew this remembrance was entirely true. For a long time, I had no idea where I was, only that I was stirred inside and out.

Robere said quietly, "It was in Jerusalem."

His voice drew me back to the present when we sat in his hermitage. Still in a state of shock, I thought his quiet voice was far too mild to speak of such a terrible thing.

I forced myself to blink and shake my head, as if movement might dispel the prepotent vision I was mired in, but it was useless. François's rasp of steel-on-stone had ceased at some point, and I felt his regard like a palpable pressure upon my back, the undeniable weight of his loving paternal concern for me.

With difficulty, I raised my eyes to meet Robere's, dispelling the vision. A cascade of impressions flooded my thoughts, and what I perceived as my innate flaws took on new meaning in light of the vision's insights. Nothing seemed improved by this new knowledge.

Instead, the memory seemed to provide the ultimate and final confirmation of my failure as a soul. There had always been a feeling in the background that I was fundamentally lacking in some significant and indelible way, despite the healing I'd received. Yet, I had woefully underestimated the extent of my flaws.

Before me sat a man whom I now understood to be my soul's other half, in his holiness and perfection, making it as clear as crystal how far beyond I was for any possible repair or redemption. The vision made it clear that my role in our soul's relentless pursuit of victory and murderous violence—a sin by any reckoning—had added an even graver sin to my list: that I had caused our once singular soul to sunder into two.

What was I but the murderer of our soul's divinely-given unity?

Strangely, the certainty of this conclusion felt like a relief, suggesting I might as well give up all hope for myself and stop fighting for worthiness. What was the use? I now realized there was no denying the vision Robere had brought up. Nothing could ever undo the damage I had caused.

Robere waited patiently for all of this to pass through me. It was uncanny; despite how shattered I was, he remained even more profoundly silent. He looked like a vast pool of still water, deeply present and untroubled, absorbing all my chaos. I sensed that if it took days for me to sort through this, Robere would silently and steadily be there with me, though I deserved it not.

It was pointless to waste his patience on me, and eventually, I decided there was nothing for me to do but push forward. It was better to finish this engagement and escape. I had wanted to know who Robere was to me, hadn't I? Now that I knew, it had turned out to be far more terrible than I expected.

So it goes.

Well, I've faced other terrible things in my short life. Man up, Étienne, lad; you got what you came for. Now, you just have to deal with it. I took a moment to gather myself and began to straighten up. I would stand, thank Robere for our little talk, and take my leave.

Knowing my intention before I could act on it, François rose with alacrity and positioned himself closely behind me, his hands bracing my shoulders. I could not even get my feet under me, but he made it clear there was no need to. He had my back in any way I might need, conveyed without a word spoken.

With Robere's hands still holding mine, and François firmly at my back, I could do little else than consent to stay in place. For now. Not trusting myself to speak, I jutted my chin to indicate to Robere that he could proceed.

"As souls do, Étienne, ours played out the opposites over many lifetimes. Back and forth, between war and peace, victory and victim, conqueror and conquered, vulnerability and control, the Divine and the earthly. All the contrasts that can be in God's creation.

"Most souls come to a balance, or perhaps a middle way, between the extremes, though it takes eons. Some come to a blend of qualities, neither one thing nor the other. Others discover an integration to some new kind of wholeness. Some souls find a way to *transcend* opposites, revealing a higher truth. In this way, all evolve to better reflect our true and deepest nature, thereby serving the mystery of Creation.

"Yet, Étienne, *our* soul did not travel these paths. Neither the middle way nor a blend, neither integration nor transcendence, was to be our soul's solution. Within each opposite, was something so essential that neither aspect could be relinquished."

His voice had become increasingly rhythmic, like a Bard whose song naturally shaped itself to his story.

"Back and forth it went for countless lifetimes, the very warp and weft of the soul's story woven into the Great Tapestry of time. And, as these two opposing threads were woven through space and time, the weave became pulled tighter and tighter, due to its natural opposition."

Robere's voice carried all the strain and pressure of the threads he described.

"Throughout countless ages, the strands of our soul's narrative became burdened with extraordinary tension. Until at last," he uttered, the words sounding strained through a constricting aperture, "it unfolded, in the city called Jerusalem, that the tension of our souls' weave could withstand no longer."

In his pause, I realized that tears were streaming down both of our faces. With great effort, Robere gathered himself to continue his story. I could see his neck muscles corded with tension, and his face reddened from the force required to continue the story.

"Our souls' singular fabric gave and tore in two, each half left to weave its own distinct story in the tapestry of existence."

His words sounded almost poetic, like verses from an ancient Greek tragedy. But the strain in his telling made the unimaginable pain his narrative described clear. I shuddered hearing it.

Robere stared at the floor, breathing heavily and working to pull himself back from the pain of this revelation. He looked up after a moment and gave me a sympathetic look.

When he next spoke, none of that prior strain was in evidence. His voice was strikingly resonant, as if someone talking in an ancient, formal style—clearly not his own.

"Even the angels knew not how this could be," he pronounced. *"Yet, it was so!"*

His eyes widened, surprised to hear what had come from his mouth. He recognized that these words could not be his own. They had come *through* him, from the Beyond.

He sat, reflecting on this utterance's impossible implications, repeating it aloud to himself, as if trying to get his mind around it. "Even the angels knew not how this could be," he breathed, "yet… it was so…."

His face displayed perplexity and confusion, revealing the depth of the message. I could only sit and watch Robere struggle with this mystery, which was so inconsistent with my image of him as a saintly and wise person. The fact that our situation presented more puzzles than even a holy man could comprehend was astounding. And if this was a puzzle for *him*, how much more was I in the dark?

It dawned on me how this utterance must have affected him. As a man of God, how would it feel to hear that our divided souls were beyond angelic understanding? It would be a confrontation with a theological impossibility, as how can anything be beyond angelic beings, granted the power of creation and destruction to serve on the Creator's behalf? What could be beyond *them* but Divine Will itself?

And if our fracturing and bifurcation were beyond even angelic understanding, how much further beyond *mortal* comprehension might it be? Certainly beyond that of a holy man or an orphan boy.

If Divine will set this in motion, why and to what purpose? Can we ever know? It is foolish to ask, as neither mortal nor angel truly understands the Divine mind and its purpose. Faced with this conundrum, a man can only bow to the Unfathomable and accept his ignorance.

While I reasoned this through, Robere remained still, shaking his head with dismay from time to time. He'd been about to disclose his newly transformed insights of many lifetimes about our bifurcation, until that utterance cast them all to the winds.

His transformed insights about the bifurcation of our soul, drawn from lifetimes of searching, scattered like leaves by that utterance. If I felt overwhelmed, how much worse was it for him, as his understanding of seeking his other half shifted entirely? It was astounding to witness. A power washed over him, taking his strain and struggle into its care. And in an act of faith, Robere released any need to understand. I thought to myself, "So this is what it means to be devoted more to the holy than to oneself." Robere released the need to solve this puzzle and, along with his dismay, emptied himself, opening purely to grace.

When he looked at me again, this same power radiated from him to wash over me like an upwelling spring. Whereas for Robere, this grace lifted the burden of knowing; with me, it washed aside my preoccupation with unworthiness. It left me blissfully blank and, at least for a moment, without torment.

"Ah, Étienne, I realize that my perspective may not be as clear as I believed, but that will suffice for now. Finally, it seems I have gleaned everything of Mercy our soul was destined for," he stated, alluding to that principle from Jewish mysticism I recalled from my studies in the Maestro's library.

"And your piece of our soul, Étienne," he continued, "has fulfilled all the lessons that Severity had to offer. Foolish old monk that I am, I'd hoped that we could someday be woven back together now that our individual threads are done. A pity I'm not wiser after so many cycles of searching for you, my other half!" He laughed heartily, shaking his head, eyes twinkling as he confessed his mistake.

Moved by the monk's lack of pride and pretense, François and I could not help but join him in laughter, sharing this unique moment when this wise and holy man admitted that he was indeed full of folly, a holy man who was also just a human being. Our laughter relieved a tension I hadn't realized was building within me.

Robere looked sheepishly at us, continuing, "Until this moment with you, I believed I understood the meaning of our divided journey. But God, as always, has something different in mind.

"You may find it peculiar, Étienne, for me to say that our paths have essentially been directed at the same thing, but I will explain why I say this. Both are paths of love. On your part, the soul has sought understanding of love through the principle of Severity. This may sound like an outrageous assertion to you, as it's hard to understand how Severity's harshness could result in love, correct? Yet, in rough times, violence may be required to protect those we love, even to the point of sacrificing oneself. The soul learns the necessity of preserving life through aggressive means, how this differs from the will to power, and how this expresses love. This is an earthly path of love seeking to reveal the Divine principle shining through Nature's most primitive experiences.

"My part of the soul sought to apprehend Divine love directly by devotion to revealing its shine within everything. My task seemed all but complete, save for bringing everything that my part of our soul had learned together with yours. I believed that doing this would heal and complete us, but now I see that you bring much-needed insight to complete *me*."

He paused to rest as his voice had grown raspy and dry. It would be a long soliloquy for anyone, but for him, more so as he'd been under a vow of silence for thirty years.

I appreciated his pause for my own sake, as I struggled to understand what he was telling me. In the pause, I recognized that something beyond his words registered despite my confusion. I would have to rest in that, as he cleared his throat to continue.

"So, my dearest Étienne, it seems we are not to find the union I'd sought. I see now, *only* now, that there is some purpose for which we are shaped. Though we appear to face opposite directions, we serve in kind, side by side. Though I cannot fathom what or how, I'm confident our circumstance serves the Divine."

I found Robere's admission of ignorance oddly reassuring. He pointed to a greater mystery beyond any he could fathom, and therefore outside human reasoning, that my preoccupation with self-blame for our split held little weight.

If there was more for Robere to understand, this applied doubly to me. Our story remains unfinished; there was much more to be understood. The impulse to flee and lick my wounds faded considerably.

The daylight had diminished without Robere or me realizing it, and the dark was approaching. François stepped forward to rest his hand upon our clasped hands nearest him and spoke for the first time since we had sat down.

"I believe it's time to stop for the day," François said. "It would be good for us all to take nourishment and rest."

Robere and I agreed, and we released our hands, shaking our arms to get the blood circulating. I stood painfully, feeling my muscles had cramped from the tension and restraint I must have had. I had been so intent on the conversation that I hadn't realized I was bracing myself tightly.

François handed me a hatchet he had found leaning next to the door and directed me outside to chop some kindling for the fire. "The movement will do you good, lad," he encouraged. I circled the hut until I found the woodpile around the back and busied myself chopping small logs into smaller kindling.

I could sense the Moon Mother, not yet visible but a tangible presence to me as she prepared to rise, just beneath the edge of the trees. With each swing of the axe, I found myself praying in rhythm, expressing my gratitude to her, and seeking her guidance and wisdom. Despite my turmoil and confusion about Robere and our story, I knew I could rely on her to steady and guide me. A surge of response brought my chopping to a halt as tears overtook me. I sobbed from being so pent up with many emotions, then my tears turned sweet with my gratitude for her blessing and undeniable response.

When I could chop again, I did so with renewed vigor, working up a good sweat until I had quite a scattering of split wood around me. I stacked most of it in the woodshed, then gathered an armful and carried it into the hut, dumping it into a box by the hearth.

Then I carefully tended the smoldering fire, building it up for the cool evening.

We had brought provisions from the Chateau, not wishing to strain the monk's meager resources, Robere and François laid them out. Robere gave the blessing, and then we set to devouring our bread, wine, and meat as if we'd been at hard labor all day in the fields. Afterward, I banked the fire with larger logs, lay on the floor near the hearth wrapped in a blanket, and fell asleep immediately.

CHAPTER XVII:

Travels Through The Sea of Time

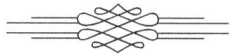

In May 2023, my wife, Lourdes, and I embarked on a two-week journey to France to celebrate my 70th birthday. My siblings and their spouses joined us for the first week of birthday festivities in Paris. Lourdes and I planned to spend the second week touring by car to gather impressions and, hopefully, stimulate more memories for Book II, which had already been underway since Book I, About Time, was published in April.

The COVID pandemic had recently been declared officially over, and the world was starting to emerge from that dark period. My wife and I were healing from family losses, and our anticipation of the trip over the previous winter glimmered with the promise of hope ahead.

Everyone had a wonderful time in Paris, affirming that life can be filled with goodness despite difficulties and loss. It was the best birthday celebration I've ever had. The three couples stayed in a historic walk-up apartment converted from a loft, featuring a ceiling reinforced by a riveted ironwork beam from Gustave Eiffel's engineering company—yes, that Eiffel, as in *Eiffel Tower!*

Our time together reminded us of how well we got along during vacations in our youth. Oh, Paris, that delightful city! We savored the cuisine and explored markets, museums, and patisseries. We even visited Monet's gardens. The grief I carried was present, but our time together, surrounded by love, highlighted a truth about grief: we grieve because we love. Life is woven with many threads, especially love. Wasn't that what my time with Édouard was about?

Planning our itinerary for the second week of car travel proved to be quite challenging. Despite the narrative detail I had managed to summon while writing the story, I only had the faintest idea about *where* the Chateau and the Abbess's convent were in France.

I had a treasure trove of mental images from that period—beautiful buildings, cozy rooms, and stunning landscapes—but none came with addresses or map coordinates. As a tech enthusiast, I eagerly dove into online resources, sifting through maps to locate the Chateau and Abbey. My searches left me feeling more puzzled than before. My problem-solving style seemed to go against my intuitive side.

I had the feeling that Spirit was intentionally keeping me in the dark about specific locations. Why? Well, in the past, they'd thwarted my over-reliance on logic to push me to trust my intuition.

It also occurred to me that perhaps satellite imagery and high-resolution overflights did not match the memories I was seeking. After all, it was a time when maps were rare and most people didn't travel farther than the next village, let alone have any sense of belonging outside of their locality. If you ask a child where "home" is, what do they tell you? That home is located, well, where *home* is. What more did an orphan need than "home " in the *Chateau?*

Still, as Étienne, I'd been educated and had travelled, so I knew exactly where the Chateau was situated. Yet, I could only get a general impression that the Chateau had been located in the northeast quadrant of France, somewhere in the Burgundy, Champagne, and Haute-Marne regions.

My clearest intuitive impression, before I even started writing, was that nothing of the Chateau remained to be found, not even ruins. Naming it "The Chateau" came from a romantic view of grateful orphans rather than an official title, and in reality, it is little more than a country house built with less-than-permanent materials. Neither as grand nor as enduring as a stone castle, it resembled more of a rustic country farm estate than a manor house. The only building made of stone was the unassuming round tower of Édouard's observatory, likely a remnant from an earlier time; everything else was constructed of timber and stucco, which were vulnerable to fire and other elements.

My main hope was that a journey through these French landscapes, even without specific locations in mind, would evoke more of the energy of Etienne's time. While I was willing to rely more on intuition, at 70, I needed more comfort than could be found in hoping my intuition would find us a place to stay each night! One has only to remember May's birthday and look up a Taurus's need for comfort and security. Exactly!

Ultimately, due to the wonders of the internet, logical problem-solving and intuition somehow found a mutually agreeable solution. It turns out that there are B&B listings for "historical stays in France," and with pictures! I searched for places whose photos evoked a resonance, regardless of their location. As I saw what stood out, I couldn't help but feel a little thrill. Even if it didn't spark any past-life connections, the grinning little boy in me was determined to fulfill his childhood dream of living in a castle!

I devised an itinerary that took us to a restored chateau in Normandy, just two hours from Paris, for our first night. Next, we'd head south to a small walled castle in the Loire Valley, featuring a guest room in a round tower reminiscent of Édouard's observatory. Then, we'd traverse France from west to east to Burgundy (Bourgogne), staying in the drawbridge house of a Templar fortress! The Templars predated Étienne's time by a long shot. Still, the pictures conveyed such rich romance and history that I couldn't resist, and it was ideally situated for exploring the region, just as my intuition suggested.

Surprisingly, I enjoyed the driving challenges of piloting the rental car out of Paris. Navigating through the insanity of Parisian traffic was an exercise in Le Mans-level driving reflexes! Eventually, we found our way onto the correct highway, and the traffic thinned out. After about an hour, we reached the gently rolling farmland of the beautiful Norman countryside.

The luscious spring greens of May met the eye with the colors of fresh new grass in emerald and viridian, halos of intense chartreuse of the emerging seed crops, and the green apple glow of leafing trees. Swaths of wildflowers in yellows and pinks spread along the roadside berm, and golden fields of winter wheat and barley stood ready for spring harvest.

The scene appeared to be taken directly from one of those classical oil paintings of French landscapes we had just seen in the Paris museums. Even the clouds drifting across the intense blue sky seemed so ridiculously dramatic in style that we joked about our certainty that the French Tourist Bureau had them painted up there to enhance the visitor experience! Only occasional farm machinery and the modern highway we traveled on belied the countryside's timeless air.

Our exit took us through a lovely medieval town, where we stopped for lunch. After that, we continued our drive, following the map's directions through villages and turning onto smaller lanes that led through farmland. We missed the small signage, "Allée du Manoir," pointing to the turn, and had to double back, alerted by the GPS. The narrow lane followed a slow river on the right, across grass-covered hills where cream-colored cows grazed in the bright sunshine.

On our left, we passed farmhouses and fields of new plantings, with soil turned and ready for seed. Shortly ahead, on the left, were the rising stone walls of a beautifully restored and substantial castle and manor house. It was set like a jewel amidst the lush farmland, looking much as it must have when first built in the 1500s.

The castle, with its friendly proprietors, circular tower stairs to the guest wing, and garden tables for breakfast, was simply glorious. Its bucolic environs became a haven where we could rest, walk, gaze, and breathe, slowing us from the frantic pace of Paris. We didn't realize how much we needed this to shift gears for our journey.

We wandered the area for two days, becoming increasingly sensitive to Spirit's subtle signs. It was the perfect place for nature to attune us to the energies of the land and the journey of our purpose. It seemed no accident that we had found a place to prepare for the beginning of our second week. We would need more openness to guidance than we might typically have.

After two nights, we had one of those mystical moments that would inform the rest of our time in France. We were walking along the road, stopping now and then to look across the river and watch the Norman cows grazing contentedly in the sun. I'm convinced the reason the French butter and cheese are so splendid is the lush grass and air of contentment we could see in their bovine faces.

The scene was so timeless that one could easily imagine it in any century past. Time, ah yes. Isn't that the essence of our whole journey through France? How can I sense my connection through time in the atmosphere of the land?

There is a meditation practice in our energy work that opens the *back* aspect of the energy centers (chakras), connecting us to the dimension of *unmanifest potential*, which includes the past. While practicing this, I sometimes had a vision of time stretching back toward the past in a line behind me. I hoped that being in the energy of France would assist me in extending my "reach" further back. Time is often depicted as a line we travel along, with the future ahead, the present as the membrane of our subjective experience, and the past extending behind us into the dim reaches.

As we gazed at this timeless rural scene, I opened and settled into the back of my upper chakras, beginning to sense time stretching back into the past. I'd just started the practice when I felt a subtle, yet familiar, tug on my collar, which I interpreted as a message of "hold on a minute, young fella," from my inner teachers. Typically, this signaled that they had something different in mind than what I was doing out of habit. I paused and realized this was from Robere and that he wanted me to approach the process differently.

He told me that trying to reach too far into the past required more energy than I had available, much like swimming against the current. Turning my impressions into conversation would be similar to this.

"Time is a sea, not a line, and you must learn to immerse your mind *in* it," Robere told me. "Don't reach back; rest back and sink *into* the space behind you. You will feel that your awareness drifts back *into* that dimension, until the invisible membrane of the 'present' between the future and the past seems to come before you as you drift back from it."

I followed his steps as best as I could as he described them.

"It will be like falling back, Robere continued, "and sinking into clear waters until you can see the shimmering surface, the boundary between water and air, above you. Everything will feel watery, and in this dream-like state of floating in the Sea of Time, cast your intention to know of that time in France. Impressions will float across your vision in this Sea, like bubbles of events from that time. They will not be in any order or sequence, and you won't control what appears."

I followed Robere's instructions and sensed his assistance, without which I doubt I would have been able to do this, as I continued gazing at the green hills across the river. As I drifted back from the "membrane of the present," the picturesque scene appeared filmy and dreamlike. Everything seemed to float, like a watery sea overlaying the current landscape. It reminded me of scuba diving in the Caribbean, where the waters were so clear that I could see the shimmering surface 50 feet above me.

I summoned enough presence of mind in this odd state to "call to" that time with Édouard. Gradually, images of bubble-like "pockets of time" floated across the landscape before my eyes. I had vague impressions of scenes within them, some of which I thought were familiar, while others featured people or places I didn't recognize.

If I tried to understand what was shown in these bubbles, I would disrupt the dreamy, fluid state of the Sea of Time, causing the vision to fade. Once again, it was like that scuba diving experience: the fish would dart away when I reached for them. I could only float idly and gather impressions.

After a while, I described Robere's instructions to Lourdes. She immediately tried it and quickly became immersed in the Sea of Time. We continued like this, gazing at the river, the sun-drenched hills, and contented cows. I gleaned no new memories as I couldn't hold onto any of my impressions, but that didn't seem to be the point. The point was to make the Sea of Time recognizable to us. It wasn't a meditation practice nor an information source; it was more like a special condition facilitated by guidance—a space to immerse ourselves in as we recognized it was happening.

I had a momentary notion that it might be an "altered state research method," but I immediately realized how this contradicted everything the Sea of Time was about. If I gleaned anything while in this state, it came only afterward, if at all. I had to trust that being in the Sea was enough. It was yet another lesson on how unnecessarily restricted I was by limiting my learning to conscious awareness alone.

The Sea of Time was so subtle that we might have missed it in our usual sightseeing mode without this first experience. I was grateful to have had the opportunity to learn about it in the quiet countryside of Normandy, as the Sea of Time became a significant aspect of our time in France.

We drove south to the Loire Valley for our next castle stay. As we approached the region, characterized by its white limestone soil and flat terrain, I realized it held no resonance with my time as Étienne. My wife had a similar reaction. It was beautiful and picturesque, but we felt only the normal curiosity typical of tourists exploring a new place.

The picturesque, walled castle we sought was nestled among fields of grapevines and fruit orchards. We parked outside the wall and met the British owners, who showed us to our tower guest room. We wandered the grounds, discovering a garden courtyard next to a small manor house and ancient walls adorned with fragrant wisteria. It was a lovely place with its own unique history, but like the Loire itself, it lacked the intuitive resonance I had hoped for from the online pictures.

Reflecting on my disappointment with this error in my travel intuition, I realized there was something to be learned from our experiences on the trip. Neither place was close to the location I had intuited for the region of the Chateau on the other side of France, but I had planned our itinerary using photos that captured the essence of Etienne's time.

I chose this lovely castle in the Loire because the images of the cylindrical tower reminded me of Édouard's observatory; however, once I arrived, the atmosphere and landscape were entirely different from those of the Château. In contrast, the chateau in Normandy resonated with something, even though it bore little resemblance to anything I remembered from the Chateau. What was that "something?" Reflecting on it, it was indistinct and fleeting, like a scent that disappears just as you reach for it, leaving you questioning its reality even as you're certain it's real.

The pressure to plan an itinerary with interesting places to stay, fitting them into the allotted days and driving time, could easily overshadow that "something." It was a wonder that it worked out at all! The art of discerning that "something" and trusting the scent, even when you doubt it, is a constant challenge to my worldly ways. Fortunately, the final leg of our journey dispelled any doubt that, despite the challenges, we were still following the scent.

We drove due east across the heart of France toward Burgundy. A little over halfway, the landscape changed noticeably. The flat valley of the Loire had receded, and we were now driving through rolling hills. With Lourdes driving, I was free to look around intently, which excited me. This landscape was familiar to me! I could envision myself as Étienne riding on horseback through it.

Along with the terrain, the colors had changed as well. No longer the unfamiliar chalky white of the Loire, the soil had transformed into a recognizable reddish-tan, accompanied by the dark green hues of hardwood trees and the blue-green of stands of pines and fir. As the drive continued, larger patches of woodland and dense forest areas covered the hills, interspersed with stretches of rich farmland. It all undeniably matched my memories as Étienne.

"This is more like it!" I exclaimed. "Much closer to what I remember."

I've visited France many times but had never been to the eastern regions before. Yet, everything felt oddly familiar as I gazed at the hills with dreamy, double vision. I saw fleeting images of thatched-roof farms and stone cottages that vanished when I blinked. Ancient cart paths seemed to intersect the modern highway but shimmered away as our car raced past.

My wife glanced at me and asked, "Have you tried the Sea of Time practice here?"

I took a moment to reflect. "No, I haven't, but it's unnecessary. When you asked, it became clear that I had been absorbed in it for about an hour without even noticing! Wow, I'm really grateful you're driving, as I wouldn't trust myself behind the wheel like this."

Eventually, we exited the highway, and I tried to stay grounded and help navigate the rural roads to our B&B. We turned off the main road onto a lane that took us through fields of crops and past a farm. The lane dipped between the trees, and there it was, the *Commanderie*, built as a frontier fortress in the 1100s by the Knights Templar.

To our right stood a long stone building with a tiled roof. Red Templar crosses adorned panels beneath several small high windows. On our left, an old stone wall was covered in blooming pink roses. Directly ahead was the drawbridge portico, the narrow lane we were on passing through its arch, and a cylindrical defensive tower attached to it.

We turned left through a gate into a parking space, where more roses bloomed. The owner lived in the restored manor house, which had another stone tower at the end that matched the one of the drawbridge house. There was a green lawn between them.

Our stay immersed us in rich dimensions of time and history. Rose bushes bloomed everywhere around the grounds, giving a sense of the place's enduring vitality. It felt as if a time pocket had been planted in the surrounding fields of crops. Our drawbridge tower suite overlooked a river that had once served as the castle's moat, spanned by the now-absent drawbridge. From our window above, we watched river otters fish and play at dusk and dawn.

The place certainly lived up to its photos on the internet! And although it predated Étienne's time by 300 years, the energy of the landscape and historic era seeped into my pores as we strolled around that afternoon after our arrival. Being there fulfilled a deep, unspoken feeling that I knew was important, even if I couldn't quite put it into words.

CHAPTER XVIII:

The Ruined Abbey

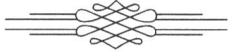

Tomorrow was the last day of our 2023 travel through France before returning to Paris to catch our flight home. Our week's journey after Paris had been rich in impressions and had stirred me profoundly in ways I didn't yet grasp. Though we hadn't been led to a specific location from my time with Édouard, I hadn't required this to feel satisfied with the journey. I had enough experience in the intuitive and spiritual realms to understand that it is exceedingly subtle, and one should not require something subtle to hit you over the head with proof to believe it.

I have come to understand that both our intellectual and emotional sides often feel unsatisfied with the mysterious realms of intuition, magic, and past lives. The mind, having ruled out intuition and past lives as unreasonable from the outset, has dismissed them outright. Similarly, our emotional self disapproves of subtlety for its reasons. Seeing Hollywood as its benchmark, anything magical must include romance and showcase realistic special effects. In the absence of these elements, our emotional self overlooks anything that falls within the delicate nuances!

I've learned that if I pay close attention, unexpected confirmations can happen and be noticed simply because they are, well, unexpected.

So, though I didn't *require* it, I *might* have had a tiny, secret hope that we'd be led to a recognizable place. I wasn't asking for Hollywood, was I? "I have to keep trusting spirit," I kept reminding myself, "no matter what." We still had one more day. How should we spend it?

So that evening, before bed, I decided to plan our last day. Despite the tower's meter-thick stone walls, it had internet! I started looking north of us to see what "lit up" to my intuition. Now and then, I'd look up from my search at the beamed ceiling, appreciating the incongruity of connecting to the whole world in a room that was 900 years old, and shake my head in wonder.

I was looking for a provisional goal, an endpoint to drive towards, knowing that we could wander as intuition prompted us. Even if we found nothing specific, we had nothing to lose as we would simply enjoy the beautiful day.

On a French-speaking travel forum, translated by the modern magic of technology, I discovered mention of the ruins of an old Cistercian Abbey north of us. It sounded atmospheric, and conveniently, it was in the direction we wanted to explore anyway. I thought it might evoke something of the Abbess's convent from Etienne's time. I knew it was not the place itself, as this abbey was attended only by monks.

It seemed farther away than I wished, and we might not have the time to drive all the way, especially if we meandered along the way. No matter. Even if we didn't get to the Abbey ruins, it would be a lovely way to end our spiritual quest.

The next day, we drove north, stopping in a picturesque village for a stroll and a leisurely lunch at an outdoor cafe in the little square. We left to continue to the Abbey ruins at about two in the afternoon. I didn't want to drive in the dark to return to our lodgings and wondered if we had left enough time. I fussed about this and other uncertainties as my wife drove us north.

I felt uneasy and anxious as we progressed toward our destination, overwhelmed by uncertainty and doubt. At times, I would make remarks to my wife about how this entire trip might not lead to much, but that was fine. It could just be a pleasant drive.

"We don't have to go all the way if we don't want to," I said. "The Abbey might be too far, but the countryside is so beautiful, isn't it?"

And another time, I said, "We can always trust our intuition and take a different turn along the way."

Lourdes, focused on driving, didn't appear to require my reassurances. In fact, she looked increasingly pleased and excited, in exact proportion to my growing restlessness.

When, for the one time too many, I repeated my excuses, Lourdes glanced at me and responded.

"Why do you keep saying that?" she said, sounding bothered by my hedging. "Of *course*, we are going all the way there! That's been clear to me for a while now."

Why *do* I keep saying this? Indeed. Who did I think I was talking to with my excuses? I thought I was saying this to comfort her, but I must be saying these things to comfort myself. While I had been listening solely to my mounting anxiety, it turned out that she had been listening to the spirit guiding her. I finally quieted down and surrendered to my wife's greater wisdom.

It took effort to calm my churning thoughts, but I succeeded. Only then could I recognize the familiar charged atmosphere of spiritual presence surrounding us, now palpable and evident. This charged atmosphere had been building for a while, likely contributing to my feelings of anxiety. It was curious that Lourdes responded to the charged atmosphere with excitement, while I reacted with nervousness and anxiety. It was true, and I had no idea why.

Exiting the highway, we drove through an exquisite French countryside, dotted with lush farmland and distant rolling hills adorned with darker green forests. The broad road prompted a turn onto a local route. Next, the GPS guided us onto a narrower village lane and eventually onto a paved, single-track farm road. The road continued to narrow as we progressed, winding through cultivated fields and patches of dense woods. Each bend led us into an increasingly isolated landscape. I noticed that we no longer had cell phone service and was grateful I had thought to download the map, ensuring we still had navigation.

As we approached our destination, something took hold of us. We felt breathless as a dense energy field grew within and around us. Pressure built in my chest, as if something was about to unfold that was bigger than my small heart could hold. My wife felt the same when I described it. I wondered how much more I could endure.

We were driving down a narrow lane in a densely shaded forest when we suddenly emerged into a bright, sunlit scene. Just ahead of us, across a cultivated field, stood an old stone tower at the corner of crumbling stone walls. The walls extended at right angles from either side of the tower, and we faced one stretching to the right for a couple of hundred feet to another tower anchoring its end. The scene was so stunning that Lourdes stopped the car, allowing us to absorb the sight in quiet amazement.

We arrived at the Abbey, its crumbling walls surrounding a compound of partially ruined buildings. The enclosure, guarded by the towers, was topped with vines swelled with greenery. Our narrow farm lane crossed the field, continued past the tower, and then ran along the wall of the enclosed compound.

In that moment, I truly felt the strong and distinctive presence of Robere around us. I told this to Lourdes, who nodded excitedly.

"Oh yes," she nodded, "he's been with us for quite a while now!"

I was stupidly surprised.

Robere was with us? What was he doing here? I didn't know he talked to my wife, but now he's guiding her for the drive? I thought this was about gathering impressions about the Abbess's convent, you know, from the story? What would Robere, a monk, not a nun, have to do with all that?

It felt like a light had switched on, and suddenly, everything became clear to me. How clueless can I be? Well, very, *very* clueless. I'd thought this Abbey was just a direction to follow while we listened to intuitive indications as we went.

All this time, it had really been about Robere all along. I controlled the impulse to smack my palm against my forehead in dismay. Instead, as we slowly drove along the long stone wall, my heart bloomed open, and tears streamed down my face. What a clever act of spirit misdirection, to keep me from overthinking a perfectly good intuition.

Coming to terms with the fact that Robere had brought us here was mind-bending, I thought, but then I realized that wasn't the problem. The real challenge was accepting that Robere had led us to *his* own place—the Cistercian Abbey, or an earlier version of it—where he had once been a monk. Somewhere in the forest surrounding the Abbey, his solitary hermitage was hidden, where I visited him as Étienne.

I'd never considered that his hermitage might be linked to a larger Abbey. Now that I'm here, it makes sense that he took orders to become a monk from somewhere. A hermit monk would greatly benefit from the protection, provisions, safety, and spiritual guidance offered by such an institution.

And here I stood, having accepted that finding an actual location from Etienne's time was unlikely, astonished by being led to a real location, just not the one I expected.

We rolled slowly along the wall, catching glimpses through crumbling gaps of the ruins of buildings within the compound. The wall ended, and the lane turned right. The lane continued between a slow river and the partially reconstructed entrance to the Abbey before veering left across an old stone bridge to intersect with a road.

We pulled off the lane and parked in front of the scaffolded 18th-century Abbey entrance facing the bridge. Walls made of stones from older constructions gave the comparatively recent facade a sense of greater age. A profound sense of the sacred imbues the place, one that has persisted through different eras, each contributing to the whole, perhaps even long before the Abbey's Christian foundation nine hundred years ago.

As we left the car, it felt as though we had stepped into a timeless realm. I was transfixed by the surroundings. The energy of the landscape pulled me into a deep state of altered consciousness. I couldn't get over how the light and hues of the trees, water, and grass strikingly echoed the scene in Judy Marz's painting of Robere. How did she know?

And another thing was the three hawks circling lazily overhead. I'd learned over the years that hawks symbolize Édouard and often appear when he wants to get my attention. We frequently saw hawks as we drove through French agricultural areas, hunting in the croplands. They were usually perched on wires or posts close to the road, and I would reach for my good camera to take a photo. Every single time, by the time I would point the lens at them, they had vanished. It became a running joke between Lourdes and me.

I was sure that Édouard was telling me, "They are here as heralds, not photo opportunities!! When you see them, I'm asking you to pay attention, Étienne, not to be a photo-tourist!" Eventually, I stopped grabbing for the camera when we'd see a hawk and attended to what was around us.

And now, three of them circled above the Abbey, calling loudly as they wheeled around, waiting for me to take my pictures as if to underscore their point.

"You finally listened, silly man! You reached the place we've been pointing you to. Go ahead and take your pictures now."

So, I did. As soon as I had a few pictures, the hawks flew off, leaving me thankful for Édouard's patience with me. I'm slow, but I get there eventually. I turned back to the Abbey to continue my explorations.

To the left of the entryway, the trees parted to reveal a lush field where a herd of cream-and-tan Charolais cattle grazed. The herd ambled toward a breach in the wall, where their farmer loaded hay with a pitchfork into their feeding station, parked within the protective Abbey walls. Behind him, stacks of hay were visible in an intact stone building.

Spotting us watching them, they all paused outside the Abbey walls, the mammas calling their calves closer to them protectively. We were an anomaly in their otherwise routine feeding schedule, making them cautious. As a result, they stayed in the field and grazed, waiting for us to leave.

Lourdes and I stood there, gazing at the scene in wonder. It was so absurdly bucolic, as if it had been recreated by a movie set designer from a museum painting for a period film. Bright sunlight highlighted the rich green hues of new grass, while the gentle burble of the river flowing beneath the stone bridge provided a musical accompaniment. Cows drank from its waters as it meandered through the meadow.

The herd grazed while calves nursed, cowbells clanking occasionally, as they always have. The gap between the trees, arched by boughs, framed a portal through which we peered back in time, witnessing what could be this spring day or one of the nine hundred springs that have passed since the Abbey was built.

Lourdes walked over to the partially reconstructed 18th-century entrance edifice. She took pictures and videos with her phone, looking wide-eyed; her smile was huge as she photographed every informational placard displayed. The placards, in French, discussed the Hildegard medicinal garden and the Abbey's history, including details about the Cistercian Order. They described the land grant given by the local aristocracy around 1121, which included vast swaths of forest and several villages. An Abbey has stood here since its construction, though it has been destroyed and rebuilt more than once over the centuries. Its resources made it both a haven and a target during times of conflict.

The ruins before us, dating back to the 1700s, were at least 200 years after my time with Édouard, but this did not lessen their evocative power. The entire site was like a layered pastry soaked in honey; many strata of history infused with the constant nectar of prayer and devotion.

And Robere is here with me in his layer, and I am with him in mine.

I walked to a spot where I could see into the compound within the Abbey walls, Robere beside me as we gazed companionably at the ruins. Then, it felt as if we were no longer next to each other, but instead we had overlapped in some odd way. It wasn't that we had merged, exactly, more that we had aligned to the same axis, each in our dimension and timezone.

It was curiously distinct. On the one hand, I could feel him all around me, as if his energy body occupied the same space as mine. We were both looking at the Abbey together, but it was clear that I wasn't looking through his eyes, nor he through mine. I had a shadow-like sense of what he saw through his eyes, a place much different from the one I was seeing. In turn, he had some understanding of what I was seeing of these ruins after his last visit.

This strangely layered experience profoundly moved me, leaving me deeply shaken. There was something about being so close to him, yet so distinct, that stirred both longing and… I didn't know what else to do, but I was deeply affected and stirred.

I had no recollections of seeing him at a monastery, only his forest hermitage. But two things made being here so affecting. It revealed something about his story that I hadn't known, which was shocking in itself, given it happened in a real place.

The second was that the landscape felt achingly familiar to me. I had lived with Judy's painting of him for years, observing how she crafted it as a window frame into his place in the spiritual dimension, a place revealed to her because he sat for the portrait. I didn't realize that it was a place in my earthly world, painted so I would recognize it when I eventually arrived here.

It had never occurred to me that, as a monk, he was part of a larger institution. I was undeniably ignorant of how these things worked. Perhaps such a thing was not memorable for Étienne, who simply took for granted that monks, even hermit monks, were part of a monastery. And if not of note to Étienne, then it is likely not memorable to me. I don't remember much of Etienne's day-to-day meals either.

I wandered, taking it all in. The photos my wife took of me there show me with quite an intense expression; I appear both preoccupied and serious, here and not here at the same time. In contrast, my wife looks smiling and joyful in photos. When I see my images, I feel vaguely embarrassed, as I think I look like I'm on drugs. My wife disagrees with this assessment. "No, no!" she says, "You don't look like you are on drugs. This is how you look when your heart is blown open."

Wise woman. Go figure.

Naturally, I was not experiencing a chemically induced state, but one caused by my neatly organized categories dissolving in the face of an undeniable reality. To understand my bond with Robere, I had to set aside disbelief and embrace uncertainty, thereby avoiding requirements that blocked my intuition. In this resonant place, my usual strategies all fell away, leaving me vulnerable and unsettled.

We walked around the ruined walls to view the various buildings and grounds, as they were fenced off to prevent entry into the compound for safety. We took numerous photographs, hoping to capture something of the mystical atmosphere we felt. Drawn back to the entry portico, we crossed the lane and made our way through the weeds and remnants of masonry to the river.

The river widens just before flowing beneath the bridge, creating a slower and deeper pool. Dense vegetation leans close to the water, overhanging the banks, whose surface mirrors the dark green leaves of the surrounding trees and the bright chartreuse of the underbrush. We observe, once again, that it is a striking match for the color palette, tone, and atmosphere of Judy's painting of Robere. I thought about how he'd come to Judy for his portrait sitting, opening a window to this place for her so that the landscape would be recognizable when I arrived many years later.

Lourdes points excitedly to the water, saying that she sees Robere, as plain as day, hovering over the pool in front of us. His appearance is so real to her that she is compelled to record the scene, as if digital video tech could capture him floating there! Of course, electronics can't register an ethereal presence.

Yet, in a photo she took just after the video clip, there's… something. It's a photo of me standing before a split-trunk oak tree, whose moss-covered trunks rise behind me. As in many pictures taken that day, my expression is intensely serious, reflecting how overwhelmed I felt.

To my left, you can see across the river to the opposite bank, perhaps thirty feet away. In a curious trick of perspective, the typically receding view of the far bank seems instead to push forward toward the observer, as if an invisible presence beside me were guiding the eye to focus on the same visual plane I occupied, rather than on the more distant bank behind. Curious indeed.

Lourdes had brought cornmeal and tobacco to make an offering in the tradition of her heritage. She took me to a place by the water and guided us in a ritual to express our gratitude to all the spirits of this place and those who had led us here.

Amidst this, I recalled reading about the indigenous Neolithic sites in this part of France dating back to 3000 BC. It struck me that this area was a sacred place long before it was Christianized. In the tradition of the Indigenous peoples of the Americas, her way of offering was like a bridge through space and time, linking the ancient peoples of one continent to those of another.

By now, it was late afternoon, and the sun was skirting the tops of the trees over the forested hills. It was time to return to our lodgings from last night before dark. Once I closed the car door, I realized I was emotionally exhausted and quite hungry.

It was a Sunday evening, and we overlooked that neither restaurants nor groceries were open for dinner in rural France. Even the modern grocery store —a box store we passed at a highway junction with contemporary hours —was locking its doors as we arrived. I reluctantly grumbled that we would have to scrounge the few snacks left at our B&B for supper.

Lourdes drove us home as the sun approached the horizon. Suddenly, she veered into the empty parking lot of a large home improvement store. I asked her what she was thinking on earth. Didn't she realize everything was closed? I admit that it wasn't a question.

Lourdes ignores me and continues steering through the parking lot without answering. As they say, she looks like she's "on a mission from God." We pass by the darkened front of the box store, and she takes a sharp left to circle to the back of the empty parking lot.

Behold! There is a food truck in all its splendor! It is positioned in the expansive grassy area between the parking lot and the main road. Lourdes parks us right behind it and turns to me with a grin.

"I saw a sign," she says, "but we were going too fast to read it. I just knew that something would be here!"

There was a scattering of outdoor tables and chairs, and a group of twenty-something hippies was hanging out at one of the tables, drinking wine and conversing pleasantly in the dusk. A dog slept beneath one of the chairs, and Beatles music wafted from the truck's speakers—our kind of oldies music. I couldn't imagine a better way to end this wondrous day.

A chalkboard menu showcased galettes—those savory, hearty buckwheat crepes typical of Brittany and Normandy, popular throughout France—and sweet crepes for dessert. We ordered a galette with onions and ratatouille and another with mushrooms, cheese, and ham. The galettes were delicious, made even better because this unlikely feast reflected how Spirit had guided and cared for us throughout the day.

Local families stopped by from time to time for snacks or dessert. It was wonderful to watch them enjoying their Sunday evening treat, filling the air with the warm, convivial tones of French. We indulged in a couple of delightful sweet crêpes for dessert and a glass of wine, reminiscing about our fantastic day and the surprising discoveries we encountered, especially the most astonishing twist of being guided to find, right in front of a home improvement center, the elusive unicorn of a Sunday night dinner in the French countryside!

I drove us the rest of the way back to our B&B in the Templar fortress for our last night there. When we turned onto the farm lane leading through cultivated fields and towards the old chateau, I had to slow down the car to better absorb the magical scene before us. It seemed spirit was not done with us yet.

The full moon rose above the horizon into a cloudless night sky. The moon always appears most immense when closest to the horizon, and the greater visual impact seemed to amplify our sense of her native power.

We parked next to the stone walls of the keep and walked under the portico of the drawbridge house, but bypassed the door to the circular stairway that led to our rooms. Instead, we exited on the other side of the portico to find an unobstructed view. We discovered one down the lane, where we could stand in the soft summer air and watch the moon as she spread her silvery sheen over the fields surrounding the castle. The ancient walls of the castle glowed with her luminescence, just as they had for thousands of full moons since it was constructed.

CHAPTER XIX:

The Soul's Double Time

***

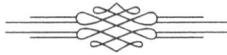

15th Century, Northeast France—Morning of the second day of François and Etienne's visit with Robere.

I awoke at dawn, still wrapped in my blanket and lying on the cool dirt floor of Robere's hermitage hut. I rolled onto my back and stared at the dim thatch overhead, gathering my thoughts about yesterday's events. I reviewed Robere's revelations until I felt that my reflection was yielding no further insights. It was time for me to get up. I folded my blanket, grabbed my boots, crept outside barefoot, put them on, and went to relieve myself.

After stretching, I walked around in the forest surrounding the hermitage to warm up my stiff muscles. I found a clearing where I could do the Old Man's practices. It was ideal, being under the open sky yet surrounded by trees. I connected my bones to the rocks as he'd taught me, working outward from there. These practices always left me feeling solid and fortified —just what I needed to start the day —and I walked back to Robere's hermitage.

François awaited me, his whipcord musculature looking ready to spring into action. He seemed to have just stepped outside the door, carrying our weaponry. He looked me over carefully in his particular way and remarked, "A lot to digest, eh?"

I agreed.

"Well," he informed, "I have just the medicine to improve your digestion."

I needed no leap of imagination to know that his digestive remedy would be a hefty dose of hard, physical training!

I bowed to him and said, "Oh, my physician! I require your expert treatment!"

I led him to the clearing I'd found earlier.

Once there, we commenced blade drills. As the morning warmed with the sun, we worked up a sweat and paused long enough to strip off our blouses before continuing.

Shortly, Robere emerged from the woods where he'd been doing his morning prayers. He sat on a log at the edge of the clearing and watched as François and I continued our weapons drills.

We completed our set and paused to wrap blade edges with a unique leather hardened for sparring. They safely covered the blade's edge and point, but were much lighter than a full sheath. Starting slowly, we began to fight. As our movement became more fluid and concerted, we moved rapidly. After a round or two, we naturally entered the fighting trance familiar to the Way.

In the unique state of fighting trance, a different way of seeing emerges: battle sight. The opponent appears as a bundle of glowing threads of light, and their intention to move appears as a strand of light flashing across the combat space. This strand *precedes* their physical movement, if only by a mere hairsbreadth, allowing one trained in the Way to anticipate, intercept, and attack before the opponent has moved.

With most opponents, this gave the fighter of the *Way of the Straight and the Curved* a distinct advantage. However, with a master such as François, this only worked if I also had flawless technique.

With the average fighter, my counters and attacks sought to exploit the gaps in the lines of light I perceived from battle sight, but with François, such gaps were rare. By the same token, I was advanced enough to be a worthy sparring opponent for him, as I had fewer gaps for François to exploit, and our sparring sequence had become more drawn-out and challenging.

As we started the set, Robere sat behind me on the log. In due course, our turns and maneuvers brought him within the frame of my fighting sight. Intent on the ball of light that was François to my battle sight, I only glimpsed Robere in the background. What I glimpsed was enough to break my rhythm, which François took immediate advantage of.

His blade flashed, slicing across my neck; a killing blow if not for the leather-wrapped edge. Then, he reversed and dropped the pommel in a blow to my sternum. The blow brought me to my knees, and I yielded, breathless, raising my hands out to my sides while gasping painfully.

After a moment of us both huffing and puffing from our exertions, François must have understood the cause of my hesitation.

"Ah, yes," he observed, still breathing heavily. "A remarkable sight, isn't it?" he puffed.

"Certainly...," I agreed between gasps, as I was far more winded than my teacher. "Well... not exactly... more it's...," I gasped, shaking my head, "It's impossible!" I finished.

"Ha!" François agreed. "It speaks volumes, does it not?"

I simply nodded, recalling what I'd seen.

Battle sight reveals much about the mind in a broader sense, informing the method's mystical philosophy. At rest, most people appear as a tangle of light strands, reflecting their mess of conflicting and incomplete intentions. We call this tangle "my thoughts," revealing the average mind as a mess of intentions, counter-intentions, and trial runs. All this without ever having taken action! You may believe yourself to have a singular thought, action, and plan, but battle sight reveals otherwise.

Of course, there are a few exceptions. The truly disciplined—François and the Maestro being the exemplars—will show light bodies at rest that are organized with few tangled strands. This mirrors their singular and decisive minds, which differ from the mind of the average person.

But when our maneuvering brought Robere into my fighting sight, His light body looked as smooth and uniform as an eggshell. There seemed to be no distinct strands of intention whatsoever, that is to say, of thought. This implied that his mind was perfectly empty as he sat observing us. Robere indeed and quite simply witnessed our practice. And nothing more.

As I said to François, "Impossible."

Of course, everyone likes to believe that they can "simply witness" events. But this is false. It is obvious in battle sight that so-called "observers" are nothing of the kind, as they look like seething and tangled strands of light, demonstrating that, even while "observing," they have a constant stream of thoughts, opinions, and reactions.

Robere was of another order entirely. I'd never seen the like before. He was truly witnessing, without any other thoughts — impossible, as I said. My glimpse of the impossible might make me hesitate, yes?

Robere, feeling our attention was upon him, spoke up.

He smiled sunnily and said, "I wanted to see you unencumbered by your understandably churning thoughts, Étienne. François's art is such a demanding practice that I felt you would shed everything extraneous, revealing your untrammeled nature. Most illuminating."

François and I looked at each other. "Illuminating?" François laughed, "I'm sure it was. For you as well, Étienne, I believe?"

I could only shake my head, wondering still what kind of creature this monk was.

Robere rose from his seat and gestured to us to follow him, walking us back to the hut. He gestured to a bucket outside the door and told us, "Kindly wash up, gentlemen, and join me when you are done. I shall prepare a breakfast, after which we still have much to talk about."

We did as he asked, and I drew water from the spring. We washed with an herb-scented soap and dried ourselves with a cloth provided by Robere. Once dry and dressed, we carried the table and benches outside at Robere's request, as he preferred to eat outdoors, where we could enjoy the autumn air and sun. I guessed that Robere did almost everything in nature so that the energies remained unattenuated by human structures. In this way, he somewhat resembled the Druids.

The monk rendered grace over the meal in a sonorous chant that was more than mere formality. His voice soared to the Divine in a way that felt like he was directly conversing with whom he was thanking. Compared to this, the prayers of thanks recited by priests in church were little more than rote formulas.

We broke bread in silence. Watching François eat, I realized this was how he preferred to eat. I had only seen him with our loud group of boys, where he maintained order at the table. It was a moment of transition from childhood to adulthood, allowing me to appreciate the sacrifices he made for us. It added to my already high admiration for him.

Robere cleared the table after we finished, gesturing for François and me to stay seated. He quickly completed the task and returned to his stool. While eating, we sat nearly side by side, gazing out at the woods with the hut behind us, soaking in the tranquility of nature. This arrangement allowed Robere and me to sit comfortably next to each other while we chatted, unlike our face-to-face meeting the previous day.

The monk asked me how I fared with all that had been revealed. I reflected on his question and offered my best answer.

"I'm still struggling to grasp it," I told him. "I don't have much to say yet. Frankly, there was so much to sort out, and my emotions are so confused that I don't know what to say."

Robere nodded in sympathy, saying that the whole thing must seem outlandish and shocking, coming all at once like this.

"True enough, but that's not what's so difficult, Robere," I said. "It's not how outlandish it all sounds that's the problem; it's that, outlandish or not, I know it to be *true*. I'd rather dismiss out of hand what you've told me as ridiculous and be done with it. But I feel so strongly that it is true, and that brings a view of myself I can hardly bear."

We conversed, almost idly, while gazing at the beauty of the woods. I felt no pressure from Robere or myself to understand or know more, only to converse and be together as we shared this story we had in common. Even my first comments were spoken in a dispassionate tone, simply observing that I was struggling and emotional, just so. Perhaps it was the peacefulness of the scene around us, or, more likely, the peaceful influence of Robere himself. Still, after talking for a time, I felt less tortured inside by yesterday's disclosures, as if his loving presence helped things find a place to settle in me.

Without thinking, it prompted me to speak more of the terrible shame I felt yesterday in his presence—still felt, to be completely honest. I told him how I couldn't help but feel responsible for the fracture of our soul because of my allegiance to Victory and violence, and confessed my impulse to flee after I'd heard his, or rather *our* story.

Oddly, as I spoke about this, none of these feelings held sway in the moment. It was a bit like talking about something difficult that happened many years ago, yet time has given it perspective. Something about him made it possible for me to speak frankly without being so overwhelmed, though I sensed that my feelings were still there, under the surface. Something had grown between us in this short time together.

I asked myself what, among all this tumult, could have changed. I saw now that there had been a barrier inside me and, much as water from a hidden spring softens the earth to reach the surface, simply being in Robere's presence had similarly dissolved this barrier. I had been so guarded against so much, perhaps for eons—my kinship with this monk and, especially, my need for him. Only now, in his presence, could I sense how much had been missing in ways that defied comprehension.

Spontaneously, Robere and I turned to face each other. I reached out to clasp his forearms, and he responded in turn to clasp mine. We braced each other. Like strands of rope pulled apart yet still coiling to entwine, I understood why Robere longed to join again. A wrenching desire to be whole overwhelmed me, and I felt another barrier dissolve within.

Images flooded my mind in a sudden rush, like a dam breaking. It felt as if I might be overwhelmed, so I tightened my grip on Robere's arms, seeking stability in his steadfast presence. His firm grasp assured me he wouldn't let me sink, prompting me to yield to the surging waters.

The scenes unfolding were familiar: key moments from many lifetimes, as shown to me by the alchemical Phoenix Egg years ago, when Édouard had used it to address my fear of death and life. Now, with the knowledge of my bifurcated soul, everything is reshuffled, framed by my soul's engagement with Severity and Victory principles.

I saw many lifetimes engaged with violence and aggression, in a search to understand the nature of these principles woven through Creation, as avid a search as Robere's for divine union and love. It was the conundrum embedded in the very fabric of God's creation: violence, catastrophe, and destruction.

Nature partakes of it, as storms, earthquakes, and volcanoes attest. Life could not exist without death and destruction. The lion commits violence to hunt and kill its food, and even takes pleasure in the act, as a house cat plays with the mouse before devouring it, or leaving the carcass as a gift for its master.

Then, there is that unique human contribution to Nature's fury. Only human creativity and passion could turn violence and destruction into art and science, the study of war.

Each aspect of our soul was equally compelled, one part towards the ultimate of the Creator's love, and the other towards the passionate mystery of divine destruction. And if love and violence, sublime peace, and righteous aggression are intrinsic aspects of the Creator's plan, then to what end?

When is violence harmful, and when not? Violence always entails harm, but is there such a thing as *measured* harm? Where is the line crossed into *unmeasured* harm? And, what of the violence in the surgeon's art: painful, severe, yet necessary to serve life? The surgeon amputates a limb to save a life, just as a warrior kills to protect the tribe and family. Tyrants must be destroyed to preserve the tribe and to shield the weak, lest the warrior serve the needs of power alone. No line marks where violence serves only power or where we've yielded to the power of wanton destruction for its own sake.

And what of my ultimate act of violence? That tore apart the very fabric of the soul itself? Had my severed half learned nothing through its multitude of ensuing, lonely incarnations in my pursuit of Severity? Had my obsession with piercing this mystery become consumed by its own wanton destructiveness?

It seemed that I had stripped my half of a soul of all its goodness in my unrelenting pursuit of this obsession. A soul cannot find its way to wholeness with only a sword as its tool. A sharp blade can cut away the bad, but cannot create good.

I remained convinced that I had carelessly and irreparably harmed our spirit by dismissing its finest aspect. I couldn't envision a means by which my deliberate severing of the soul's God-given completeness could be forgiven. How could there be pardon for rejecting the Divine's most precious gift?

I blinked, realizing I was staring at Robere, who had somehow pulled me out of the maelstrom of shame and guilt that the vision had drawn me into. I would likely have fallen off my stool if our still-clasped forearms hadn't kept me from losing my balance.

I felt conflicted. His grip was reassuring, yet I was grateful it maintained enough distance to ease my fear that I might contaminate him with my closeness. Maybe our fracture had served a greater purpose, letting my obsession with violence no longer impede Robere's pursuit of peace.

No sooner had these thoughts formed in my mind than I saw Robere's face shift from an expression of love and warmth to one of horrified concern.

"Oh, my dear! No, no! That's not what this is about!" He shook my arms firmly, as if to rouse me from my daze, and reiterated his disagreement. "I have allowed you to bear so many misunderstandings, Étienne. What a terrible burden I've left you with! Our fracture was not more your fault than mine.

"What you perceive as a flaw in your soul, Étienne, arises from your feeling of incompleteness. It is *true;* you are not whole; you are indeed lacking...."

Whatever else he was to say about this mattered not. The moment he said, *"It is true; you are not whole...,"* it was like hearing the confirming death knell, my final sentencing. A numbing cloud descended over me.

"Oh, horrors!" Robere exclaimed in despair, "Please forgive me, Étienne, that is not what I mean! Thirty years of silence have rendered my tongue awkward. Don't you understand, Étienne, I feel exactly the same! I, too, feel constantly like I am *lacking.* Like you, *I feel I am never whole!* It's the same for me! It's the very same for me!"

The absurdity of his declaration was enough to jar me enough that my anger at him shook off some of the numbness. I snorted at his ludicrous claim.

Ridiculous! The saint claims he is just as flawed and incomplete as the murderer. It was like a contest for piety among priests, each claiming more sins to out-humble the other.

I glared sullenly at Robere's beseeching eyes, daring him to explain why he'd say such a thing.

"Yes, *really*, Étienne, this is no ploy to create a false parity between us, I swear it. But think about this a moment longer," Robere insisted. "By necessity, I would have the same sense of incompleteness and inadequacy as you! How could it be otherwise? How could I *not* share in *our* incompleteness?

"You're only surprised due to your conviction that my portion of our soul has achieved perfection. You evaluate yourself against this incomplete standard, assuming that a holy monk must inherently be whole and unflawed? Yes?"

Robere understood my unspoken reasoning perfectly.

"But," he continued, "Don't you see, I, too, sacrificed my other half!"

I was unable to imagine how shedding the dead weight of my half of our soul could be such a sacrifice. It could only have freed him, I thought. It left me unmoved by his argument.

Robere searched my eyes questioningly before staring off to the side, deep in thought as if in an inner conversation. Later, he told me he was praying for help understanding why I found it impossible to grasp what was so apparent to him.

But my part of our soul had carried this certainty of guilt for our bifurcation for so many lifetimes that it was no longer a conclusion, simply so.

Robere stared up into the sky for a few moments. Perhaps the Divine reminded him that all this was beyond words, that further explanations would not resolve the issue. At any rate, he was done talking me out of it. He nodded to himself and closed his eyes.

Something welled up from him. It swept through me like a great, fresh wind. My guilt and shame were dwarfed by it; *I* felt dwarfed by it. My earlier certainties resembled nothing more than lifeless, dry leaves blown away by the wind, and my mind became clear, as if restored to something more fundamental and true, before so many lifetimes of regret had been heaped upon it.

This clarity seemed almost blinding at first, like stepping from a dark room into bright sunlight. After a moment, I could see Robere for the first time without the distortion of such overwhelming emotion.

Whatever flowed through me cleared my perception of the false glow of sainthood that my guilt had imposed on him. Indeed, I saw that he was a remarkable man with an unusual and loving presence. Yet, despite his garb of holiness, he was also a man.

Robere inclined his head, looking gratified that what had stood between us was no longer the barrier it had been.

"As I was saying, Étienne, there *is* truth in your feeling that something is missing in you, just as *I* feel there is something profoundly missing in me," he repeated. "But what is missing from you is not goodness or humanity."

He paused for a breath and perhaps for dramatic effect.

"The thing that is indeed missing in you, Étienne…" Robere said, staring intently at me as his pause lengthened.

I caught my breath and braced myself against the bad news my conscience still knew must be coming.

"…is…," he said, pausing tortuously.

"…Me!" Robere finished.

What? I was so startled that I couldn't tell if I'd spoken aloud or not—unlikely since all words had fled me. I stared at him in silent astonishment.

"And," Robere went on, *"it is exactly the same for me, only the other way! That my fundamental lack is you!"*

Though I was still speechless, it didn't matter as he had more to say.

"I, too, could never feel whole," Robere explained. "No matter how much enlightenment I gained, something was still missing. Like you, I could never be more than incomplete and flawed, and, also like you, I didn't know that what was missing was the *other half* of my fragmented soul; I could only feel its shadow."

"I have spent countless lifetimes searching for the cause of this unnamed void, tracing back through the fabric of time. Ultimately, I grasped our disconnected threads and their origin. Nothing less than Divine grace revealed the way to discover my other half. To discover *you*, Étienne."

It was an astounding story. I could not imagine how Robere could be so relentlessly driven to pursue this, one lifetime after another, until our story was revealed. I realized suddenly that I was lying to myself. It was not that I could not imagine it, but that I could not imagine I was worthy of being searched for. Had we not been sundered for good reason? But despite the threads of this old certainty, I had been absorbing what Robere had been trying to tell me, and I realized that I could no longer see us or myself in the same way. For the first time, I could see that there was "us," and I could see the greater truth in this.

Certainement! Of course, we would both feel lacking. How could it be otherwise? Divided from wholeness, how could we ever find ourselves other than partial?

Robere smiled, seeing that he had gotten through to me.

"And," he went on, "all this has led us, finally, to grasp something even more profound and difficult to grasp than I had ever expected. When those words came through me yesterday, I realized that I was as limited and beclouded in my view of the nature of things, of us, as you. What had happened to our soul was so beyond understanding that we could only see it through our sense of what we lacked.

"We *must*, my dear Étienne, learn to perceive from the soul's perspective, rather *than* our self-image. From this perspective, I can assert that our soul has never truly been divided! And this provokes a very different question, 'In what way do these two aspects and their paths fulfill the goals of the soul?'"

I could say nothing to this bewildering statement, stacked atop so many others that remained unresolved and undigestible. I had only a day to accept that this seeming stranger was the missing half of my soul. I was barely starting to realize that, for countless lifetimes, I had mistaken the absence of my other half for my sense of inadequacy as a human being. Now he proposes that nothing of our soul was ever truly divided?

My pursed lips must have suggested disagreement rather than indigestion to Robere, for he leaped in quickly to explain further.

"An outlandish claim, I know," he admitted. "But we must press on lest the window of insight slam shut before it has brought fresh air into our midst.

"Your Maestro taught you to look at the manifold Creation and ask how it must serve the *singular* Creator. Yes? He said that life, all the souls inhabiting creation, are like the Divine light shining through a myriad stained-glass windows, the play of light throughout Creation, yes?"

The Maestro had spoken of it time and again. I nodded, wondering where Robere, the silent monk, had learned of Édouard's metaphor. During interminable High Masses we'd been required to attend, we'd been instructed to watch the play of light on the Cathedral floor as the sun changed its angle. I had thought it a ruse to keep us busy and quiet, though I found it quite entrancing.

The Maestro explained that each piece of glass symbolizes a soul, and that the Divine light shining through countless stained-glass windows reveals the stories of incarnation as it dances across the floor of time. He emphasized our sacred trust to discern the nature of our window and soul as we contemplate the light that represents our lives. For a fleeting moment, I saw that one of the secrets to his human alchemy was that the Maestro viewed each of us as a display of radiant divine light, revealing our true nature.

"I have been under a vow of silence," Robere said, responding to my unspoken thoughts, "But I have visited and communed with your Maestro for many years as your training prepared you to meet me. I even spent time reading in his library when you were away. I think he enjoyed that my silence allowed him to talk more! He offered this insightful metaphor to me in due course, and I found it… most illuminating!" He smiled, pleased with his play on words.

"Keep the Maestro's metaphor in mind now when I ask, Étienne, is there any reason to believe that a singular soul better serves the Creator's aims? Might not the Artist tap a piece of glass, causing it to crack and refract more angles of Divine light? I've read nothing in holy writ that requires us to see souls only through a singular lens."

I realized I was holding my breath, as if bracing myself for another change in direction. No sooner had I shed one universe of understanding than he presented me with another. It was an effort to be receptive to what he might express next.

"This is most important, Étienne," Robere said, intent on getting my full attention. There was a slight glint in his eye that belied the seriousness of his subject matter up to this moment, leaving me momentarily cautious.

"From our soul's point of view," he said, "it would be completely correct to say that the 'Robere' part was as stubbornly and relentlessly drawn to Peace as the 'Étienne' part was stubbornly and relentlessly drawn to Aggression."

Robere paused, looking pleased with his formulation and, no doubt, also pleased with its effect on me as I drew back in surprise. If I could say nothing else about him, I'd say the man kept surprising me.

He was inspired enough by the humor in his twist of phrase to step into a comedian's role, leaving me little doubt that he'd spent way *too much* time with the Maestro of high drama, and he took on a boyish air.

He off-balanced me further with a mischievous grin and *winked* at me, dissolving the dignified image I had of him. He leaned closer, like my fellows do when whispering a grand secret.

In a hushed voice, he rasped, "No one, Étienne, should be spared in our efforts to assign blame, don't you think?"

Continuing in a theatrical mode worthy of Édouard, Robere straightened up and looked around as if gathering the crowd in the village square. He raised his arms high to make his decree.

"Hear ye, hear ye!" he announced loudly. "Let it be known that the Robere part of our soul has so *violently insisted on peace*, that its violence has torn the soul in two!"

I had forgotten that François was behind me until he burst into laughter at Robere's dramatics. Robere grinned over my shoulder at him, provoking further hysterics from François. The monk nodded excitedly, like a little boy delighted by the cleverness of his joke.

I found the shift in tone during such serious discussions to be quite inappropriate. These two supposedly mature men are provoking each other like children! I cast a disapproving glare at François for supporting Robere's childish antics. Of all people, I expected more sobriety from François!

I admit that I took pleasure from my judgmental perspective. It brought me a sense of gravity and steadiness. I felt like the adult among us for a moment, countering the many recent shocks I had received. Perhaps Robere intended his dramatic gestures to support me in this way, yet they also underscored his argument about my guilt, putting us on more equal ground.

We sat for a time, the two so-called men chuckling out loud now and then, I feeling self-righteous enough to permit them. Robere gathered himself to continue eventually.

"Truly, Étienne," he said, "I am equally to blame for our bifurcation as you, if it is blame you need. From our soul's perspective, it is too simple-minded to believe that the 'bad' and violent Étienne aspect was the singular cause of our disunion, while the 'good' and pure Robere aspect carried on its divinely approved, saintly path… No matter the cost! What kind of saint is that monk, if his heart could accept everyone but his other half?

"Only if we maintain the narrowest view of *both* the soul *and* the Divine could this be so! After all that you know now, Étienne, is it not evident that to hold such a view would be silly?

Was he referring to me, the one acting so mature, as silly? I must have shown my annoyance, leading him to modify his approach.

"Étienne, are we not *both* an original result of our singular soul?" he said.

I agreed, reluctantly, that I could see how this was so.

"And," he continued, "was not our soul torn between things so essential to it that neither of these opposite principles could be renounced?"

I realized Robere was asking me to play along, as I often played the dummy for Édouard's didactics, so I nodded reluctantly.

"How could it be otherwise, yes?" Robere affirmed.

"And, if I can claim authority as resident saint," he said with a small smile, "I assure you, Étienne, that God does not give his light to souls only to set them on a path of destruction. Each soul is a spark of His light, a shining particle of divine being, charged to weave a tiny thread in creation's tapestry. Collectively, we manifest humanity's living story of the divine. Life is the Divine's gift to itself, our soul's dual story as much as any other."

We fell silent, sinking into the softness of the midday atmosphere, surrounded by the rustling of the trees and the birds calling in the forest, so sweet and true. I sensed that François, sitting behind me, had entered a meditative state familiar to me from our training together, and let myself slip into my own. Robere, whose very nature seemed a prayer, joined in, without needing to shift into any kind of meditation. In this mutually amplified state, I had the impression of an infinity of sparks shining from everything around us. It was only a moment, a glimpse, but enough to affirm all that had been said so far, and no further doubts remained for me about our story.

Robere smiled over my shoulder at François, then at me, allowing this new level of calm to support him in expressing himself more freely.

"Just as you, Étienne, I struggle with feeling at fault for our split," he said. "No matter how much of the Divine I could touch, or how much I elevated my mind and purified my body, I was still missing something that, like you, I could not know or understand. Through many lifetimes, I worked to overcome this lack by evolving a greater capacity to love, attaining my soul's greatest desire: to become one with the heart of God. It was only at the very moment this was granted that I was given the vision of our bipartite soul."

"Imagine Étienne," he exclaimed, "how it was to attain my most long-sought union, and discover that half of my soul was missing! Divine union revealing my hidden disunion, unable to reflect the wholeness I had yearned for."

"What was revealed was not only that the other half of my soul was missing, Étienne, but that by so singularly adhering to this path of Divine love, I had rejected and turned away from the Divine principles everywhere that your half symbolized!"

The monk's face revealed the depth of his anguish at this revelation. "I was confronted by the divine loving heart itself that, in my relentless pursuit of holiness, I'd chosen to break my soul's unity rather than struggle through resolving my soul's extremes? All of this so shattered me that I, who had been the paragon of forgiveness to others, found that I could not forgive *myself.*"

I could see Robere's eyes fill with moisture, conveying the pain of this lesson. I could certainly sympathize.

"But, dear Étienne, my self-blame and lack of forgiveness have been as distorted and incorrect as yours," Robere insisted. "Our greatest challenge is to see beyond our partial views and see our story as our *soul's* story, rather than your story or mine."

I had no idea what this could mean. It felt as if he were holding a bucket of water and saying that I must fit its contents into the thimble of my brain.

"Has your Maestro not said that everything is ingredients? That nothing presented is to be wasted or left out?"

Well, at least this was familiar ground for me. I nodded in agreement, hoping this might give me a basis for understanding how it applied to us.

"That means, Étienne, that you and I, together, are the ingredients, and neither one of us can be left out if we are to have a hope of understanding the divine alchemy, yes? You understand?"

I acknowledged, somewhat reluctantly, that this must indeed be the case. If I learned nothing else from Édouard, it was the importance of this principle and the art of recognizing that every situation holds its essential ingredients for transformation—nothing may be dismissed as unimportant. This was the essence of his alchemy. I thought of how, grasping it could not be suppressed, he steered Ton Ton's compulsive thievery towards a higher purpose, and how he used my fear of disappointing him to teach me to read.

"So, Étienne," Robere asked, "w*hat* are you and I the ingredients *for, n'est-ce pas?*"

What are *we* the ingredients for? I struggled with his question, as I could barely get my head around any one of us as 'ingredients,' let alone look at us collectively.

"Let me put it to you another way. " What is our soul about?" he asked. "That it was a *necessity* to maintain such seemingly opposed qualities and, by dividing, evolve them so separately?"

"How does our *seeming* division serve the wholeness of Divine intent? For our allegedly tragic shattering *must be* an essential ingredient in something greater; it cannot be otherwise. Our bifurcation has shaped our soul to be better fitted to divine intent than it would be if our soul had remained singular."

His questions completely threw me off balance. I could barely hold the words in my mind as he spoke them. Not only because they forced me to stretch my mind's grasp, but also because something in me resisted letting go of what I believed. Some part of me clung to the self-blame, shame, and guilt I'd carried as if it were a bizarre talisman against healing and forgiveness.

There was a feeling that if I eased my grip on my familiar misery to receive what Robere so purely offered, I would cease to exist altogether. For lifetimes, certainties about my nature had become something reliable, something indelible. Though horrid and relentless, I'd come to rely on them as my enduring truth. At least my proven unworthiness was *something;* without that, I would be… nothing. Fear of death, indeed.

But that was without knowledge of Robere. In his presence, I had to ask myself: Where had all my guilt and miserable self-blame led, after all? To anywhere useful? Had there been anything of higher benefit? Had it resulted in any greater purpose?

Robere waited while I struggled to work all this through before continuing.

"So, Étienne, after many lifetimes of reflection, and now, in your presence, we are offered an entirely new vision of our soul, new to us both."

Mon Dieu! What could possibly be *new* for this monk? I still had so many unanswered questions, with nothing else—new or otherwise—being added. Overloaded, my intellect gave up and simply shut down, abandoning me to an abrupt, unwritten blankness. Robere smiled as if he'd been waiting for that moment, when I'd finally be present, heedless of defenses, wounds, or concepts.

He momentarily firmed his grip on my hands, then turned them palm down to rest on my knees. Placing his own gently over the backs of my hands, he anchored us both to the weight and solidity of our warm flesh. Spirit must have been at play because a beam of sunlight brushed the edges of Robere's beard, rendering his gray whiskers into a polished and shining silver.

Then the monk, whom I still thought of as our soul's better half, despite accepting that he too struggled, uttered something I contemplate to this day.

"I can see now, Étienne, that our two halves do not make a whole," he said, "and they never shall!"

He grinned as he declared this, then continued. "Because they are so much *more* than the parts they seem to be. Whatever the Divine has in mind is a mystery, but from our soul's view, it is clear that we are called to serve in some way *beyond what even wholeness can conceive of.*"

The phrase carried much, much more than the words themselves conveyed. I was dumbfounded, repeating it over and over in my mind, as if I were memorizing a sentence in a foreign language.

Beyond what even wholeness can conceive of... Beyond what even wholeness can conceive of.... Beyond what even wholeness can conceive of....

I recited it urgently and stupidly as if I could force the words to make sense by brute force. But the phrase would not be shaped into a customary understanding. It stood by itself and insisted that sense come to *it*.

Robere's revelations had saturated every corner of my being with impossibility, yet his lucent presence called to something beyond all these impossible words. Eschewing all questions, intuition grasped what logic could not even encompass, and in the blessed absence of sense, everything I'd understood before was reshuffled. No words, explanations, or descriptions could convey the profound impact that Robere's phrase had on me. As much as the earlier utterance, "... even the angels know not...," had changed everything for Robere, this one, *beyond what even wholeness can conceive*, swept through me and altered the path of my future.

Robere watched all this work its way through me. He looked satisfied that our 'little talk,' as he put it, was bearing fruit. He appeared to relax a bit and looked about the forest with his warm and loving regard. I, on the other hand, was in a daze, staring at but hardly seeing the trees before me. I don't know how long it took for the forest scents and sounds to penetrate enough to draw me back to the present.

Robere leaned towards me again, his broad smile and sparkling eyes on display.

"And so we have arrived, Étienne," he said earnestly, "and we must celebrate the important fact that finally, as a result of our soul's *double-time*, we have been brought to this singular moment."

Robere paused, his eyes still locked on mine as if to ensure he had my full attention before continuing. I bowed slightly to acknowledge that he did. Robere's smile deepened at this, and he continued. He spoke as if declaring the attainment of a monumental achievement, such as the completion of one of the great cathedrals. I suppose it was just monumental in its way, perhaps even more so.

"In this singular moment," Robere declared, "we may be completely assured that *I, Robere, am no saint and you, Étienne, are no murderer!*"

My first response was a long silence. Whatever I thought the monk would say, this wasn't it. His pronouncement reflected how each part of our soul bore its burden, and in its simplicity, placed us on equal footing. It encompassed my burden of guilt, along with his, underscoring the depth of our mutual errors.

In a delayed reaction to everything revealed over the past two days, the acceptance and understanding I had struggled with finally clicked. I saw Robere's relief at shedding his burden of holiness, and felt mine at dropping my burden of disgrace.

Union with Divine Love could not mend Robere's missing wholeness any more than mastering Divine Chaos mended mine. Neither a saint nor a murderer, both aspects of our bifurcated soul needed each other. We were something else. What? Something we could not know, only discover.

As all this unfolded within me, Robere managed to lift us to our feet. He raised our arms above our heads, interlacing our fingers to hold each other's hands, palm to palm. We shook our clasped hands triumphantly, like champions celebrating a victory. And it was true: we had indeed triumphed over a veritable Olympia, races whose heats were held over many lifetimes.

"Hallelujah!" Robere shouted as we continued to vigorously shake our arms.

"*At last*, we have achieved the ultimate goal of *less-than-perfection!*"

At this, we burst into laughter, and François came to his feet to laugh with us. We drew him heartily into our embrace, and he affectionately slapped us both on the backs, smiling at us with such warmth and love.

Robere made his final, resounding declaration, "Thanks be to God!"

His grin was so broad that it filled me with wonder. The three of us found ourselves gently swaying, a sort of dance-like embrace. It had taken endless eons for us to arrive at this moment together. Even so, our dancing embrace seemed to go on for much longer than the journey that had brought us here.

—THE END of Book II—

Acknowledgements

These books have come into being, truly, by magic—
otherwise known as love.

My deepest gratitude is to all who have loved this story,
and me, into being.

To my communities—

the many friends and companions of my Retreat years,
my beloved Frankfurt Senior Trainers,
to my dear friends in my monthly energy group,
and my Pathways for Healing friends and students—
you have each been part of the alchemy that made these pages possible.
Your presence has been a living circle of learning, laughter, and grace.

Because the dance of feminine and masculine energies
lies so deeply at the heart of this work,
I offer my thanks in that same sacred balance.

The Feminine

To my wife, Maria de Lourdes Quiroz-Kepner—
you have joined me on this path with such devotion, courage, and
radiance
that I cannot imagine the journey without you.
In truth, I could not have made it without your love.
Muchas gracias, mi amor.

To Rosalyn Bruyere, my golden teacher,
who embodies the lineage of spiritual authority with such
luminosity,
thank you, patient Bear to my restless Crow;
to Carol DeSanto, my dharma buddy and dear friend,
who has kept me both grounded and unbound as spirit required;
to Judy Marz, whose friendship and artistry
continue to open me to new ways of seeing;
to Jackie Lowe-Stevenson, whose horse-wisdom
has deepened my trust in the living field;
to my sister Judy, whose constancy of love
has spanned every lifetime of this one;
and to Mother Moon, still and ever unfathomable—
my eternal gratitude.

The Masculine

To Rich Milne, editor extraordinaire, who midwifed both these
books into coherent and much more grammatical existence,
keeping me true to the story;

To Herb Stevenson, steadfast friend and midwife to this work,
who urged me forward when hesitation beckoned,
reminding me that a story untold is a spirit unfreed;
to Theo Kyrkostas, brother of the heart from our Retreat years and
beyond,
who continues to hold this story with warmth and faith;
to my brother Alan Kepner, for his abiding love
and willingness to travel with me through these improbable
memories;
and to Édouard and François—
may I have done justice to their truth,
and may their voices be heard through mine.

Family

To my daughter Tessa Rose,
whose own far journey mirrors the soul's unfolding;
to my son Braeden, a wonderful son and a finer father than I,
for his patient love and tolerance of his Pop's spirited obsessions;
to Carolina, loving mother of my grandchildren
and loving partner to my son;
to Eliás, who reminds me daily of wonder—
There are diamonds on the soles of his shoes;
and to the one coming—
I look forward to meeting you… again.

[1]   The Maestro, tickled by the concept of "free verse" poetry, enlisted me as his scribe.

[2]   If this is your first encounter with this story, I encourage you to begin with *Book I: About Time*. What follows continues that journey—woven from the same thread, but in deeper waters. Without the first book, this one may feel like a dream already in motion. Regardless, I'm no one to insist on any kind of sequence; read in any order you wish.

[3]   Amazon page https://a.co/d/03dJbww3

www.ingramcontent.com/pod-product-compliance
Lightning Source LLC
LaVergne TN
LVHW051357080426
835508LV00022B/2870